THOUSAND OAKS LIBRARY

THOUSAND OAKS LIBRARY

S 2052 00428 0452 ✓

D0583646

5/00-19 (2/00)

DISCARD

8-01	21	8-01
10/03	25	3/03
7/04	24-1	4/04
10/09	32-1	5/09
6/2012	34-1	3/2012

DEC 1991

PROPERTY OF
THOUSAND OAKS LIBRARY
1401 E. Janss Road
Thousand Oaks, California
(805) 497-6282

DEMCO

AMERICA EATS OUT

AMERICA EATS OUT

An Illustrated History of Restaurants, Taverns, Coffee Shops, Speakeasies, and Other Establishments That Have Fed Us for 350 Years

JOHN MARIANI

WILLIAM MORROW AND COMPANY, INC. *NEW YORK*

Sections of Chapter 5 first appeared in *American Heritage*.
Sections of Chapter 8 first appeared in *Gastronome*.

Copyright © 1991 by John Mariani

Photograph credits, constituting a continuation of the copyright page, appear on page 285.

All rights reserved. No part of this book may be reproduced or utilized in any form or by any means, electronic or mechanical, including photocopying, recording, or by any information storage or retrieval system, without permission in writing from the Publisher. Inquiries should be addressed to Permissions Department, William Morrow and Company, Inc., 1350 Avenue of the Americas, New York, N.Y. 10019.

It is the policy of William Morrow and Company, Inc., and its imprints and affiliates, recognizing the importance of preserving what has been written, to print the books we publish on acid-free paper, and we exert our best efforts to that end.

Library of Congress Cataloging-in-Publication Data

Mariani, John F.
    America eats out : an illustrated history of restaurants, taverns, coffee shops, speakeasies, and other establishments that have fed us for 350 years / John Mariani.
        p.   cm.
    Includes bibliographical references and index.
    ISBN 0-688-09996-3
    1. Restaurants, lunchrooms, etc.—United States—History.   2. Hotels, taverns, etc.—United States—History.   I. Title.
    TX909.M32   1991
    647.9573/09—dc20   91-2380
                                                        CIP

Printed in the United States of America

First Edition

1 2 3 4 5 6 7 8 9 10

BOOK DESIGN BY BARRY ZAID

For Misha and Christopher

Contents

Selling the American dream—a restaurant of one's own

Introduction

FROM THE BEGINNING there was always a gimmick.

Whether it was the novelty of serving a hot lunch in the middle of the day, as John and Peter Delmonico did in New York back in 1827, or the idea of delivering a Domino's pizza to one's door in less than thirty minutes, the story of America's restaurants and eateries begins with a snap of the fingers. Every successful—and many an unsuccessful—entrepreneur in this country has grasped the idea of food service as an opportunity to make a mark, and the need to invent and be innovative in America has always been as urgent a force in food service as it has been in the automobile, aviation, or architecture industries or in art, music, or dance.

Sometimes the gimmick was just plain good food, or even simple cleanliness, two innovations Englishman Fred Harvey launched in depot restaurants along the Santa Fe Railroad in 1876. Other times it was the introduction of extraordinary comfort, as when George Pullman designed dining cars on trains, or amazing convenience, as when two Philadelphians named Horn and Hardart imported German equipment to create the first Automat in 1902.

Lunch wagons, milk bars, diners, drive-ins, speakeasies, restaurants shaped like hot dogs, restaurants designed to look like a pirate's den, restaurants where the waiters sing opera, restaurants with wine lists as thick as family bibles—all are, in their own way, gimmicks to hook in the crowds. The American love of something new and different allowed for the creation of restaurants built around extravagant themes like ancient Rome, medieval monasteries, and fairy tale castles, while others might be set on the 107th floor of a skyscraper or at the top of a pylon at a World's Fair.

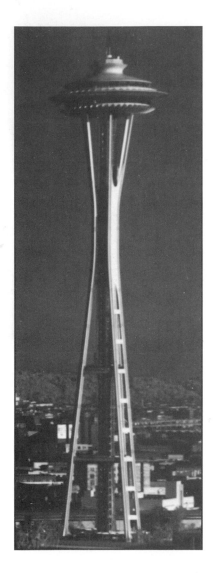

In the rest of the world, such concepts and fantasies have rarely affected dining out. In Europe, as much in the temples of French haute cuisine as in the neighborhood Italian trattorias, the quality of the food has always come before any other consideration—a notion constantly shored up by tenets of classicism codified in the nineteenth century. To veer from these tenets, to disturb the equanimity of genteel dining—or even of bourgeois eating—is considered a betrayal of the whole idea of dining out.

In France, restaurants have traditionally been of three kinds—the haute cuisine establishment where exquisite and very expensive food is prepared for the delectation of the connoisseur; the small family-run bistro serving traditional regional cooking; and the brasserie, specializing in beer and Alsatian food and which caters to working people and families.

In Italy, it is much the same, with restaurants divided between formal, international dining rooms (often set in hotels) and smaller, casual trattorias. Throughout Europe there are also pubs, beerhalls, rathskellers, tapas bars, and other varieties of eateries, but all follow cherished guidelines as to their nature and character, and the quality of the food served is what distinguishes one from another.

Quite the same can be said for eating places in Central and South America, which for the most part copy European models, and in Asia, where formal restaurants appeared only by virtue of imperialism, and where most people ate at street stalls or in tea parlors when and if they could afford to do so.

THE DIVERSITY of American restaurants ranges from the high of Seattle's revolving Space Needle dining room to the low of a rudimentary roadside eatery in Queen City, Missouri.

These cultures have, in the last two decades, begun to accept American restaurant ideas, although many see the appearance of those ideas as a travesty of gastronomy. Nothing is more disturbing to European chefs than to see the intrusion of American fast-food concepts into their culture, just as French academicians abhor the invasion of their language by words like "hamburger," "hot dog" and "self-service."

By the same token Europeans have long been suspicious of all new technologies in the kitchen, while Americans' inbred love of a whizbang manifests itself as much in our restaurants as in our steel mills or oil fields. As restaurateur Charles Rector observed at the turn of the last century, "The introduction of steam and electricity, refrigerator cars and cold-storage made the abolishment of time and distance, and of climate even, possible. Then American genius, responsive to the opportunities, evolved the Oyster House."

SPICK-AND-SPAN CLEANLINESS has since the nineteenth century been a hallmark of even the least pretentious American restaurants, like New Jersey's Sterling Café.

The oyster house as an American institution has its own lively, raucous history, which shall be dealt with in these pages, but it is but one of a dizzying array of restaurant types to which this country has given rise since the late eighteenth century—a scant two hundred years ago, when there were no restaurants as we know them yet in existence. The cornucopia of raw ingredients, the irresistible charm of technology, the waves of hungry immigrants, and the incredible wealth of America have given us every kind of eatery imaginable—taverns, pubs, barbecue pits, crabshacks, soup kitchens, rathskellers, chop suey parlors, Japanese steakhouses, ice cream parlors, salad bars, restaurants that spin atop buildings, restaurants that float on barges, restaurants that move on wheels, and restaurants that fly at thirty thousand feet—and there still seems no end in sight.

One mustn't take the history of restaurants too lightly. Modern historians who pore over the shipping records of sixteenth-century Venetians or the number of oxcarts owned by a feudal lord have shown us that it is the incidentals of history that inexorably lead to major social changes, and restaurants have long symbolized the fertility of the American imagination,

BOSTON'S Ye Olde Union Oyster House, opened in 1826, is a classic American genre restaurant whose popularity has never waned.

ADAPTABILITY to the market is the hallmark of American restaurateurs, as shown on the signage of the Swan River roadside eatery in Minnesota, where customers could get anything from Italian spaghetti to hamburgers.

the range of our fantasies, and the power of our institutions. There is as much to be read into the concept of the "power lunch" in New York as there is into the segregation of lunch counters in the South, and we learn a great deal about ourselves simply by bending Brillat-Savarin's dictum to read "We are where we eat."

So much of our culture is explained by its being set in restaurants—the diner in Hemingway's short story "The Killers"; the demimonde world of Truman Capote's "La Côte Basque"; the exclusion of the police detective from the doors of a deluxe French restaurant where rich drug dealers take their meals in the film *The French Connection;* the provocative sexuality of the barroom in beer commercials—all tell us as much about ourselves and our fantasies as do the grand schemes of manifest destiny and the New Frontier.

For the history of restaurants in the United States is tied up intimately and completely with our vaunted mobility, both geographically and sociologically. When an American goes on the road, he is off on an adventure, part of which is the discovery of new foods in unfamiliar, sometimes bleak, sometimes breathtaking landscapes where a restaurant may be as much an idiosyncratic expression of the region's culture as it is a signpost along the way. The Golden Arches of McDonald's, as familiar and beckoning as the Statue of Liberty, act like beacons in the night. The ride to the 107th floor of New York's World Trade Center is a thrilling ritual consummated by entrance into a restaurant called, quite aptly, Windows on the World. And the scent of hickory curling upward from a barbecue shack alongside a highway in Missouri can break over an American with the bittersweet realization of something lost and found all at once.

There's always the gimmick, the draw, the come-on in American eateries. The American restaurant is never merely a place to eat. It is a place to go, to see, to experience, to hang out in, to seduce in, and to be seduced. Good taste has as much to do with it all as bad taste, and there's plenty of both to go around in this story.

A FINE EXAMPLE of Programmatic architecture—the Tail o' the Pup hot dog stand—was due to be razed to make way for a hotel but instead moved two blocks away, where it is still one of Los Angeles's most beloved landmarks.

The American ideal—a square meal for a square deal

Chapter 1

Potluck

Food Service in Colonial and Revolutionary America

FOR MOST AMERICANS, the thought of removing oneself for a weekend to a quaint country inn is to revel in an ideal that depends far more on fantasy than fact. The restored beauty of a country inn, with varnished floorboards, antique quilts, down pillows, and a cozy candlelit dining room serving a varied menu of chowders and roast turkey, sweet potatoes and pecan pie is not so much a myth as it is a distortion of the realities of America's early taverns and inns, where the basic amenities of heat and hot water were as hard to come by as good, wholesome food.

Typical of comments by eighteenth-century travelers on the food served at country inns are those of Sarah Knight, who remarked on the meal she was served at a coach stop in Rhode Island in 1704:

> Here, having called for something to eat, the woman bro't in a twisted thing like a cable, but something whiter; and laying it on the bord, tugg'ed for life to bring it into a capacity to spread; which having with great pains accomplished, shee serv'd in a dish of Pork and Cabbage, I suppose the remains of Dinner. The sauce was of a deep Purple, which I tho't was boil'd in her dye Kettle; the bread was Indian, and every thing on the Table service agreeable to these. I, being hungry, gott down a little; but my stomach was soon cloy'd, and what cabbage I swallowed serv'd me for a Cudd the whole day after.

15

Not all reports of food served in colonial inns and taverns were as dreadful. Many visitors praised the bounty of American tables, heaped with fresh and preserved food. In his 1787 diary Samuel Vaughan ticked off the following offerings he found on his travels: "Ham, bacon & fowl pigeon of one sort or another always to be had upon the road & often fresh meat or fish, dried Venison Indian or wheaten bread, butter eggs milk, often cheese, drinks Rum, Brandy or Whiskey, resembling Gin."

But food service, such as it existed in colonial times, was a hodgepodge of taverns, inns, boardinghouses, grog houses, coffeehouses, brandy shops, and ordinaries, few of them distinguishable from each other until well into the eighteenth century. Indeed, the idea of a restaurant, where one could go in and order a meal from a menu, was still unknown in Europe and far off in the future of the young country.

Yet almost from the moment the first English and Dutch immigrants landed on these shores, the service of food and drink to those willing to pay for it became a part of everyday life in the colonies. By 1629 Virginia had two beer brewhouses, and the Puritans at Plymouth Colony licensed their first in 1637, although within two years the General Court of Massachusetts enacted a law against the "abominable practice" of drinking toasts. The popularity of breweries and the houses that dispensed their products soared, so that by 1648 nearly a fourth of all the buildings in New Amsterdam were, according to director-general Peter Stuyvesant, "Brandy shops, Tobacco or Beer houses" and by century's end Boston had dozens of taverns.

These establishments were little more than places where men would gather to drink and to drink heavily, and many of the earliest laws passed by colonial governments were attempts to curb the consumption of alcohol and the merrymaking that went along with it. But taverns were vital to the life of the community, serving as meeting houses and rallying rooms for political discourse, and later, rebellion. In New Amsterdam the proliferation of taverns was encouraged, because they paid excise taxes to the city government, and many taverns were in fact used as district courts, with fines sometimes paid in drinks for the Court, the judge, and the attorneys.

Many taverns were owned and run by the town's most prominent citizens. In New Amsterdam in 1642 Governor Kieft, weary of entertaining visitors at his home, built the Staat's Herberg tavern, then leased it to Philip Giraerdy, on condition he sell only liquors made by Kieft's West India Company. More often than not, these early taverns were the only place travelers and visitors could get something to eat, and as the colonies' wealth expanded, so too grew the stature and prominence of the tavern.

In many taverns the kitchen doubled as the common room, the fireplace of which served as both sole cooking source and heating unit. One New Amsterdam tavern, owned by Wolfert Webber, was reputed to have a fireplace large enough in which to roast a whole ox. But most were rudimentary structures serving rudimentary meals that offered customers no choice in the matter of what they would eat. The meal consisted of whatever came out of a large pot set above the flames of the fireplace. Whatever the tavernkeeper ate for his dinner, so did the traveler, and that meant pretty much anything thrown into that pot. More often than not, food was of secondary importance to drink in such places, and, since no one expected much culinary talent at these new establishments, there was little need to change, as long as the liquor, beer, and cider flowed.

And flow it did. In New Netherland, tavernkeepers were forbidden to serve anything but the larger Dutch measures of liquor rather than the smaller English ones, and the enforcement of anti-drinking laws was generally lax throughout the colonies. By the end of the next century the average American over the age of fifteen was drinking nearly six gallons of alcohol each year, mostly beer and cider, but a good deal of liquor and wine too.

Toward the end of the seventeenth century the fashion for coffee and chocolate houses of the kind then the rage in London (which had two thousand of them by 1698) hit American shores as a diversion from the more ruffian taverns. In 1670 Dorothy Jones of Boston announced she would be serving coffee and chocolate at her new establishment, and the idea caught on fast. In the same year the New York Merchants' Coffee House opened, later earning the reputation as being "birthplace of the American Union." Coffeehouses were considered somewhat more civilized than taverns for gentlemen to meet in, although alcohol and food were served in both. In the next century coffeehouses grew into lavish establishments, like New York's Tontine Coffee House, which was built in 1794 on the corner of Wall and Water streets. It housed the stock exchange and insurance offices, where every ship's arrival and departure was logged. Set up by subscriptions at two hundred dollars a share, the Tontine had water closets, a bath, a tearoom, a dining room, mahogany furniture, and crystal chandeliers, all of which drew

"NOTHING FANCY" might well describe the offerings in most early eating houses, like Old Tom's Chop and Steak House in New York City.

a rising middle class whose expectations of comfort were increasingly a matter of competition among tavernkeepers.

Respectability became a selling point for taverners in the eighteenth century, and establishments like the Tontine in New York, the Blue Anchor in Boston, the City Tavern in Philadelphia, and others vied for the new wealth ready to be spent by the emerging middle-class businessman. Such taverns attracted the most powerful men of their day. Indeed, the oldest men's social and cooking club in the world was the State in Schuylkill, established in Philadelphia in 1732, four years before London's Whyte's was formally organized. The American Philosophical Society was also founded in Philadelphia, in 1743, where menus were built exclusively around oyster dishes.

French émigré Jean Anthelme Brillat-Savarin, author of a seminal gastronomic treatise entitled *La Physiologie du Goût* (1825), spent two years in New York (1794–96) as a French teacher and musician. He later recalled the hospitality of American taverns and told of the time two Englishmen from Jamaica challenged him and two French friends to a drinking bout at Little's Tavern. The dinner consisted of roast beef, turkey, vegetables, salad, fruit tart, cheese, and nuts, all accompanied by copious quantities of claret, Port, and Madeira, followed by rum, brandy, and whiskey. Brillat-Savarin, who disliked such shows of gluttony, won the day, as the Englishmen were carried out singing "Rule Brittania."

Traveling in America was becoming easier by the year. The first road guide was issued in 1732, and by 1771 one could board a "Flying Machine" coach that covered the distance from New York to Philadelphia in a day and a half—with food and lodging included in the twenty-shilling fare. Taverns sprang up along the newly built routes like mushrooms in the forest. Thus, while the inns and taverns in the backwoods were crude in the extreme, the city taverns were becoming increasingly appealing to travelers.

The food, too, was improving rapidly, and there was always plenty of it. Henry Gignilliat's tavern in Charleston, South Carolina, put out a spread of forty dishes, and New York's Tontine eventually offered at least a dozen dishes a day. The availability of meat and game exemplified America's bounty, so that venison, pigeon, turkey, ducks, bear, and other game were not unusual in a large tavern, both in the country and in the city. Pork was the principal meat, beef not as easy to come by. Vegetables were not much eaten in those days, and shellfish was preferred to fish.

One of the most successful entrepreneurs of his day was Samuel Fraunces, who in 1763 opened a tavern on Dock (later Pearl) and Broad streets in New York that became a central meetinghouse for every important personage who came through New York in the late eighteenth century. The three-and-one-half-story structure had an ale room, game room, seating for seventy, five bedrooms, and elegant furnishings. Fraunces was also one of the first entrepreneurs to offer off-premises catering (he often sent meals to General George Washington's home) and take-out service for families desiring pastries and desserts or for sea captains and their passengers. Fraunces even exported his own pickled and fried oysters, lobster, and "beef alamonde" as far as the West Indies. Fraunces Tavern still exists and flourishes on its original site, albeit in reconstructed form, with only a small section of the original building still extant.

Most of the food served at taverns, especially those in the country, bore little resemblance to the kind of fancy cookery Sam Fraunces featured. Yet few ever complained about the huge portions offered at even the most remote inn, and a breakfast of several eggs, game birds, pancakes, and coffee or tea was ubiquitous throughout America. A Scotsman named John Melish stopped for a meal in a backwoods inn, where his hostess began making his breakfast by wringing the necks of two chickens.

> I told her to stop [he wrote in his Travels in the United States of America (1811)], and she gave me a look of astonishment. "Have you any eggs?" said I. "Yes, plenty," replied she, still keeping in a stooping posture, with the chicken in her hand. "Well," said I, "just boil an egg, and let me have it, with a little bread and tea, and that will save you and I a great deal of trouble." She seemed quite embarrassed, and said she never could set down a breakfast to me like that.... She detained me about half an hour, and at last placed upon the table a profusion of ham, eggs, fritters, bread, butter and some excellent tea.... I mention the circumstance to show the kind of hospitality of the landlady, and the good living enjoyed by the backwoods people.

By far the most common dish served to travelers was ham (usually so heavily salted as to shock the first-time consumer) and, in the South, chickens.

FOOD SERVICE IMPROVED markedly in the cities of the new republic, with the establishment of gentlemen's dining rooms like Fraunces Tavern (shown here reconstructed on its original lower Manhattan site), where General George Washington bade farewell to his troops in December 1783.

AMPLE VARIETIES of pork, game, fish, and poultry were available in the city markets, like New York's Fulton Market, which replaced the unsanitary Oswego Market in 1821.

"Have had either Bacon or Chicken every meal since I came in to the Country," wrote visitor Nicholas Cresswell of his sojourn through Virginia. "If still continue this way [I] shall be grown over with Bristles or Feathers."

Pork had to be preserved, and salt was the cure used after a winter slaughter, when the blood was collected to make "black puddings." The innards and other parts were consumed fresh, either fried or boiled, but the ham was locked in a smokehouse and kept for eating throughout the following year. Fish, too, was smoked or packed in brine. Turtles, including sea turtles imported into Virginia, were considered a delicacy. Vegetables were not much appreciated, though the white potato was an everyday accompaniment. Fresh fruit was, of course, seasonal, though there is a record from 1751 of twenty-five thousand limes being brought in at Yorktown from the West Indies. Milk, cream, and butter were plentiful, as was cheese in the north. Breads were mainly of two kinds—cornmeal or Indian, which was for everyday consumption, and wheat bread for special occasions. Pickled items and sauces like catsup were used liberally and helped cut the saltiness of the country ham. Desserts might include cakes, jellies, trifle, and, later, ice cream.

Despite the savoriness such a list implies, it is improbable that the average traveler in the colonial era would have much enjoyed whatever it was he was eating. Culinary excellence may have been held in high esteem at some homes or in the finer city taverns after 1750, but most inns and taverns served food of a very low, if stomach-filling, order. Some communities set minimal standards for food service, even distinguishing between a "good meal" and a "common one." Meals were served at a set time and fixed price (often included in the price of the room) to the public; hence, the term "ordinary" for any such establishment that was not a club or discriminatory about who ate there.

The food had a numbing sameness to it, and, depending upon the location of the tavern, it would stick pretty close to what was most readily available. Although he describes a much later period, the narrator of Herman Melville's *Moby Dick* (1851) gives a good indication of the kind of menu one faced at a tavern in a seaside town like Nantucket. After speaking with rapture of the "juicy clams, scarcely bigger than hazelnuts, mixed with pounded ship biscuits, and salted pork . . . the whole enriched with butter, and plentifully seasoned with pepper and salt!", Ishmael seems less enamored of the entire menu, which consists of "Chowder for breakfast, and chowder for dinner, and chowder for supper, till you begin to look for fishbones coming through your clothes."

Things were hardly better, and probably worse, at the boardinghouses, which sprang up throughout bustling industrial cities for increasingly large numbers of workers who needed immediate lodgings. Boardinghouses also let rooms to travelers, and the interaction of low-class workingmen and -women with middle- or upper-class travelers probably caused as much indigestion as did the food.

Breakfast was usually at nine in the morning, followed by the main meal of the day at two in the afternoon. Guests sat at long, communal tables, and the food was consumed rapidly and with little sophistication. Those who dared to arrive even a few minutes late to the table were likely to find nothing left to eat. The so-called "boardinghouse reach" derives from the thrusting attempts of boarders to get to the food before anyone else did.

In his book *From Boarding House to Bistro* (1990), Richard Pillsbury notes that Philadelphia listed 203 boardinghouses in its city directory for 1799. Most were jammed in along the Delaware River waterfront and attracted sailors in for a night on the town as much as they did city workers, and it is not hard to imagine the standards of food preparation observed at such establishments.

Many customers couldn't have cared less about the food; they came for news, good talk, and companionship. News arrived first at and was dispatched quickly from taverns before and during the Revolution. It was at these establishments that dissidents—most of them rich merchants and landowners—met, debated, and fomented the rebellion against the Crown, and a good part of the Declaration of Independence was written by Thomas Jefferson at Philadelphia's Indian Queen Tavern. That city's Tun Tavern was the birthplace of the Marine Corps in 1775.

During the Revolution many taverns remained loyal to the Crown and served more British soldiers than American patriots. But when it was over there was all the more reason to celebrate the victory and to mark the end of hostilities by lifting a cup of cheer at a public house. So it was appropriate that George Washington, on saying farewell to his troops on December 4, 1783, did so at Fraunces Tavern (where in 1774 the Sons of the American Revolution and the Vigilance Committee had met to protest the tea tax) in the free and independent city of New York, where before long the first true restaurant would be opened in the new republic.

Delmonico's in the Gilded Age, 1891

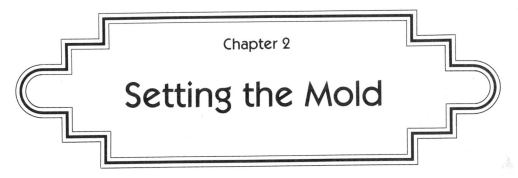

Chapter 2

Setting the Mold

Fine Dining Comes to America

WHEN THIRTY-SEVEN-YEAR-OLD sea captain Giovanni Del-Monico stepped off his boat for the last time in New York in 1825, he could not have imagined that he would become one of the richest and most important men in the city, much less the most celebrated restaurateur in American history.

He must certainly have believed, however, that this was where his fortunes lay, no matter what he chose to do. If anyone had ever been in the right spot at the right time, it was Giovanni Del-Monico in New York, at the dawn of an era of conspicuous prosperity and social change.

A native of Ticino, Switzerland, Del-Monico had plied the West Indies–New York trade route for years and had tired of the work. He decided to open a modest wineshop on the Battery, a location sure to attract his sailor friends as well as the merchants whose offices were near the piers. At first John Delmonico (he Americanized his name) offered his customers nothing out of the ordinary, but the amount of business generated by the little shop triggered in him a sense that these free-spending but naïve Americans were fast developing an appetite for the finer things their money could buy—and seemed willing to be educated on the subject.

Delmonico returned to Switzerland to convince his older brother Pietro, a confectioner, to go with him to New York, where, in 1827, they set up a pastry shop on William Street serving European-style desserts, ices, coffee, and wine.

This was not a novelty in New York (a Frenchman named Guérin had opened a confectionery on Broadway in 1815), but the Delmonico brothers did it all with a sure degree of sophistication, flair, and an uncommon attention to cleanliness that made quite an impression on those whose acquaintance with such gentility was small. The little shop prospered, and it became quite fashionable to go to "Del's" for their delicate European confections—and to ogle at another innovation, a lady cashier, who was Peter Delmonico's wife.

The Delmonicos knew they were onto something: If their clientele responded with such giddy enthusiasm to a mere pastry shop, how might they react to a place that served full meals in a setting patterned after the new "restaurants" then fashionable in Paris? So, in 1831, they bought the premises next door and took the revolutionary step of serving businessmen hot food in the middle of the day. And it was cooked by a real French chef and served on good china and linen to a public charmed by the experience and fascinated with all the new foods, like eggplant and endive. Up until then, working people ate their lunch on the street, at home, or in taverns, so the idea of sitting down to "dine" was a remarkable thing indeed.

Banker Samuel Ward reported of his first visit to Delmonico's, "I remember entering the café with something of awe.... The dim, religious light soothed the eye, its tranquil atmosphere the ear.... I was struck by the prompt and deferential attendance, unlike the democratic nonchalance of the service at Holt's Ordinary, in Fulton Street, at Clark and Brown's, in Maiden Lane, and at George W. Brown's in Water Street.... We dined perfectly for half a dollar apiece, if not less."

In desperate need of more like-minded help to handle the crowds, the Delmonicos sent for their nephew, Lorenzo, and, in short order, his brothers, Siro, François, and Constant. A second Delmonico's restaurant was opened in 1832 on Broad Street, and, when the first was destroyed by fire in 1835, a third, more opulent, Delmonico's followed in 1837 on the corner of South William and Beaver streets, where they served up menus with dozens of hors d'oeuvres, meat and game dishes, seafood, and vegetables, many based on the most sophisticated French recipes of the day. The family enjoyed fabulous success, became millionaires, and in the bargain served as social arbiters for an affluent American middle and upper class easily able to afford luxury but desperately in need of refinement.

Yet the Delmonicos were not, as is often claimed, the first to open a restaurant in America or even in New York. What the Delmonicos did was to capitalize on an undeveloped idea and to expand the possibilities. As a result, their entrepreneurial accomplishments during this era changed American dining outside the home forever.

One must go back a bit—though not very far—to find the origins of the "restaurant," a term not even recorded in English until James Fenimore Cooper wrote of "the most renowned Parisian restaurants" in his novel *The Prairie* in 1827. For centuries taverns in France had served meals at the host's table—*la table d'hôte*—while in the cities cookshops, called *traiteurs*, sold take-out food, which might be eaten at a table outside the shop. In 1765 a renegade Parisian *traiteur* named Boulanger, whose irreverent Latin motto was *Venite ad me omnes qui stomacho laboretis, et ego restaurabo vos*

("Come to me all whose stomachs ache, and I shall restore you"), offered for sale a soup of sheep's foot in white sauce that he called a *restaurant.* This brought on a lawsuit from competitors who insisted the dish did not meet the formal guidelines for a *restaurant,* a word used since the sixteenth century for a rich, restorative soup. Boulanger took good advantage of the publicity surrounding the suit, which he won, and, as one might have expected, his new *restaurant* became the rage of Paris. His idea was immediately adopted by others, including a *traiteur* named Beauvilliers (former chef to the Comte de Provence, later Louis XVIII), who in 1782 took things a step further when he began serving individual groups at small tables rather than at the typical long communal ones and offering customers a choice of several dishes at his establishment, La Grande Taverne de Londres.

The French Revolution encouraged the growth of restaurants by abolishing the monopolistic cooks' guilds and by forcing the aristocrats' former chefs to find new, proletarian uses for their talents. In 1789, at the beginning of the Revolution, Paris already had a hundred restaurants; by 1804 there were between five hundred and six hundred, all catering to a public for whom gustatory excess was no excess at all.

Travelers to France excitedly brought the news of these Parisian restaurants to an American public that already enjoyed a spiritual kinship with France ever since that country allied itself with our own Revolution. French culture had already had a considerable effect on our own. Hostesses of the period worked hard to imitate French service, French decor, and French recipes (which were called "made dishes"), especially in Washington society, leading Patrick Henry, with his usual distemper, to complain that Thomas Jefferson, on his return from France, had become so enthralled with Gallic cuisine that "he abjured his native victuals."

This affinity for French cooking convinced a former cook to the archbishop of Bordeaux to open his own French-style eating house in Boston in

THREE MEMBERS of the Delmonico family—*(opposite, top to bottom)* Lorenzo, Charles, and Siro—whose namesake restaurant set the standards for fine dining and who hosted every great personage of the day, including Mark Twain *(above)* on his seventieth birthday, December 5, 1905

1794. His name was Jean Baptiste Gilbert Payplat, and he called his establishment by his nickname, "Jullien's Restarator," where he became known as the "Prince of Soups," echoing the original meaning of the word "restaurant." Even French gastronome Jean Anthelme Brillat-Savarin lent his support by giving him recipes.

But the growth of the concept of freestanding restaurants depended ultimately on a large enough number of people willing to accept it and pay for it. In 1800 the total population of New York, Philadelphia, Boston, Baltimore, and Charleston combined was only 200,000, but soon it began to soar. New York grew fastest—160,000 inhabitants by 1825—largely because it became the principal port and most important stock exchange in the new republic. Oliver Wendell Holmes, Sr., called New York a "tongue that is licking up the cream of commerce and finance of a continent," and by 1825, traffic was so bad that an elevated railway was proposed to relieve the congestion. By 1805 New York had four coffeehouses, four oyster houses, four tea gardens, two victualing houses, and a cookshop, as well as forty-two combination boardinghouses and taverns, and these increased rapidly to absorb the new prosperity. The population was swollen with workers, merchants, and immigrants who needed to be fed.

The food available in these new eating houses—which went in and out of business at an amazing rate of failure—continued to be for the most part coarse, heavy, and of mediocre or poor quality. Game was plentiful, including venison, pigeon, raccoon, and elk. Turtle was considered a delicacy, but obtainable with little difficulty. One of the gimmicks used to attract customers at the Bank Coffee House was to wheel in a whole standing bear, fully cooked and ready to be sliced.

Fresh meat went bad quickly, so many workers slaughtered the pigs that freely roamed the streets consuming refuse, and Broadway was lined with vendors selling roast pork. Others hawked oysters, fast becoming a passion with Americans. Even those of little means could treat themselves to a platter of enormous Long Island Blue Points at one of the popular oyster cellars, identified by their lighted, red-and-white striped balloon signs. As soon as the Erie Canal opened in 1825, canal boats began bringing fresh, live oysters to the very edge of the frontier.

New Yorkers reveled in their bounty and did so with the kind of headlong gusto characteristic of the young nation. Although illustrations of the period depict spotlessly clean, sedate eating houses with gentlemen dining in what seems like a relaxed, calm atmosphere, writers of the period tell a different story of pell-mell service and breakneck consumption of crude food and tankards of strong drink. Eating houses served enormous numbers of people at a pace foreigners considered barbarous. Englishman Basil Hall wrote of his visit in 1827 to a New York eatery called the Plate House:

> We entered a long, narrow, and rather dark room or gallery, fitted up like a coffeehouse, with a row of boxes on each side made just large enough to hold four persons. . . . Along the passage, or avenue, between the rows of boxes, which was not above four feet wide, were stationed sundry little boys, and two waiters, with their jackets off—and a good need, too, as will be seen. . . . There was

ALL CLASSES MINGLED at common eating houses, as depicted in *Harper's Weekly* for September 27, 1873, by illustrator C. S. Reinhart.

an amazing clatter of knives and forks; but not a word audible to us was spoken by any of the guests. The silence, however, on the part of the company, was amply made up for by the rapid vociferation of the attendants, especially of the boys, who were gliding up and down, and across the passage, inclining their heads to one box, then to another, and receiving the whispered wishes of the company, which they straightaway bawled out in a loud voice, to give notice of what fare was wanted. It quite baffled my comprehension to imagine how the people at the upper end of the room, by which a communication was kept up in some magical way with the kitchen, could contrive to distinguish between one order and another. It was still more marvelous that within a few seconds . . . the things we asked for were placed piping hot before us. It was really quite an Arabian Nights' Entertainment, not a sober dinner at a chophouse.

Once the food was set on the table, the customers tore into it with what one observer called "inconceivable rapidity," and another defined as a technique of "gobble, gulp and go."

This was pretty much the standard procedure in most eating houses and taverns. Even in the grand, new, modern hotels like New York's City Hotel (1794), a service philosophy of "come-and-get-it" was accepted as normal, and communal dining rooms serving up fixed meals at set hours were still the rule, although the splendiferous Tremont House in Boston, which opened in 1828, inaugurated "French service" in its two-hundred-seat dining room, where guests might dine at individual tables and use the new four-tined fork. By the 1830s the "American Plan," by which travelers were forced to pay for room *and* board whether they ate the meal or not, was becoming standard in the hotel industry. In lesser hotels and taverns, it was not so much a question of "come-and-get-it" as it was "try-to-eat-it." An English traveler named Thomas Hamilton characterized hotel hosts as "the most rigorous and iron-hearted despots . . . [who feeds his guests] in droves like cattle. He rings a bell, and they come like dogs at their master's whistle. He places before them what he thinks proper, and they swallow it without grumbling."

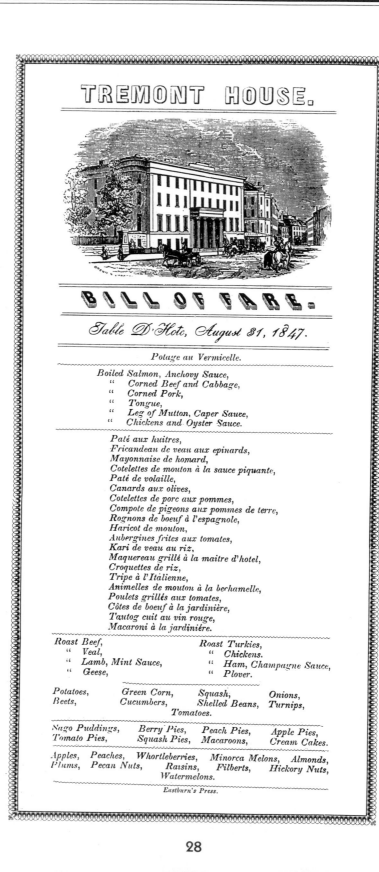

TREMONT HOUSE.

BILL OF FARE.

Table D'Hôte, August 31, 1847.

Potage au Vermicelle.

Boiled Salmon, Anchovy Sauce,
"   Corned Beef and Cabbage,
"   Corned Pork,
"   Tongue,
"   Leg of Mutton, Caper Sauce,
"   Chickens and Oyster Sauce.

Paté aux huîtres,
Fricandeau de veau aux epinards,
Mayonnaise de homard,
Cotelettes de mouton à la sauce piquante,
Paté de volaille,
Canards aux olives,
Cotelettes de porc aux pommes,
Compote de pigeons aux pommes de terre,
Rognons de boeuf à l'espagnole,
Haricot de mouton,
Aubergines frites aux tomates,
Kari de veau au riz,
Maquereau grillé à la maître d'hôtel,
Croquettes de riz,
Tripe à l'Itàlienne,
Animelles de mouton à la bechamelle,
Poulets grillés aux tomates,
Côtes de boeuf à la jardinière,
Tautog cuit au vin rouge,
Macaroni à la jardinière.

Roast Beef,   Roast Turkies,
"   Veal,   "   Chickens.
"   Lamb, Mint Sauce,   "   Ham, Champagne Sauce,
"   Geese,   "   Plover.

Potatoes,	Green Corn,	Squash,	Onions,
Beets,	Cucumbers,	Shelled Beans,	Turnips,
		Tomatoes.	

| Sago Puddings, | Berry Pies, | Peach Pies, | Apple Pies, |
| Tomato Pies, | Squash Pies, | Macaroons, | Cream Cakes. |

Apples,	Peaches,	Whortleberries,	Minorca Melons,	Almonds,
Plums,	Pecan Nuts,	Raisins,	Filberts,	Hickory Nuts,
		Watermelons.		

Eastburn's Press.

It was precisely this kind of thing the Delmonicos labored to change, and in so doing set the mold for what the American restaurant was to become—a spanking-clean, well-appointed dining room serving a choice of meals at convenient hours to the public. By doing so in New York, the Delmonicos established that city as the crucible for fine dining in America.

Fortunately for the Delmonicos, the industrial revolution helped them achieve their goals, and the family took full advantage of new technologies and improvements in sanitation. The filthy Oswego Market became outmoded the moment the new Fulton Market opened in 1821, of which the *Gazette* reported, "It was ornamented with the handsomest exhibition of beef, mutton, pork &c., ever presented to the public [and] several gentlemen from Europe . . . were unanimous that they had never seen anything of the kind to equal it, in all respects." Thus, each morning, Lorenzo Delmonico would be found at the market to purchase the best and the newest foods available, and the family set up a twenty-acre farm in Brooklyn to supply them with the freshest vegetables and fruits.

In 1815 in Troy, New York, a patent was granted on the James cookstove, which replaced the open hearth as the sole cooking medium and soon revolutionized the ways food might be prepared. Ice became readily available in the 1820s, which helped maintain freshness and opened up possibilities for all sorts of new dishes, and especially desserts.

Manners and customs were also being modified by novelties. The introduction of the four-tined fork altered the way Americans ate their food, by switching the fork to the left hand and using it more like a spoon than as a utensil with which to spear peas.

And, in addition to the *amount* of wealth pouring into New York, more and more of it was in hard cash, as more workers earned wages and more merchants dealt in United States–backed currency rather than in trade, as had long been the practice.

NINETEENTH-CENTURY AMERICAN ingenuity was applied to every aspect of food service, including newly popular carbonated water. John Matthews's 1832 "Street Spa" dispensed three "aerated" beverages and eight flavors of syrup.

When the Delmonicos opened their new establishment on South William Street in 1837, their restaurants had already achieved a reputation for being the most fashionable meeting places in New York. No important visitor could avoid coming to the booming metropolis without dining at Delmonico's, and foreigners were as astonished as any backwoodsman by what they saw. When Charles Louis Napoleon (later Napoleon III) visited Delmonico's he was presented with a seven-page *Carte du Restaurant Français,* printed in both French and English and offering nine soups, eight side dishes, fifteen seafood preparations, eleven beef items, twenty kinds of veal, eighteen vegetables, sixteen pastries, thirteen fruit dishes, and sixty-two imported wines, including the finest *premiers crus* of Bordeaux.

One of the most famous dinners ever given at Delmonico's was in 1868 to honor Charles Dickens, whose remarks on American dining on his first visit to the United States in 1842 were highly negative. This time, after being treated to nearly forty sumptuous dishes, Dickens announced that he had been received with "unsurpassable politeness, delicacy, sweet temper, hospitality [and] consideration," then, apologetically added, "This testimony . . . I shall cause to be republished as an appendix to every copy of those

FRENCH RECIPES and native American provender gave Boston's Tremont House, which opened in 1828, its reputation as one of the finest restaurants in the nation. It offered patrons the option of ordering their meals separately on the "European Plan," instead of charging for both room and board on the well-established "American Plan."

two books of mine in which I have referred to America . . . because I regard it as an act of plain justice and honor."

François Delmonico died in 1840; John a year later. In 1845 a second fire burned much of lower Manhattan to the ground, including the Broad Street Delmonico's, but within a year Peter had opened a new hotel and restaurant on Broadway, then retired from the family business. Lorenzo lifted Delmonico's to its greatest glory, taking control of the burgeoning empire and serving for the next thirty years as one of New York's most powerful men. He drew up a blacklist of those he wished to keep out of his restaurants and welcomed those he wanted to attract with unbridled enthusiasm. As competing restaurateurs vied for this same clientele, Lorenzo threw his considerable fortune into play, stealing away the brilliant young chef Charles Ranhofer from the upstart Maison Dorée in 1863. Ranhofer ran Delmonico's kitchens for thirty-four years with an autocratic control over both staff and customers that made it foolhardy for anyone even to suggest an alteration in the way he wished everything to be done—which was to perfection, no matter how large the party or how grand the event.

Everyone came through Delmonico's marble portals (brought from Pompeii)—every President of the United States after 1832 dined there, singer Jenny Lind, Tammany Hall Boss William Tweed, English novelists William Makepeace Thackeray and Charles Dickens, the Prince of Wales, and any other notables who happen through town. In 1855 a new Delmonico's opened at Broadway and Chambers streets opposite City Hall, ensuring a steady stream of politicians. Five years later the most grandiose Delmonico's debuted at Fifth Avenue and Fourteenth Street. It was from a table there that Samuel F. B. Morse sent the first cablegram across the Atlantic. Forty minutes later the answer came back to the wild applause of 350 assembled guests.

Said one observer of the new restaurant's place in New York social history, "To lunch, dine or sup at Delmonico's is the crowning ambition of those who aspire at notoriety, and no better studio for character does the city afford than that expensive resort at almost any hour of the day."

The importance of Delmonico's to New York life at mid-century may best be gauged by the response to Lorenzo's announcement just prior to the Civil War that, owing to some bad oil investments, Delmonico's had to be sold. Wall Streeters sprang to his rescue, lent him money to see him through, and proclaimed, "Delmonico's is an institution and shall not be sold."

As New York expanded northward, Delmonico's followed the crowd uptown. In 1876 they opened at Madison Square. Of this seventh Delmonico's the *New York Tribune* commented, "The great increase of American travel in Europe, and familiarity with the most famous restaurants of the old civilization, have taught our citizens to appreciate their debt to the Delmonico family. . . . There is now no restaurant in Paris or London or Vienna which can compete with our Delmonico's in the excellence and variety of its fare."

Nearly every innovative change made in American fine dining in America was first considered, then effected by the Delmonicos. Throughout the nineteenth century only women of questionable repute accompanied men to dinner at restaurants. Then on April 20, 1868, Delmonico's opened a second-floor dining room to the Sorosis Club, whose membership included many of New York's most prominent women. After a moment of outrage passed (during which some hus-

bands forced their wives to resign from the club), the idea of women dining alone became quite fashionable, and, soon thereafter, respectable. By the 1890s Delmonico's allowed women to have dinner in the evening too, thereby lending a propriety, even a cachet, to a previously suspect activity.

Delmonico's was a touchstone for changing tastes and classic form for nearly a century and a training for generations of chefs for service in the expanding restaurant industry. "There is hardly one hotel in New York today whose chef did not learn his cooking at Delmonico's, every one of them," contended Leopold Rimmer in his *History of Old New York Life and the House of the Delmonicos* (1898). So, when chef Charles Ranhofer left Delmonico's and published a massive, 3,500-recipe cookbook called *The Epicurean* in 1893, he was excoriated by many for giving away his former employer's secrets.

The Delmonicos went on to open other restaurants—they had four running at one time in the 1870s—even after Lorenzo's death in 1881, each one more grandiose than the previous one. The last Delmonico's, opened in 1897 at the corner of Fifth Avenue and Forty-fourth Street, was the grandest of all, with a Palm Garden, Gentlemen's Elizabethan Café, and a Ladies' Restaurant. It thrived until 1923; then, Prohibition shut it down and closed the books on a fairy-tale story that had entertained America for an entire century.

IN 1868 DELMONICO'S gave its stamp of approval to the idea of women dining unaccompanied by men, which prompted the widespread popularity of ladies' luncheons. Not until the 1890s, however, was it considered socially acceptable for women to dine alone in the evening. This photo shows the interior of the Delmonico's on Fifth Avenue and Forty-fourth Street in 1902.

*   *   *

It is important to put into perspective what was happening in food service in New York and other cities before the Civil War, when Delmonico's was still quite a novelty. For most Americans living in cities between 1830 and 1860, eating out was never so lavish as it was at Delmonico's or at some of the opulent new hotels. But tastes and standards of service were changing. Coffeehouses had begun to disappear and many taverns had degenerated into saloons. In New York the oyster cellars were more popular than ever, especially those around Canal Street, which offered a gimmick called the "Canal Street Plan," by which sixpence bought all the oysters a customer could eat. Proprietors rarely lost any money, because, as food historian Meryle Evans has pointed out, "if a customer became too greedy a bad oyster slipped onto the plate soon curbed his appetite!" Some of the oyster cellars, like Thomas Downing's, owned by a black man, were quite luxurious and catered to politicians and businessmen, who relished the unusual variety of his oyster dishes.

Eating houses were improving slowly. Most food was fried (still a predominant cooking technique of fast food in America) and overcooked, but it was cheap and filling. Some New York establishments were called "sixpenny eating houses," where main courses like roast beef, pork, and veal went for sixpence. Englishman Basil Hall delighted in his first New York breakfast: "We had merely asked for some fresh shad . . . but a great steaming juicy beefsteak also made its appearance, flanked by a dish of mutton cutlets [and] a splendid arrangement of snow-white rolls, regiments of hot toast, with oceans of tea and coffee."

Such largesse was to be found in other cities' eating houses, like Boston's Durgin-Park, opened in 1827, next to the Faneuil Hall Market and nearby Boston Harbor. In its family-style, bare-bones atmosphere, with its long communal tables and waiters (now waitresses) barking orders, Durgin-Park has always served the kind of simple New England fare that keeps body and soul together but offers little in the way of either novelty or luxury—chowders, fish cakes, fried shrimp, oysters, lobsters, and plenty of baked beans, corn bread, and Indian pudding make up the menu items today just as they did more than a century and a half ago.

Eating houses were becoming cleaner, too, and more consistent in quality. A not inconsiderable attraction for customers who dined at the new Marston & Sampson eating house in Boston in 1848 was, in the words of one chronicler, the "unprecedented cleanliness of every inch and corner of this little place [which] caused it to be a most popular eating place." Later it would become a hallmark of the Marston Restaurants in that city.

Food service in the South progressed little from the days of the colonial taverns until well into the twentieth century. Except in New Orleans, where, within its melting pot of French, Spanish, Indians, Blacks, Creoles, and other ethnic cultures, good food had long been at the heart of the good life. As Southern food historian John Egerton has written, "Eating in New Orleans was both a private and a public luxury before 1800, and it has remained a consuming interest of residents and visitors alike down through the years."

The steamboats that plied the Mississippi River were themselves outfitted with grand dining salons, and there was no let-up in gastronomic revelry when passengers disembarked in New Orleans. Creole society flourished alongside of and entwined with the lower classes, and the incorporation of French *haute cuisine* and country cooking with the ingredients and food cultures of the bayous and farm people made Louisiana cookery a rich stew that became the first truly American immigrant cuisine. Lusty and well-seasoned, exceptionally rich and satisfying, Creole cooking combined an enormous array of fresh Gulf seafood with the spices of the Caribbean, all served in prodigal portions at the inns and taverns of New Orleans, which by 1840 had become the fourth largest city in the United States.

New Orleans was ripe for good restaurants. The St. Louis and St. Charles hotels, both opened in the 1830s, brought a style to public rooms that rivaled the best in the North. Then, in April 1840, Marseilles-born Antoine Alciatore opened Restaurant Antoine on the Rue St. Louis, later relocated to St. Peter Street, where it stands today. Antoine's, like Delmonico's in New York, set the pattern for restaurants to follow in New Orleans, and, as it grew increasingly larger and more celebrated, it, too, became the obligatory meeting place for every important personage who passed through the city. The chefs created some of the first classic American dishes, like pompano en papillote and oysters Rockfeller (so-called back in 1899 because this dish of oysters, vegetables, and white wine was said to be as rich as John D. Rockefeller, then one of the wealthiest men in the world). A hundred and forty-five years after the restaurant's opening, *Times-Picayune* food critic Gene Bourg would write, "New Orleans without Antoine's would be like Giza without the Great Pyramid."

While no other restaurants on the order of Antoine's opened in New Orleans before the end of the Civil War, a number of more modest eating houses brought a gastronomic vitality to the city that has never abated. In 1856 Guillaume Tujague, a butcher in the French Market, and his wife, Marie, opened Tujague's on Decatur Street, catering to the workingmen of the area. The food was simpler than at Antoine's, but more characteristic of the average New Orleanian's diet—stewed chicken, bread pudding, and a famous boiled brisket of beef with horseradish, which is still on the menu today.

In 1863 a Bavarian woman named Elizabeth Kettering and her husband, Louis Dutrey, took over an old Spanish arsenal in the French Market and turned it into Dutrey's restaurant (where Tujague's now stands). It had sixteen-foot-high ceilings and a massive cypress bar with a mirror said to have been shipped from Paris. After Dutrey died, Elizabeth married the bartender, Hypolite Begué, who gave his name to the restaurant, and Madame Begué became one of the city's most beloved chefs and author of one of the classic Creole cookbooks, *Mme. Begué and Her Recipes,* issued in 1900 and still available in a facsimile edition. She also pioneered the large midmorning breakfast that was the forerunner of the now ubiquitous New Orleans brunch.

But the history of these celebrated few restaurants tells only a small part of the story of eating out in America in the nineteenth century. However influential these new restaurants were on the dining habits of eastern city dwellers, the real innovations in American food service were to come in the West, as bold, young entrepreneurs followed fast in the footsteps of the pioneers, the miners, and the railroad builders, ready to feed them all.

ONE OF THE MOST influential restaurants in America both before and after the Civil War was New Orleans's Antoine's, opened in 1840, which set the same standards for fine dining in the South as Delmonico's did in the North.

A relaxing meal aboard a turn-of-the-century Pullman dining car

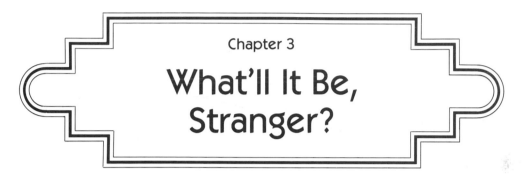

Chapter 3

What'll It Be, Stranger?

Eating Out in the West

THE VISION OF THE AMERICAN WEST was romanticized so early on and with such fervor that the rigors of expansion toward the Mississippi and beyond were themselves regarded as a form of catharsis. "This gradual and continuous progress of the European race toward the Rocky Mountains has the solemnity of a providential event," wrote Alexis de Tocqueville. "It is like a deluge of men rising unabatedly, and driven daily onward by the hand of God." The key words in this romantic conceit are "gradual" and "continuous," for the saga-like treks across the plains and onward to Oregon and California were few in number and very much out of the ordinary. "The cowards never started—and the weak died along the way," snarled one who made it across.

A resettlement fifty miles west of one's previous home was more the norm for families before the Civil War. Others moved on foot or by wagon, in small increments through the valleys of western New York, Ohio, Kentucky, and the other new territories open to any who would tame them, with few romantics among those brave pioneers. And as soon as a settlement sprang up, so did an eating house of some crude kind.

Certainly the notion of coming upon a country inn serving wholesome country food was little more than an idyll in those new territories. When landscape architect Frederick Law Olmsted traveled through the western territories in the 1850s his first meal at a Kentucky inn was nothing more

GENTEEL MANNERS were not requisite at most American hotels of the nineteenth century, but a strong constitution was.

LIFE IN AN AMERICAN HOTEL

than corn bread and bacon, which he consumed "without a thought that for the next six months I should actually see nothing else." Charles Dickens, visiting The Bradley House in Lebanon, Ohio, in 1842, was exasperated to find it a "temperance hotel," a not uncommon establishment in America, of which he wrote, "I never discovered that the scruples of such wincing landlords induced them to preserve any unusually nice balance between the quality of their fare and their scale of charges; on the contrary I rather suspected them of diminishing the one and exalting the other, by way of recompence for the loss of their profit on the sale of spiritous liquors." And when the future king of France, Louis Philippe, showed disdain for a Cincinnati tavernkeeper, the man summarily tossed him out into the gutter as he would an unruly backwoodsman.

One English tourist described the experience of dining at a Nashville inn in 1831 with disgust:

> The door was unlocked, and we all rushed into a long hall, like a squadron . . . charging the enemy, and found tables covered with meat, vegetables, preserved fruit, tea, coffee, and bread, both of maize and wheat, and soft hoe and waffel cakes. Down the company sat in a hurry—noses were blown to one side—cotton handkerchiefs were spread on the knees—cuffs were turned back, and then commenced "the crash of the crockery and the clash of the

steel." No ceremony was used; each man helped himself with his own knife and fork, and reached across his neighbor to secure a fancied morceau. Bones were picked with both hands; knives were drawn through the teeth with the edge of the lips; the scalding mocha and souchong [tea] were poured into saucers to expedite the cooling, the cup deposited in a saucerette on the right. Beefsteaks, apple tart and fish, were seen on the same plate the one moment, and had disappeared the next.

Many Americans reveled in their yahoo-ism when it came to gastronomy and saw it as a mark of their no-nonsense, buckskin spirit. When New Yorker Martin Van Buren occupied the White House, Whig congressman Charles Ogle of Pennsylvania regularly lambasted the President's fastidious manners, proclaiming Van Buren too vain to eat "those old and unfashionable dishes, *'hog and hominy,' 'fried meat and gravy,'* . . . [and] a mug of *'hard cider,'*" preferring instead to dip his "tapering soft lily white fingers" into "Fanny Kemble Green finger cups" after dining on "fricandaus de veau and omelette soufflé." In the 1840 election Van Buren was beaten by Benjamin Harrison, from the western state of Ohio, who campaigned as a "hard-cider man."

By the same token, the existence of a decent restaurant in a western city was cause for great civic pride. Indeed, when Yankeetown (later, Montgomery) and Wetumpka vied to become the capital city of Alabama, legislators were swayed in Yankeetown's favor, when, after a horrible meal at a Wetumpka hotel, they received a splendidly printed, delectable-sounding menu from a hotel in Yankeetown.

The completion of the Erie Canal in 1825 brought a tumultuous emigration westward (Buffalo grew into a city of twenty-five thousand by 1839), and steamboat travel was soon rife up and down the Mississippi. At first the boats' food service was elementary in the extreme, and passengers had no alternative but to subsist on the cheap fodder plopped down in front of them by boatmen for whom cookery was not a required skill. Coarse meats, salt pork, beans, and bad coffee was the diet on those early steamboats, all served with a maximum of dispatch and a minimum of manners.

But before long steamboat companies were competing for the patronage of free-spending plantation owners, industrialists, merchants, and gamblers, and the boats grew opulent with dining rooms far grander than any found in the shore towns of the Mississippi. Good food became a good marketing tool—abundant, fresh food, made with provender picked up along the route, served in splendiferous dining halls that would have been considered extraordinary in any American city of the 1840s. Some boats had combination wine room and gambling dens for the gentlemen, while the ladies took tea in more sedate quarters.

Most of the passengers on these floating palaces were settlers on their way west who had never seen nor eaten anything like the meals steamboat kitchens offered, and they gobbled it all up with their customary disregard for manners. The *J. M. White* served 250 passengers at a time, and they dined sumptuously off Sèvres china, Irish linen napkins, and silver flatware.

The M. S. *Mepham*'s menu offered a choice of fifty meat and fish entrée and scores of cold aspics and elaborate *pièces montées* of ornamental pastrie set the length of the table. There was a distinct pecking order when it cam to food service onboard, which preserved the proprieties of that era's clas system: Cabin passengers dined first, then the ship's officers, white dec passengers, white waiters, black passengers, and, finally, black waiters.

The decline of the steamboat came swiftly, as faster, more modern form of transportation eclipsed it, and although steamboats plied the rivers into the twentieth century, by the time Mark Twain published his *Life on th Mississippi* in 1883 they were already anachronisms. "Mississippi steam boating was born about 1812," he wrote sadly. "At the end of thirty years it had grown to mighty proportions; and in less than thirty more, it wa dead! A strangely short life for so majestic a creature." Yet while the lasted, there was nothing like them, and they introduced Americans to gastronomic splendor few had ever imagined.

Farther to the west food service kept pace with only the most basi needs of those cowboys, trappers, and miners who roamed the prairies an mountains of Arizona, Colorado, Nevada, Utah, and California. In th Southwest a cowboy might find a Mexican cantina where the menu con sisted mainly of tortillas and cheap liquor.

Everyone who passed through the West was amazed by the abundance o native foods, from wild berries to buffaloes, and such delicacies as elk, grizzl bear, and salted buffalo tongues were shipped back East to be served at restau rants like Delmonico's. But cowboys and miners were neither gatherers no hunters and depended for their food on chuckwagons, whose cooks scavenge for anything they could find to put into the common pot, and lizards taste not much different from jackrabbit when cooked for hours with red hot chil peppers. Otherwise it was a diet of salt pork, sourdough biscuits, and plent of beans. Having told young men to "Go West," Horace Greeley also note that what the West really needed was "a thousand good cooks."

Most of the cow towns and miners' camps were grim assemblages o shanties and tents, yet there was usually an eatery of some kind in thei midst. Poet Bayard Taylor wrote of eating at a tent "restaurant" in Sacra mento, where the floor was uncovered, the tables made of planks, and th food bountiful—elk steaks, venison "fattened on mountain acorns," mutton and fat salmon-trout that, "when made into a chowder or stewed in clare ... would have thrown into ecstasies the most inveterate Parisian gour mand." In Hangtown, California (now called Placerville), a miner wh struck it rich entered the Cary House and told the chef to make a dish wit the most expensive ingredients he had. The result was a sauté of eggs bacon, and oysters, thereafter known as Hangtown Fry.

Even the more established towns like San Antonio, Texas, had little t offer the famished traveler. "Chili queens" sold tamales in the streets Writer Stephen Crane, reporting on a visit to that city in 1895, observed "Upon one of the plazas, Mexican vendors with open-air stands sell foo that tastes exactly like pounded fire-brick from hades—chili con carne, tama les, enchiladas, chili verde, frijoles."

Whatever eating facilities greeted travelers in the West, there was al ways a saloon to be found. "The Americans possess a most singular tast

THE ROUGH-AND-TUMBLE saloon of Western myth had its roots in real-life, makeshift miners' camps like this Colorado example with the farcical name "Ocean Grove Dining Room."

THE REDOUBTABLE JUDGE Roy Bean dispensed both justice and whiskey at his Jersey Lily Saloon, named after British actress Lily Langtry, for whom Bean harbored a lifelong infatuation.

for marring the beauty of every place which can boast of any thing like scenery," wrote traveler E. T. Coke in 1833, "by introducing a bar-room into the most romantic and conspicuous spot."

These saloons, in towns with apt names like Gomorrah and Delirium Tremens, became central to the vivid, violent mythology of the Old West, the sets for countless shoot-outs, romances, crooked card games, and swift frontier justice. The fistfights and gun battles depicted in Western novels and movies were based on reality. In one saloon in the little mining town of Tin Cup (population, six thousand, saloons, twenty) back in 1882 more than one hundred shots were fired during a single Saturday night brawl. And the legendary Judge Roy Bean, who held court out of a bar room in Langtry, Texas, would dispense his rulings with the smack of a gavel and the pronouncment, "I'm fining you $45 and a round of drinks for the jury!" The introduction of the "free lunch" was designed to bring men into saloons so that they'd drink more. In the East this bit of lagniappe might consist of Hudson River sturgeon caviar; in the West it was anything to soak up the booze.

But people did settle down, the camps grew into towns, and more savory restaurants followed. Typical of the mining towns that grew up around the discovery of the Comstock Lode in 1859 was Virginia City, Nevada,

among the first structures of which was a tent saloon where flavored raw alcohol was sold in tin cups as "brandy." A year later, with laid-out streets and corner lots selling for a thousand dollars each, Virginia City was home to thirty-eight stores, a theater, eight hotels, twenty-five saloons, and nine restaurants. Wealth poured in, so that by 1872 an enthusiastic reporter for the New York *Daily Tribune* praised its restaurants "as fine as any in the world" and called the saloons "more gorgeous in their appointments than any in San Francisco, Philadelphia or New York," adding that "the number of diamonds displayed in the windows quite overwhelms the senses." And in the frontier town of Leadville, Colorado, the Saddle Rock Restaurant even imported a chef from Delmonico's to please a multi-millionaire customer for whom only the best would do. The promotional value of alluding to the kind of food served in the best Eastern restaurants was immediately evident, and many rather rough-house Western restaurants printed up menus full of French-sounding dishes, sometimes copying verbatim the menu cards of Eastern restaurants. Western novelist Owen Wister told the legend of the traveler who ordered *"vol-au-vent"* at a Texas eatery, only to be told by the proprietor brandishing a six-gun, "Stranger, you'll take hash."

But the mining town that grew fastest was San Francisco. The discovery of gold in 1848 swelled the population of eight hundred people to two thousand five hundred in just two years, including a wave of Chinese immigrants who came to work the railroads, often employed as cooks. The first eating establishments along the Barbary Coast were rough and basic, like The Iron House, built entirely of sheet metal, the Fly Trap (so-called because of the flies that gathered on the meat out back), and Monkey Warner's Cobweb Palace, decorated with stuffed animals and whales' teeth. But those who struck it rich wanted to spend their new money on good food, good wine, and fine surroundings, and restaurateurs responded almost overnight to the demand. Only a year after gold was discovered, the Poule d'Or (later renamed The Poodle Dog) was dispensing French cuisine, and Tadich Grill, opened the same year, was known for its seafood; two years later the Irving House served eighty different dishes at a banquet there. "Grill" restaurants popped up all over town: Jack's, opened in 1864, was known for its elegance and refined menu; and Sam's Grill, opened in 1867, renowned for its steaks and chops. Later on, Coppa's Restaurant on Montgomery Street attracted the literati who chronicled the West, including Jack London, and owner Joe Coppa's walls, tablecloths, napkins, and walls were covered with sketches by the artists who ate and drank there. Said one visitor to San Francisco in 1877, "Whatever other ingredients may enter into merry-making in this capital of the Pacific, it is obvious that love and gluttony come first."

San Francisco may have been an anomaly in a Western landscape nearly bereft of decent places to eat, but things were changing fast. New forms of transportation gave a powerful impetus to cross-country travel. In 1850 a stagecoach left Independence, Missouri, and arrived in Santa Fe two weeks later, making the arduous wagon train crossing obsolete. But the stagecoaches themselves were obsolescent as soon as they went into service, for the railroads were hard on their wheels. By mid-century trains were fast

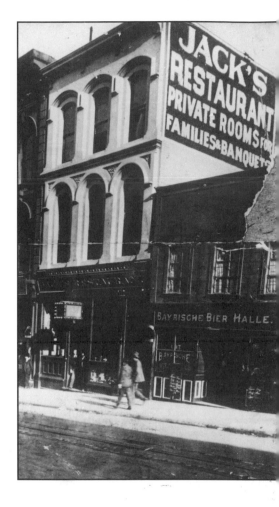

ONE OF SAN FRANCISCO'S earliest grills—Jack's—opened in 1864. Shown here in 1904, Jack's survived the devastating 1906 earthquake and still thrives today on its Sacramento Street site.

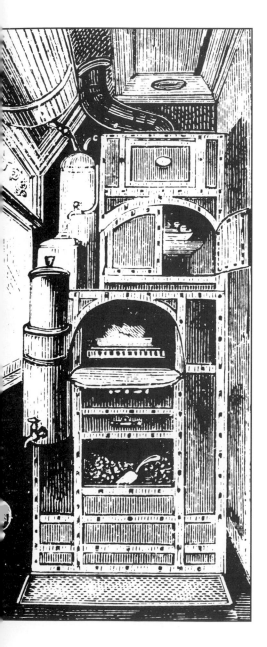

THE UP-TO-DATE, wonderfully compact Pullman dining car kitchen of 1872. Note the extensive exhaust system and the water tank for hot water.

forming a network culminating in the completion of the transcontinental railway in 1869, effectively closing out the romantic era of the pioneer by providing cross-country travel in a mere eight days.

At first railroad cars were not outfitted with any means to feed passengers, so guidebooks of the period counseled passengers to pack their own dry or preserved food to be consumed on trackside picnics when the trains stopped. The first railroad dining cars, put in service on the Philadephia, Wilmington, and Baltimore Railroad in 1863, had only buffets, divided for either stand-up or sit-down eating. They were crude and merely serviceable, the food precooked and simply heated up en route.

Only five years later, however, George Mortimer Pullman of Palmyra, New York, whose sleeping cars had just revolutionized train travel, put into service a true dining car on the Union Pacific Railroad. With an unerring sense of showmanship, he called it the "Delmonico" and outfitted it with fine linens, a complete menu, wines and spirits, and food prepared by a professional chef right onboard. Within five years Pullman cars were rolling examples of sumptuous Victorian luxury, with Turkish carpets, French mirrors, tufted velvet chairs, and the finest inlaid woods. Chinaware had patterns distinctive to the individual railroads—the Pennsylvania used a keystone symbol, the Wabash a blue-and-red flag, the Chesapeake & Ohio a reproduction of Gilbert Stuart's portrait of George Washington.

Chefs picked up fresh produce along the way, and passengers were treated to California figs, Oregon Dungeness crabs, and Idaho trout. By 1877 the Chicago and Northwestern Line advertised a one-dollar menu of thirty-five main courses and twenty-five desserts. So it was not unexpected to dine on *fricandeau de veau à la Richelieu* one night and roast saddle of antelope the next, all accompanied by the finest wines from America and Europe.

But the Pullman cars were mainly in the East, and train passengers headed farther west had meager access to even the most elementary food service. Chugging through the night, the train would arrive at a way-stop and disgorge its human cargo into decrepit eating rooms or saloons serving sub-standard grub. These forlorn railroad towns were called "hell on wheels," often torn down as the railroad workers moved on down the line. In *Food & Drink in America,* Richard J. Hooker described the scene: "The conductor would call out, 'Twenty minutes for breakfast,' but it was hard to enter the restaurant because of the crowd and to get a seat was even more difficult. Those who were successful could buy weak coffee, a piece of tough fried beefsteak, some fried potatoes, and a heavy sour biscuit. Two muscular men were posted at the door to collect payment, and the passengers were often indignant." There was a high probability that prairie dog stew would be on the menu on any given night.

Into this bare-bones landscape came the next great figure in American food service, an Englishman named Frederick Henry Harvey, who would be the first restaurateur to understand and capitalize on the restless mobility of Americans.

Born in London in 1835, Harvey came to the United States when he was fifteen; seven years later in St. Louis he owned his own café. This failed during the Civil War (his partner absconded with the money), so he began working odd jobs, including that of mail clerk on the Hannibal and St. Joseph Railroad, later absorbed by the Chicago, Burlington, & Quincy. By 1875 the enterprising young man had enough capital to open cafés in Wallace, Kansas, and Hugo, Colorado, along the Kansas Pacific Railroad route, while at the same time holding down employment as western freight agent for the Burlington and Quincy, and as newspaper ad salesman for *The Leavenworth Solicitor.* Despite problems maintaining standards at his faraway cafés, Harvey was encouraged in the belief that the real goldmines in the West were to be found in food service. After being turned down by the Burlington-Quincy with the idea of setting up cafés along their route, Harvey approached the owners of the struggling Atchison, Topeka, & Santa Fe Railway, who took a chance on this young Englishman with an eye on the future. Together with railway superintendent Charles F. Morse, Harvey opened a small restaurant above the depot in Topeka, Kansas, in the spring of 1876, agreeing to provide the equipment and expertise, while the railroad delivered his supplies free of charge.

The two men set to work, with an eye not only to improving the quality of food available to travelers but to changing completely the image of the railroad eating room from something dirty, makeshift, and ramshackle to that of an immaculate, beautifully appointed restaurant. As Lesley Poling-Kempes points out in *The Harvey Girls* (1989), "Unsanitary lodging, poor food, and the risk of illness from one or both, made Harvey's time away from home an ordeal and discomfort. He lost two [of his six] children to scarlet fever, . . . and with his own health scarred from typhoid and yellow fever he was not tolerant of what seemed to be a widely accepted standard of inadequate and even sordid traveler's services. . . . Harvey believed he might be the person to introduce good food and clean service to the traveling public."

The little restaurant was a success from the moment it opened its doors, and word of this new enterprise spread rapidly up and down the line, forcing the railroad to open more Harvey restaurants along the route—Newton, Hutchinson, and Dodge City, Kansas, followed, then La Junta and Trinidad, Colorado. Next came Albuquerque, then it was on to California. By 1887 there was a "Harvey House" every hundred miles along the twelve-thousand-mile long Atchison, Topeka, & Santa Fe line, and "Meals by Harvey" became a respected slogan and selling point of the railroad. Elbert Hubbard, America's self-appointed bohemian philosopher, wrote of Harvey's fame in 1901:

> *Where the name Fred Harvey appears, the traveling public expects much. It may be on the desert of Arizona, a hundred miles from water, but if it is a Fred Harvey place, you get filtered spring water, ice, fresh fruit and every other good thing you can find at the same season in the best places in New York City or Chicago. How the miracle occurs, you do not know—it is a Fred Harvey concern—that is enough.*

Menus were varied and made from the best local ingredients. In the 1880s meals cost the not-inexpensive sum of seventy-five cents, for which a customer had a choice of fresh oysters, sea turtle, roast beef, olives, cheeses, pastries, ice cream, and charlotte of peaches with Cognac sauce. A breakfast of steak, eggs, hashed browns, six wheatcakes, apple pie, and coffee cost thirty-five cents. And, since no passenger should have to eat the same meal twice, Harvey offered completely different meals at every stop, with menus changed every four days and recipes rotated from restaurant to restaurant. He used local provender and even ran his own dairy farms to ensure the quality of his milk, cream, eggs, and butter.

The Harvey House restaurants would have been welcome in any town in the United States, for in addition to the fine linen, good silverware, and scrupulously clean dining rooms, they were the first attempts at providing the American public with consistently well-prepared food and dependable service. The Harvey House restaurants established the guidelines for the success of every restaurant chain to follow, including Howard Johnson's, Schrafft's, and McDonald's.

Harvey was manic about his own impossibly high standards, and he expected his customers to respect what he was trying to do. Even in rough western cow towns Harvey demanded men wear jackets in the dining room. His managers quaked when they saw an inspector—often Fred Harvey himself—enter their dining room. As one railroad chronicler put it, Harvey's inspectors looked over a restaurant "as if he suspected a murder had been committed and the search was for clues." If a manager failed inspection he was summarily fired; on occasion, he was tossed out into the street in front of the astonished customers. The customer was *always* right, and the tougher to please, the harder Harvey expected his staff to work to please him. No excuses were accepted, no deviations from the formula allowed.

From his offices in Kansas City and Chicago, Harvey kept tabs on every detail of his operations, including the requirement that they *lose* money. When one of his hotels cut losses from one thousand dollars to five hundred per month by decreasing portion size and other amenities, Harvey fired the manager and replaced him with someone who would go back to losing the original amount. If that seems like a strange way to run a successful business, it was. For it was not by volume that Harvey made his money; it was by being subsidized by the railroad itself, which was happy to lose money on the restaurants if the Harvey name and image attracted more passengers to purchase tickets on the Atchison, Topeka, & Santa Fe. Which is exactly what they did.

And he attracted something else whose presence had a direct effect on the civilizing of the West: women. Starting in 1883 and continuing on into the 1950s, the Harvey organization hired more than one hundred thousand young women to be waitresses in his restaurants at a time when men outnumbered women by more than two to one west of the Mississippi.

The Harvey Girls, as they were called—never "waitresses"—were chosen to represent the most impeccable standards of cleanliness, mannerliness, and hospitality—qualities in severely short supply in the West. Harvey had already established his restaurants as beacons of civilization in a savage environment, and the introduction of the Harvey Girls had a further mellowing effect on the settlements they worked in.

The idea of using women in his restaurants came after Harvey learned of fights breaking out among male waiters in a Raton, New Mexico, Harvey House. Harvey, of course, fired the manager, replacing him with one who suggested women might be far easier to manage and less likely "to get lik-kered up and go on tears."

And so Harvey began advertising in Eastern magazines and newspapers for "young women 18 to 30 years of age, of good character, attractive and intelligent." The response was overwhelming. With the zeal of a missionary, Harvey imbued these young women with the belief that they truly were nurturers, bearers of manners and morals, and a combination of beauty, strength, and femininity that could tame the wilderness. In their black skirts, high "elsie" collars, and starched white aprons, their hair carefully netted atop their heads, forbidden to wear makeup or chew gum, they were icons of Victorian propriety. They were inspected for absolute cleanliness. A spot of gravy or smear of butter forced an immediate change of uniform, which was shipped back to either Newton, Kansas, or Needles, California, for proper laundering.

The women signed a promise not to marry while under the usual year's contract, and, although fraternizing with men was permitted, they lived un-der strict curfews in Harvey-run dormitories. Salaries were approximately $17.50 per month, plus tips—about average for waitresses then—with room, board, laundry, and travel expenses totaling about $210 annually. They worked twelve-hour days, six or seven days a week, and, argued one Harvey Girl, the work was so time-consuming that "we didn't have *time* to do all the bad things people claimed we were doing!"

THE PRIM AND PROPER—some would say grim—demeanor of the Harvey Girl waitresses brought a semblance of civilized standards to the West, at least in those western towns along the Santa Fe Railroad route fortunate enough to have a Fred Harvey depot restaurant.

Harvey did not employ these women to endorse or further the cause of equal rights, but purely as a business decision, based on a codified, conventional, and stringent feminine ideal of high virtue and virginal demeanor. Those who could not, or would not, abide by his standards of behavior and dress were chastened or fired. He did not hire blacks or Hispanics to be Harvey Girls. Yet among those he did hire, Harvey encouraged initiative, promoted some to managerial positions, and ennobled the profession of waitering to the point where the Harvey Girl became a model of gentility, sophistication, and refinement at a time when Americans were becoming more self-reflective and were developing their own identity based on popular idols drawn from the masses.

Fred Harvey died on February 9, 1901, leaving the management of fifteen hotels, forty-seven lunch and dining rooms, and thirty dining cars to family members, who continued in partnership with the Santa Fe Railroad until December 1968. By 1930 the empire had extended into major cities and served up to fifteen million meals each year. By the end of the decade Harvey House restaurants were in decline, owing to faster train service that made frequent stops unnecessary along the route. (The company was offered the first contract for in-flight food service in 1939 but declined, believing there was no future in it.) In many cases, the towns the railroad created had been sustained by the business and the employment opportunities at Harvey House restaurants, and the Depression further ensured their demise.

Seventeen-year-old Mary Lou Lewis Urban worked as a Harvey Girl in Waynoka, Oklahoma, in 1935 and, in an interview with Poling-Kempes, recalled how the town went into decline:

> It hurt Waynoka when the Harvey House closed. We didn't have much anyway; it was a big deal here to go down and see people getting off the train. Everybody went there to eat. . . . And they all wanted to know about the Harvey Girls: what kind of life we had, how we lived. Just ordinary American folks talking with other folks.
>
> After the Harvey House closed, there were still trains coming through here, but the stops weren't for meals. People would just get off and then right back on. Eventually the passenger trains didn't come here at all.

As railroad business dwindled after World War II, so did the Harvey House restaurants and hotels. By the end of the sixties they were all gone. They were mourned out of nostalgia for something that had been so beloved for so long and seemed so much a part of the American landscape. But Fred Harvey's dream thrives in every chain restaurant in the United States.

Clearly, like the Delmonicos, Fred Harvey was at the right spot at the right time to make his fortune. But if the Delmonicos' influence was gradual and limited to the Eastern cities, Harvey's effect was immediate, populist, and spread through the entire country. He had, quite literally, an open field all to himself in which to set the course of culinary history. As the dispensers of what we now call "road food," Fred Harvey restaurants were as imbedded as the gas station in the American landscape and a haven for millions of travelers who were headed West.

A CLASSIC CONFRONTATION of good girl versus bad girl in the Old West was dramatically depicted in MGM's 1946 film *The Harvey Girls,* in which Harvey Girl Judy Garland (*in print dress*) battles with dancehall hostesses led by Angela Lansbury (*far left*).

Millionaire C.K.G. Billings's horseback dinner at Louis Sherry's, 1903

Chapter 4

The Age of Gluttony

Conspicuous Consumption in the Late Nineteenth Century

AMERICANS LIKE NOTHING BETTER than to be criticized for their excesses—as long as the excesses last. And for many Americans in the post–Civil War period, the excesses went on and on. "The American does not drink at meals as a sensible man should," observed Rudyard Kipling. "Indeed, he has no meals. He stuffs for ten minutes thrice a day."

The phrase "conspicuous consumption" was coined by Norwegian immigrant Thorstein Veblen in his 1899 treatise, *The Theory of the Leisure Class,* to describe this new class of Americans for whom the acquisition of more goods was an affirmation of both their social position and their self-esteem, no matter how much wealth was wasted in ways that did "not serve human life or human well-being on the whole." Earlier, Mark Twain and C. D. Warner had used another, more telling term for the era as the title for their 1873 novel, *The Gilded Age.*

After the Civil War, America became a very large, very rich country, despite all that speculators, scalawags, carpetbaggers, crooked politicians, and rank greed could do to stunt its growth in a series of scandals, recessions, and stock market crashes. Industry promised a brave new world. Expansionism was destiny. Technology shrank time: The transcontinental railroad brought the West to the doorstep of the East. The telegraph made instantaneous international communication possible. And the McCormick reaper produced a bushel of corn in less than fifteen minutes, where once it took three hours.

Proud cities mounted magnificent World's Fairs to showcase Yankee ingenuity. At the Philadelphia Exposition of 1876 an icebox with ammonia as a refrigerant was displayed; the 1884 World's Industrial and Cotton Centennial Exposition in New Orleans blazed with thousands of electric lights and had the largest number of elevators in the world; the Ferris wheel was the big attraction in Chicago's 1893 World Columbian Exposition; and St. Louis's 1904 Louisiana Purchase Exposition featured fifty-three restaurants, including a 2,500-seat Italian Café, and novelties like iced tea and ice cream cones.

Most people had money to spend and leisure time in which to spend it, even though in 1890 a mere 1 percent of the population possessed more than half the nation's wealth, and poverty was as blatant in the industrialized North as in the war-scarred rural South. This was due, however, more to an inequitable distribution of goods and services than to an excess of mouths to feed. In fact, the United States desperately needed a larger population to work the factories, lay the railroads, erect the buildings, dig the sewers, plow the fields, and slaughter the cattle, which would create more wealth, more jobs, and a more efficient way of distributing them.

And grow the population did: In 1880 Americans numbered fifty million; by 1890, sixty-three million; a decade later, seventy-six million, and ten years after that, ninety-two million, most of them new immigrants from Europe and Asia. By 1900 urban dwellers made up 30 percent of the population, doubled since the end of the Civil War. Despite the poverty, social injustice, and corruption that plagued the new Union, it was nevertheless a time of upward mobility for most Americans, an era when anything seemed possible, an age when wealth proved God's favor. The new popular heroes were educated, moral, self-made men like William Dean Howells's Silas Lapham and Horatio Alger, Jr.'s Ragged Dick.

But wealth created its own problems for those who had it, because freedom from want too often boiled over into profligacy and excess among those who had too much. Nowhere was this more evident than in the restaurants of the Gilded Age, rococo palaces that catered to this new leisure class in extravagant dining rooms where conspicuous consumption was not only accepted but encouraged and marveled at.

The most conspicuous consumer of them all was financier James Buchanan Brady, known as "Diamond Jim," who personified the gluttony of the age both in his physiognomy and in his carefully cultivated public image. With actress Lillian Russell by his side, Brady would march through twelve-course dinners like Sherman through Georgia, consuming everything set before him, then calling for more. He'd begin his day with a hefty breakfast of eggs, breads, muffins, grits, pancakes, steaks, chops, fried potatoes, and pitchers of orange juice. He'd stave off mid-morning hunger by downing two or three dozen clams or oysters, then repair to Delmonico's or Rector's for a lunch that consisted of more oysters and clams, lobsters, crabs, a joint of beef, pie, and more orange juice. (Brady was, for all his excesses, a teetotaler who never touched wine or spirits; neither did he smoke.)

An afternoon snack of more seafood would be followed by a nap, so that he might be in good shape for the main event of the evening—dinner.

Settling his girth four inches from the dinner table, he'd stop eating when his stomach touched the rim. Brady would stuff a napkin into one of his multiple chins and begin the onslaught, as people watched in amazement. According to restaurateur George Rector, Brady would consume three dozen oysters (the largest Lynnhavens were saved for him), a dozen crabs, six or seven lobsters, terrapin soup, a steak, coffee, a tray full of pastries ("He selected his cakes carefully," said Rector, "in handfuls."), and two pounds of bonbons. This was replenished with another pound or two on his way to the theater, basing his choice of candy on what play he was seeing: "Shaw was more tolerable with bonbons," he remarked, "and Ibsen was best with *glacé* fruit." By curtain's drop, Brady's stomach was growling again, so he repaired for a late-night supper of a few game birds and more orange juice. And so to bed.

"Diamond Jim's stomach started at his neck and swelled out in majestic proportions," observed Rector, "gaining power and curve as it proceeded southwards." In fact, when Brady died, at the age of fifty-six, his stomach was said to be six times larger than the ordinary man's. Incredibly, Lillian Russell was said to keep up with her Pantagruelian paramour morsel for morsel, maintaining her famous hourglass figure by continual tugs on her corset.

Diamond Jim reveled in his role as champion gourmand, and, in his good-natured way, came to symbolize all that was prodigal and fabulous about the late nineteenth century. He had risen from the lower classes, worked as a bellboy on the New York Central Railroad, and made a fortune selling railroad supplies, amassing a collection of jewelry worth a million dollars. Brady knew how to have a good time and put on a good show. He once threw a party on the roof of the Hoffman House at which he and his guests consumed five hundred bottles of Champagne and enormous quantities of food in under five hours, at a cost of $100,000, which, to be fair, included $60,000 worth of diamond jewelry as party gifts for his guests. "Being a sucker is fun," said Brady, "if you can afford it."

If Brady held claim to being the greatest trencherman of them all, there were plenty of competitors who packed the grand dining rooms of New York like Delmonico's, Rector's, Maison Dorée, Louis Sherry's, Lüchow's, and the Waldorf-Astoria each night to consume prodigious amounts of food on a regular basis. In 1848 the *New York Weekly Herald* pronounced Delmonico's the "only complete specimen in the United States" of an "expensive and aristocratic restaurant." But by the turn of the century *The New York Times* wrote of the restaurants on Fifth Avenue, "One has now just as one had in the old days in Paris, as they say in French, 'an embarrassment of riches' from which to choose." Decked out in the finest oak, mahogany, and Italian marble, hung with velvet draperies, and festooned with ferns and potted palms, New York restaurants tried to outdo each other in the amount of Victorian clutter they could pack into their mammoth dining rooms.

Louis Sherry's, which opened in 1882 at Fifth Avenue and Forty-fourth Street, was the most direct competitor of Delmonico's and was known especially for its superb cuisine. But it was not above mounting its own fantasy evenings, as when the New York Riding Club held its famous Horse Dinner in 1903 on the fourth-floor ballroom. Horses were brought up in freight elevators, harnessed to a large dining table, and fed oats, while in their saddles guests consumed a fourteen-course dinner and sipped champagne out of bottles set in saddlebags. The tab for the event was fifty thousand dollars. Louis Sherry's specialized in bachelor dinners and was the scene of a notorious banquet held by playboy Herbert Barnum Seely, featuring the gyrations of the scandalous belly dancer Little Egypt (some reports said she'd danced naked).

Sherry, who was born in Saint Albans, Vermont, shamelessly catered to his rich clientele. Once the kitchen was asked to make up a special cake embedded with gold bracelets for shipment to an upstate banquet. As the time drew short, the cake and two chefs boarded a Pullman car specially chartered so that the final decorations could be affixed as the train made its way north. "Never disappoint a patron" was Sherry's motto. "Get a special train, a special boat—anything—but never disappoint a patron." For the next decade Delmonico's and Louis Sherry's would wage, in the words of the *Illustrated American,* "a fight to the death" for preeminence in the fast-moving New York social world.

New York, the population of which topped two million by 1880, led the way and set the fashions for the rest of the country, leading Wall Street banker Henry Clews to proclaim, "New York is the immense domain of the American Republic, a natural stage . . . for the great drama of civilization on this Continent." One of the most popular pastimes of the era was the "political chowder," held in July and August to gain voter support for local candidates. The biggest ever given was by Big Tim Sullivan of the Bowery, who led a parade of seven thousand potential voters to the docks where they boarded the steamer *Grand Republic,* then repaired to Donnelly's Pavilion on College Point, Long Island, for a breakfast of clam fritters, ham and eggs, fried potatoes, and all the trimmings. This was followed by games, beer bouts, and a lavish dinner of chowder, roast beef, lamb, and ice cream.

The 1890s was the great era of these dining palaces. Broadway rang with extravagant new restaurants—Churchill's, Murray's Roman Gardens, Shanley's, The Knickerbocker Grill, Maxim's, and others that catered to the theater crowd. When things got rowdy at Jack Dunstan's chophouse, the waiters formed their famous "flying-wedge" to drive out unruly customers.

Others went the route of elegance. The Café Martin, opened in 1899 on Twenty-sixth Street and Fifth Avenue, introduced banquettes to the restaurant dining scene. When the Waldorf-Astoria opened in 1893, its Palm Garden was lined with mirrors that allowed diners to ogle each other throughout the evening, while its haughty maître d', Oscar Tschirky (who had risen from position of busboy at the Hoffman House to Diamond Jim's favorite waiter at Delmonico's), coddled his most eminent customers while keeping others at bay behind a velvet rope. "Oscar of the Waldorf," as he was known, became the model of the imperious maître d', who represented everything snobbish and undemocratic about deluxe restaurants to the average American. In addition to simply seating his patrons, he delighted in putting them in their place. He would grovel when he had to in order to ensure his most celebrated customers' favor and gratuities, but he also set

standards for dining room service that affected every deluxe establishment to follow. Oscar was not a chef, though he is given credit for creating the Waldorf Salad, and he demanded his captains and waiters be impeccable at carving roasts and flaming desserts at tableside. He also inaugurated the idea of the electrical buzzer by which he gave commands to his service staff as to when dishes would be served. On a given night the Waldorf might serve three hundred partridges and a thousand portions of lobster newburg.

A far more convivial restaurateur of that era was George Rector, whose namesake restaurant in New York was known for its ostentation, showmanship, and not a little scandalous behavior—all marketing gimmicks he'd learned from his father, Charles, who in 1884 had opened the first restaurant in Chicago to serve lobsters and once brought in a three-hundred-pound turtle on whose shell customers carved their initials. Charles's second restaurant, the Café Marine at the Columbia Exposition, became notorious as the site where a woman first dared to smoke a cigarette in public.

The younger Rector opened his own, namesake restaurant on September 23, 1899, at the intersection of New York's Fifth Avenue and Broadway, immediately drawing crowds who wanted to take a spin in the city's first

THE ARCHETYPE OF the imperious maître d', Oscar Tschirky of the Waldorf (here photographed in 1918) was an arbiter of New York society for more than four decades.

revolving door. Once through it, customers were greeted with a splendor to surpass anything at Delmonico's. The decor was Louis XIV, the tables covered with Irish linen, and much of the food was imported from Europe—*foie gras* from Strasbourg, truffles from the Périgord, beluga caviar from the Caspian Sea, peaches from Algeria, quail from Egypt, and strawberries from Europe that costs fifty cents apiece. One employee was paid the princely sum of fifty dollars a week just to oversee Rector's humidors and was each year sent to Cuba to choose a supply of the finest cigars.

George Rector prided himself on providing the best at the most reasonable price and refused to serve common dishes like ham and eggs, Welsh rabbit, or sandwiches (although he admitted to substituting halibut for crab, rabbit for terrapin, and lamb for venison on occasion). His clientele was finicky, demanding, and famous—everyone dined there, including writers O. Henry and Stephen Crane, actress Sarah Bernhardt, and, of course, singer Lillian Russell and Diamond Jim Brady, who Rector called "my twenty-five best customers." It was very much a businessman's restaurant, and, he said, many fortunes were won and lost over dinner at Rector's.

His was also the first restaurant to introduce dancing, an activity explicitly designed to appeal to those gentlemen who sought to show off their new mistresses or showgirls, and the *New York Tribune* took note of a new species in the city—the "man about town"—who stayed up past 1:00 A.M. carousing at the new restaurants and cafés, and calling for a "hot bird and a cold bottle," a not-very-subtle double entendre of the period.

Another innovation of the *fin de siècle* was the open-air restaurant, which in the hot, stifling New York summers made good business sense. The first was the Café Boulevard, which opened about 1880, soon to be followed by the Casino in the Park, which was considered "a trifle bohemian." Possibly the earliest garden restaurant set atop a roof was the United States Hotel, followed by the Hoffman House and the St. Regis, which was the first to serve full meals. The idea of the roof garden caught the public fancy, so that before long hotels were competing to come up with bigger, more elegant examples: The Waldorf-Astoria spent fifty thousand dollars a year on flowers for its rooftop garden, and the Hotel Astor could seat a thousand people amid ivy pergolas, honeysuckle, and cascades of water. "The reason for the roof garden's sudden rise in popularity is not far to seek," observed a writer for *Town & Country* magazine in September 1906. "Metropolitan society, after holding aloof for years, has suddenly set its seal of approval upon these high perched, airy Edens provided by many well-known hotels and clubs, and where society leads an extensive following is assured." Ironically, three months earlier, on June 25, millionaire Harry K. Thaw followed society architect Stanford White to the Madison Square Garden Roof Theater (which he'd designed) and, during a performance of a revue called *Mamzelle Champagne,* pumped three bullets into White's head for allegedly having an illicit affair with Thaw's beautiful young wife, Evelyn Nesbit. Yet in 1907 New York's Hoffman House refused service to the unescorted Mrs. Harriet S. Blatch, who filed suit against the hotel and lost, the courts determining that the hotel was within its rights to maintain its own form of propriety.

Somewhat below the roof gardens and a few rungs down the social

ladder were the gigantic urban oyster houses and lobster palaces, evolved from the oyster cellars of the early nineteenth century into quite lavish institutions of their own. Every major city had one by the end of the century, owing to advances in refrigeration and cold storage that allowed seafood to be shipped anywhere in the country. Oysters from the East Coast would be shelled, packed in milk containers, and shipped westward, where restaurateurs would place them back on the half shell. In fact, Americans had become oyster mad. Annual consumption was 660 oysters per person, against 120 in the United Kingdom and only 26 in France. And the bigger the better: A British visitor to New York in the 1880s wrote of how he consumed a plateful of Cow Bay oysters with shells 10½ inches long.

The oyster house had far outgrown its original simple design and function, however. "The real Oyster House is a specialized restaurant," explained the author of an 1897 souvenir booklet about Rector's Oyster House in Chicago, "the specialties of which are, in general, sea-food, game, salads, certain delicatessen, and the choicest wines, brandies and ales. In greater detail it is a place where, in their season, the finest and freshest oysters of

THE ONCE-HUMBLE OYSTER BAR was brought to grandiose proportions with the opening in 1913 of the Grand Central Oyster Bar on the lower level of New York's Grand Central Terminal.

THE OPULENCE OF THE GILDED Age extended even to soda fountains, like this 1872 example called "The Snow Queen," which had a polished marble exterior and silver-plated fittings. It sold for $4,250 and could dispense $80,000 worth of confections in a single year.

a dozen varieties are to be found; where lobsters, and every variety of edible sea-food, from the hard-shell crab or the delicate soft-shell to the fragile, almost transparent shrimp are daily served."

The apotheosis of the oyster house was New York's grandiose Grand Central Oyster Bar & Restaurant set underground in Grand Central Terminal. With its graceful arched ceilings done in a herringbone pattern of tiles by Rafael Guastavino (who later did the tilework at Ellis Island), the Oyster Bar opened in 1913, serving more than a dozen species of the bivalves each day.

Fine restaurants were springing up throughout the United States, so that even George Rector acknowledged the comparison of his own restaurant with places like The Parker House in Boston, the Planters in St. Louis, the Brown Palace in Denver, the St. Francis in San Francisco, the Palmer House in Chicago, Harvey's in Washington, D.C., Green's in Philadelphia, the Seelbach in Louisville, and the Sinton in Cincinnati.

Chicago's Palmer House set the standards for deluxe dining in the Midwest when it opened in 1871, known especially for the variety of its game dishes. Florida's Hotel Miami, opened in 1896, featured local fresh seafood. The Windsor in Denver—the first Western restaurant to cater to unescorted women—specialized in the foods of the prairie: buffalo, antelope, venison, and bear's paw *"en gelée,"* while the chefs at The Antlers in Colorado Springs boasted they could prepare any dish a customer might ask for on short notice. San Francisco's The Palace (1875) was particularly renowned for its inventive kitchen, and dishes like oysters Kirkpatrick were as famous in their day as Antoine's oysters à la Rockefeller.

The popularity of the "European Plan" (which originated in France), by which guests could choose from à la carte menus rather than be forced to eat set meals at set times on the American Plan, was growing rapidly by the 1870s. The European Plan was first adopted at New York's Tammany Hall Hotel in the 1830s, and explained to customers at the Washington Hall Hotel in 1840 with the announcement, "The restaurant will remain open from 7 o'clock in the morning till 11 o'clock at night, during which time the guest can always be accommodated from the daily bill of fare, and charged accordingly. This plan of hotelkeeping leaves the guests at liberty to dine when and where they please." Although the European Plan was more amenable for the guest and encouraged creativity among chefs, some Americans pronounced it undemocratic and unacceptably aristocratic.

While American restaurants may have copied European models in both design and menus, the preparations were always based on indigenous American provender, and chefs proudly listed the provenance of his products, like Little Neck clams, California salmon, and Bermuda onions. Most chefs followed the French repertoire established by Delmonico's, and the arrival of the great French classicist himself, Auguste Escoffier, for the opening of New York's Ritz-Carlton Hotel in 1910 help solidify the hotel dining room tradition in the United States for decades to come. But just as many new dishes were fast becoming *American* classics—even if written up in franglais on the menus. Thus, a diner at a deluxe restaurant might choose from a menu of simply prepared chops and seafood, with Saratoga potatoes, clam chowder, and Catawba white wines as well as delicacies like "salmis of prairie chicken chasseur," "shad maître d'hôtel," "terrapin à la Baltimore," and "lobster à la Newburg" (a Delmonico's creation named after a patron named Ben Wenberg but changed to "Newburg" after he had a squabble with the management). In the main the food was based on what was locally available and cooked rather simply. The menus of the period show a new regard for vegetables and salads and a voracious appetite for all sorts of French pastries, ice creams, and sherbets.

All of this would strongly suggest that generally the food at these establishments was a cuisine of high caliber, but it is, from a distance of a hundred years later, difficult to judge. That the meals were lavish and generously proportioned is evident from reading menus of the period, but just how well the food was cooked is another matter entirely. At the very least it must have resembled the kind of overly elaborate cooking and presentation done to this day in casino hotels in Las Vegas and Atlantic City, but, as in those two cities, the sophistication level of free-spending customers might well have favored ostentation over delicacy of taste.

One can say with confidence that technology had radically increased the odds of getting a good meal and the food products available were a vast improvement over what was available before the Civil War. Indeed, the cast-iron stove virtually made possible the restaurant as we know it. When clean water was brought to New York via the new forty-five-mile-long Croton Aqueduct in 1842, it was considered a true miracle of the age. Refrigeration made the work of cooks easier than ever before, allowing for the storage of foods that once would have gone bad overnight, and the availability of year-round ice from New England had ceased to be a novelty by the 1850s.

Steel-rolled flour, which was of a more consistent texture than mill-ground flour, made bread and pastry-making more consistent and artful than ever before, and hermetically sealed canned foods could be brought in from all over the world, thereby increasing the larder of the average cook who once had to depend entirely upon local, seasonally available ingredients.

Dairy products were suspect until late in the century, although New York was getting fresh milk shipped in by railroad from upstate Orange County by 1843. Condensed milk was invented by Gail Borden in 1856, but it was not until the 1890s that pasteurization was widely adopted in the United States, and by 1908 only 25 percent of New York's and 33 percent of Boston's milk was being pasteurized.

REFRIGERATION TECHNOLOGY dramatically improved the prospects for sanitary, fresh foods, as shown in this 1895 solid oak lunch cooler.

Corned and salted pork was still popular, but there was an increasing appetite for beef, which had became readily available after the Civil War. Yet, despite advances in cold storage, unsanitary conditions prevailed in the stockyards, as Upton Sinclair showed in his exposé novel *The Jungle* (1906), which led to the passage of the Pure Food and Drug Law that same year.

Of game, however, there was great abundance and little to fear. It is amazing, now, to read nineteenth-century menus featuring dozens of game dishes on an everyday basis. An 1889 menu for the Grand Pacific Hotel in Chicago lists "turkey, mountain sheep, antelope, venison, pheasant, goose, blue grouse, mallard duck, red head duck, quail, prairie chickens, spotted grouse, jack rabbit, black tail deer, plover, canvasback, black bear, wood duck, squirrel, opossum, ruffled grouse, coon, elk, partridge, brandt, cinnamon bear, widgeon, teal, snipe, marsh birds, blackbirds, reed birds, partridge, and rice birds." A San Francisco restaurant named The States even imported frozen Alaskan reindeer.

Seafood was not quite so readily available, but in those cities proximate to teeming lakes and rivers, the variety was remarkable. The Hotel Nicollet Café in Minneapolis offered patrons mackerel, crappies, striped bass, black bass, white fish, shad, wall-eyed pike, blue fish, finnan haddie, salmon, sardines, cod, fish cakes, and brook trout.

Chefs, though restricted by convention and popular taste, felt free to utilize what was available in new and creative ways. Thus, in 1899 the Florentine Hotel in Huntington, West Virginia, served its guests soft-shell crabs à la tartare and suckling pig with candied yams, pineapple fritters, and rum sauce. San Francisco's Bohemian Club was known for its Golden Gate Crab Casserole, and in 1900 chef Victor Hirtzler of that city's St. Francis Hotel concocted a dish of pheasant stuffed with truffles and woodcocks with a champagne, Cognac, and Madeira sauce.

The luxury that was commonplace in such restaurants may have appealed to a greater number of Americans in the late nineteenth century than ever before, but obviously most people could never afford to dine in so Lucullan a fashion even once in their lives. The rising middle class in America, fearful of the barely contained rage of the lower class and envious of the high-living amorality of the upper class, had been rapidly drifting into a conservatism charged with a crusading impulse to stamp out wickedness and excess.

The Temperance Movement grew in strength in the late nineteenth century, even as Americans' consumption of hard spirits dropped significantly after the Civil War (although beer consumption tripled between the 1860s and the 1890s). The Women's Christian Temperance Union, founded in Cleveland in 1874, and the Anti-Saloon league, founded in Washington, D.C., in 1893, grew more and more vocal and popular with middle-class Americans, and their wrath was turned not only on the woe-begone workingman's saloon but on the deluxe restaurants where drinking was nearly as rampant.

Hotels and restaurants were regarded by many as proximate occasions of sin, and scandalous incidents such as Stanford White's murder did not help matters. Wealthy society women, by then addicted to the freedom of dining out, had begun to enjoy afternoon tea as the epitome of refined propriety. But during World War I the fashionable new *thé dansant,* or tea dance, was soon turning into what one wag of the period called "booze dansants," at which cocktails were served in teacups.

The exquisitely coiffed Gibson Girl was fast giving way to the flapper, but as young American boys died in the trenches of France, the lavish show of wealth and disregard for public morals seemed ill advised. In New York the competition for customers at Louis Sherry's, Rector's, the Waldorf-Astoria, and Delmonico's was no longer cause for bigger parties and more lavish dinners, but rather for reconsideration of the folly of the whole idea. During World War I anti-German feelings ran high against restaurants like Lüchow's on Fourteenth Street, and, in any case, New York society was moving uptown. In 1916 the oldest Delmonico's, which had opened in 1836, closed for lack of business. Louis Sherry's followed within three years.

The reputation of Rector's—never unassailable in the first place—was seriously and openly besmirched by the popularity of a racy French farce called, in its English version by Paul Potter, *The Girl from Rector's;* at first the publicity caused a profitable splash for the restaurant, but, ultimately, moral outrage took its toll, and business suffered. It was not much helped by a 1907 *Ziegfeld Follies* song entitled "If a Table at Rector's Could Talk." Entertainer George M. Cohan tried to bring business back to the failing institution, but, after an initial closing, the restaurant reopened as a shadow of its former self, jammed with tourists eating food even George Rector admitted was not at its previous high standards.

But more than any other factor, the onset of Prohibition in 1919 sealed the fates of the restaurants of the Gilded Age. Fine dining and lavish entertaining was powered by wine and liquor, and such license was no longer legal nor publicly tolerated. The parties went on, but they were in private homes or in the new, illegal "speakeasies." On New Year's Day, 1919, two weeks before the Eighteenth Amendment was ratified, Rector's closed its doors for the last time, its elegy penned in a ditty by Clarence Harvey:

> And we motored down to Rector's,
> Where all was gay and bright;
> And by the way, dear empress,
> Who took you home that night?

Delmonico's, no longer under the family's management, held on until May 21, 1923, when the last of the chain, at Forty-fourth Street and Fifth Avenue, served its last meal.

Perhaps another piece of doggerel, by a Delmonico's habitué named Arthur Nies, puts things in better perspective at a time when the common man, rather than the insatiable glutton, would determine the direction American dining would take:

> No more the grape with fire divine
> Shall light the torch of pleasure gay,
> And where the gourmand paused to dine,
> Hot dog and fudge shops have their day.

An Italian-American cook prepares the day's antipasto orders.

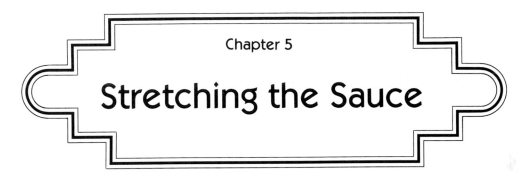

Chapter 5

Stretching the Sauce

Immigrants Enrich the Broth

SHOULD THE SMITHSONIAN INSTITUTION ever wish to display an example of a prototypical Italian-American restaurant they could do no better than to move Mario's, lock, stock, and Barolo, from its situation on Arthur Avenue in the Bronx, New York, to the Institution's halls in Washington, D.C. In every detail—from the thickly varnished mural of Mount Vesuvius (done by an uncle sixty years ago), the diminutive reproduction of Michelangelo's "David," the photos of the owners' grandchildren over the entrance, and the mustachioed, tuxedoed waiters to the thin-crusted pizzas, steaming pots of mussels, broccoli di rape with sausage, garlic, and white beans, crisp-shelled cannolis bursting with ricotta cheese and candied fruit, and ink-black espresso with lemon rind and a shot of Sambuca—Mario's evokes every American's image of what an Italian-American restaurant should look, taste, and smell like.

Mario Migliucci's food is very good, and the portions are hearty and not very expensive. Mrs. Migliucci still makes her peppered carrots for customers to nibble on with bread, and Mario, with his son Joseph, still makes pizzas and oversees the dining room with the fervor of someone who's just had a grand opening.

Yet Mario's opened in 1919, and since then has entertained generations of New York Yankees, movie stars, politicians, and other celebrities in quarters considerably expanded since the days when it was nothing more than a neighborhood pizzeria. Italians who moved away from the neighbor-

FOOD SERVICE IN steerage class was of distressingly poor quality, but European immigrants brought with them their own varied food culture, which they adapted to the American larder they found upon landing in the New World.

hood—one of the safest in New York City, although surrounded by urban blight—still drive an hour or more from New Jersey or Connecticut to eat at Mario's, not just because the food is so good but because the place buzzes with a timelessness unreproducible outside of this four-block market street, where singsong southern Italian dialects blend with brisk Bronx English.

On second thought, without reproducing Arthur Avenue itself, the Smithsonian could never really capture the essence of Mario's, or, for that matter, of the Italian-American restaurant as Americans have come to know it. Superficially Mario's thrives on a stereotype Americans have long cherished—the triumph of an immigrant culture comfortably fitted to the idea of the high-spirited, hard-working Italian—the spaghetti benders, pizza makers, garlic eaters. Indeed, in lunch counter patois garlic has long been called "Italian perfume" and "Bronx vanilla," while in the South some people still order a plate of lettuce, olives, oregano, capers, anchovies, garlic, and oil by saying, "Gimme a Wop salad."

Despite the picturesque, sentimentalized ethnic imagery, restaurants like Mario's are nevertheless part of an immigrant food culture grown so successful that American supermarkets now stock more Italian-American food items than any other ethnic kind. And Italian-American restaurants by far eclipse all Chinese, Mexican, French, and Spanish eateries in number. Truly, as dramatist Neil Simon has observed, "There are two laws in the Universe: The Law of Gravity and Everybody Likes Italian Food."

Italian food, like the Italians themselves, was assimilated into American culture slowly, simmering in the Melting Pot, absorbing other cultures as it

was dispersed and dispensed over decades from the days when Americans regarded "going to a spaghetti joint" as something of an adventure in exotica. Yet the Italian immigrants who came to this country after the American Civil War would never have heard of most of the dishes Americans think of as standard Italian restaurant fare: menu items like fettuccine Alfredo, clams Posillipo, Caesar salad, pasta primavera, shrimp scampi, veal parmigiana, chicken Tetrazzini, even spaghetti and meatballs were unknown to Italian immigrants by such names and were, instead, dishes concocted for American customers through adaption, corruption, and sometimes sheer self-promotion. They were certainly not the dishes first-generation Italians ate when they arrived on these shores. For one thing, most of these impoverished immigrants had never set foot in a restaurant back in the Old Country.

This was true largely of all the immigrants who came to America after the Civil War up through the 1920s. They did not come seeking "streets of gold" but streets of markets overflowing with the kinds of foods they had scraped the earth to get at back in the Old Country. This was as much the case with the Italians as it was with the Germans, the Jews, the Irish, and Chinese, the Norwegians, the Finns, the Poles, the Greeks, and the Russians who emigrated to America on nearly empty stomachs, hoping that the tales of bounty were true and that there was work and freedom to build new lives. Many were disillusioned or crushed underfoot by prejudice and violence, and a large percentage returned home, after either having made their fortune in America or having failed to be assimilated into the culture. Most stayed on.

THE READING TERMINAL MARKET, opened in 1893 in Philadelphia's Reading Terminal, has long been a showcase for an enormous variety of immigrant foods.

Alla Carte

Spaghetti and Maccheroni

Order Spaghetti or Maccheroni to Your Taste . . .
("Al Denti" is Hard — "Expresso" is Medium)

Fettuccine (Egg Noodles), Melted Butter	1.00
with Meat or Marinara Sauce	1.25
Manicotti alla Romana with Ricotta	1.25
Stuffed Cannelloni with Meat	1.50
Ravioli (Cheese)	1.25
Ravioli (Meat)	1.00
Pasta col Pesto, Genovese Style (Green Sauce)	1.50
Gnocchi	1.25
Potato Dumpling with Meat Sauce	
Lasagna al Forno	1.50
Wide Egg Noodles Stuffed, Meat, Ricotta, Mozzarella Cheese and Eggs with Tomato Sauce	
Risotto alla Milanese (30 minutes)	1.50
With Chicken Livers and Mushrooms	2.25
Ditali with Ricotta (Red or White)	1.25
Maccheroni or Ravioli au Gratin	1.25
Baked Maccheroni alla Siciliana	1.25
With Eggplant, Meat Sauce and Cheese	
Spaghetti alla Caruso	1.75
Chicken Livers, Mushrooms, With or Without Tomato Sauce	
Spaghetti, Mushroom Sauce	1.25
Spaghetti, Cacciatora	1.25
With Onions, Mushrooms and Wine Sauce	
Spaghetti, Meat Balls	1.00
Spaghetti, Italian Sausages	1.25
Spaghetti, Chicken Livers	1.50
With or Without Tomato Sauce	
Spaghetti, Meat Sauce	.90
Spaghetti, Filet of Tomatoes	1.50
With Prosciutto and Onion Sauce	
Spaghetti, Butter Sauce	.80
Spaghetti, Tetrazzini	1.75
Baked with Cream Sauce, Mushrooms, Diced Chicken and Cheese	
Spaghetti, Tomato Sauce	.70
Spaghetti, Tomato Sauce alla Picciolo	1.00
Plain Tomato with Garlic Flavor and Sweet Basil	
Spaghetti, Bolognese	1.50
Beef Prosciutto, Mushrooms, Grated Onions	
Spaghetti, Meat Balls, Meat Sauce	1.25
Spaghetti, Tuna Fish Sauce, (Red or White)	1.25
Buitoni, Linguine or Spaghetti	1.00
Tagliatelle, Verdi (Spinach Noodles)	1.25
with Butter or Tomato Sauce	
Rotini, Tomato, Marinara or Meat Sauce	1.00
Rigatoni, Tomato, Marinara or Meat Sauce	1.00
Farfalloni	1.00

(Extra with Maccheroni Orders—Meat Balls .30; Sausage .55)

For almost all these people—and there were millions upon millions who came during that period—the idea of a restaurant was as alien to them as words like "Susquehanna" and "Cincinnati." Few of these people knew anything at all about running an eating house, although all came from countries with highly developed, traditional gastronomies.

More than any other ethnic people, the Italians were exceptionally successful in adapting their food culture to America's, and in so doing created a hybrid—Italian-American cookery—which today is more easily identifiable to most Americans than are dishes like Boston cream pie, chicken fried steak, gumbo, or red-eye gravy.

Key to understanding Italian food culture in the United States is knowing where the Italian immigrants came from: Eighty percent were from south of Rome—the region known as Mezzogiorno—and particularly from Sicily and Naples. Between 1890 and 1910 five million Southern Italians entered the United States; between 1880 and 1920 one out of every four immigrants to this country was a Sicilian.

These were people whose gastronomy was far more influenced by Mediterranean cultures than by European, and, given the poverty of the region, depended largely on vegetables, grains, and fruits, with very little meat in the diet at all. The tomato, which came to dominate Italian-American cookery, was brought to Italy from Central America only in the sixteenth century and was little consumed elsewhere in Europe because, as a member of the deadly nightshade family (Solanaceae), it was thought to be poisonous.

Also, these southern Italians were overwhelmingly agrarian—*contadini*—with very few emigrating from the cities. Yet, for the most part, they disembarked and settled in the teeming cities of America's Eastern seaboard, with 97 percent of them disgorged through New York's Ellis Island. By the 1920s there were more Italians living in New York than there were in Florence, Venice, and Genoa combined. Although about half eventually returned to Italy, millions stayed to begin a new life, which had very little to do with life back home, where they had tended farm, lived off the land, and, often, slept outside. Chefs and restaurateurs were few and far between among steerage-class travelers.

The poor immigrants who arrived in the Eastern cities found wretched conditions, with cramped tenement quarters, disease, filth, and prejudice rampant. Tenement apartments had no room for food storage. Food was expensive in America, though much less so than in Sicily, where up to 85 percent of one's income went to feed the family, compared to only 50 percent in the United States.

A greater disappointment was not being able to own enough land on which these former *contadini* might grow their own tomatoes, eggplants, and herbs, making them dependent on unfamiliar varieties of store-bought American vegetables and fruits that looked, smelled, and tasted quite different from what they'd been used to.

"[Southern Italians'] nostalgia for the food of their homeland paralleled their nostalgia for their patron saints," notes gastronomic historian Massimo Alberini. "They sent to Italy for cases of macaroni, and they managed to provide reasonable substitutes for missing ingredients." Mexican chile was used in place of Calabrese *peperoncino,* mozzarella cheese was made with cow's milk instead of the traditional buffalo milk, and strong red wines were made from American grape varieties or zinfandel, which non-Italians often called "Dago red." With considerable justification the immigrants mistrusted whatever was not fresh. "The [Italian] believes that the commercial method [of canning] removes all the goodness from food," noted a 1907 report on *Wage Earner's Budgets in New York,* "and a minimum of processes should intervene between harvesting and consumption." Pasta sauces were mostly tomato and vegetable based, while meat sauce—a Northern Italian luxury called *alla bolognese* ("in the style of the Bolognese")—was a mark by which Italian women measured their culinary prowess.

"There were no restaurants in our neighborhood," wrote Jerry Della Femina in his memoir, *An Italian Grows in Brooklyn.* "We didn't go out to eat. We ate either at our house, or Cousin Ronnie's, or Uncle Dom's, or wherever. My grandmother would start making her meat sauce at seven in the morning on Sunday and within five or six hours that smell would be all through the house, covering everything—clothing, furniture, appliances—and then it would go out the front door and into the streets, to mix with the aroma of neighboring meat sauces."

The food was simple, substantial, and, nutritionists now tell us, extremely healthful, based on copious amounts of carbohydrates like pasta and beans, grains products, vegetables, and fruits. Yet at the turn of the century such a diet seemed completely at odds with conventional ideas about good nutrition. Turn-of-the-century social workers in New York would report of a family, "Not yet Americanized, still eating Italian food," despite the fact that the Italians seemed to thrive on it.

Macaroni, spaghetti, lasagne (usually spelled "lasagna" in this country), manicotti, and myriad other forms of Italian noodles were curiosity dishes for Americans. While most cookbooks of the period made a travesty of supposedly Italian recipes, Charles Ranhofer, once chef at Delmonico's, offered a number of authoritative recipes in his cookbook, *The Epicurean* (1893), including gnocchi, polenta, ravioli, risotto, and "Macaroni, Neapolitan Style," made with a tomato and beef stock sauce.

Other Americans were learning to eat Italian foods too. From the Italian bakery ovens came the first pizzas, which had been strictly a Neapolitan item back in Italy. The pizza as we know it had its origins in the flat yeast breads of the Mediterranean, and the word *pizza* probably derives from an Old Italian word meaning a "point," which evolved into *pizzicare,* "to pinch" or "to pluck," with *pizza* itself first appearing in Neapolitan dialect.

In some sense the pizza symbolizes the way Italian food was modified and promoted in this country into a staple of the American diet. This humble item, unfamiliar to most Italians until after World War II, would become as identified with Italians in America as French fries were with the French, chop suey with the Chinese, and lox with Jews—even though none of those dishes originated in the home country. Originally poor people's food from the slums of Naples, the pizza idea traveled with the Neapolitan immigrants to America, where its traditional size was enlarged and sold as finger food, in contrast to the plated pizzas customarily eaten with knife and fork in Italy.

Specials alla Picciolo

Pasta E Ceci	1.25
Pasta E Broccoli	1.50
Escarole E Fagioli	1.25
Pasta E Fagioli in Olive Oil	1.25
Pasta E Piselli	1.25
Rice with Red Beans	1.25
Polenta, Plain	1.50
Polenta, Ragout Sauce or Chicken Liver	2.50
Combination Platter (Chicken Cacciatora, Sausage, Ravioli, Meat Ball, Veal Scalloppine, Spaghetti and Tomato Sauce)	2.25
Rollatine alla Picciolo (Veal), Mushroom Sauce	2.25
Sliced Filet Mignon, Mushrooms and Peppers	2.75
Braciole (2) (Rollette of Beef)	1.75
Eggplant, Parmigiana	1.25
Trippa alla Pizzaiola	1.25
Stuffed Pepper (Rice and Meat)	1.00
Roast Stuffed Pepper (Eggplant, Caper, Olives and Onions)	.75
Pork Chops and Vinegar Peppers	1.85
Italian Sausages (3)	1.00
Italian Meat Balls (3)	.75
Artichokes and Peppers Saute	1.25
Sliced Filet Mignon Saute with Artichokes	2.75
Stuffed Artichoke	1.00
Italian Sausages and Peppers	1.50
Scungilli, Red or White Sauce	1.50
Spedini alla Romana (Mozzarella en Cavallo)	2.00
Mozzarella Carrozza	1.50
Rabbit in Bianco	1.75

Italian Specialties

Veal and Peppers	2.35
Veal Chop or Pork Chop, Pizzaiola	2.50
Veal Scalloppine with Peppers and Mushrooms	2.75
Veal Scalloppine alla Francese	3.00
Chicken Parmigiana, Boneless	2.75
Chicken alla Cacciatora	2.65
Chicken (Half), Southern Fried or Broiled	2.50
Chicken alla Picciolo	3.00
Chicken Saute with Mushrooms (Red or White Wine)	2.95
Veal Cutlet alla Parmigiana	2.60
Veal Cutlet alla Milanese	2.50
Braciole— (2 Rollette of Beef)	2.75
Italian Sausages with Peppers	2.50
Sliced Filet Mignon with Mushrooms and Peppers	3.50
Trippa, Pizzaiola	2.25
Eggplant alla Parmigiana	2.25
Stuffed Pepper	1.65
Fettucine (Egg Noodles) with Meat Sauce	2.25
Lasagna (Baked Home Stuffed Noodles)	2.50
Gnocchi with Meat Sauce	2.25
Ravioli (Homemade), Tomato Sauce	2.25
Rigatoni or Mezzani, Meat Sauce	2.00
Stuffed Cannelloni with Meat	2.50

A TYPICAL ITALIAN-AMERICAN menu, from Picciolo restaurant, established in 1936 on Collins Avenue in Miami Beach, Florida

The first known pizzeria in the United States was G. Lombardi on Spring Street in New York's Little Italy, which opened in 1905. (Deep-dish "Chicago-style pizza," cooked in a black skillet, didn't come along until 1943, when it was created by Ike Sewall and Ric Riccardo at Pizzeria Uno in Chicago.) Pizza became synonymous with Italian food, especially after returning World War II GI's brought back a hunger for pizzas and other foods they'd first tasted during the liberation of southern Italy and, especially, Naples. The pizza also fit in conveniently with the postwar fast-food boom, helped along by Dean Martin's 1953 hit "(When the Moon Hits Your Eye Like a Big Pizza Pie) That's Amore."

Pizzerias may have been among the first Italian-American eateries, but even at the turn of the century distinctions were clear-cut as to what constituted a true *ristorante*. To be merely a pizzamaker was to be at the bottom of the culinary and social scale; so many pizzeria owners began offering other dishes, including the "hero" sandwich (also, depending on the region of the United States, called a "wedge," a "hoagie," a "sub," or a "grinder") made on an Italian loaf of bread with lots of salami, cheese, and peppers. Many of these pizzerias evolved into full-fledged restaurants whose owners eventually shut down their pizza ovens entirely in a meaningful and deliberate move away from the low-class image of the pizzamaker.

Most Italian restaurants in the early part of this century were small family operations—*trattorie*—although there were also a number of sprawling Italian restaurants in New York serving thousands of meals each day. Joe's Restaurant at Fulton and Pierrepont streets in Brooklyn (opened by Joe Balzarini in 1909) took up six buildings and offered everything from homemade ravioli to hot turkey sandwiches. Barbetta, opened in 1906 by Sebastiano Maioglio on West Thirty-ninth Street (still going strong after its removal to Forty-sixth Street in 1925), served deluxe Piedmontese cuisine to Enrico Caruso, Feodor Chaliapin, Arturo Toscanini, and every other musician who ever played the nearby Metropolitan Opera House, while Sardi's and Mamma Leone's became landmarks known to every tourist visiting Broadway.

Mamma Leone's growth from family restaurant (it opened in 1906 in a little room above a wine cellar near the back of the Metropolitan Opera) to baroque institution to gargantuan tourist trap mirrors what happened to Italian-American restaurants. With its nude statuary, singing waiters, enormous chunks of mozzarella on each table, and red-checkered tablecloths, it came to represent Italian dining in its most outrageous form—overdone, overcooked, and, after a while, half baked. More inevitably meant better, so portions were extremely generous.

Like Mamma Leone's, most Italian-American restaurants served a diluted form of Southern Italian cookery modulated for the American palate, which demanded far more meat dishes and less spiciness. So meatballs were added to spaghetti, veal cutlets became a standard item, and steaks and chops were included on the menu, along with several eponymous dishes named after the towns the cooks came from—clams Posillipo, seafood Golfo di Napoli, and veal Sorrentina—none of them a classic Italian dish but each created to evoke an image of the Bay of Naples or some romantic locale the cooks longed to see again. "Shrimp scampi" (shrimp done in white

wine and garlic) was actually an adaptation of the Venetian word *scampi,* meaning "prawns," which were not available in the United States.

New dishes came from many sources—rarely from Italy. Clams casino was not Italian at all: It was created by headwaiter Julius Keller at the Casino at Narragansett Pier in New York at the turn of the century. Turkey Tetrazzini, a dish of turkey with cream sauce served over spaghetti, was named after Italian coloratura Luisa Tetrazzini (1871–1940) by some enterprising Italian-American cook; and spaghetti alla Caruso (with chicken livers) was named after the great tenor. Caesar salad was actually the invention of one Caesar Cardini, who concocted the dish on the Fourth of July, 1924, weekend at his restaurant in Tijuana, Mexico, for some visiting movie stars who popularized it back in Hollywood until it became a nationally known dish. Fettuccine Alfredo—a mixture of very rich egg noodles, butter, and Parmesan cheese—was "created" by a Roman restaurateur named Alfredo Di Lelio to restore the appetite of his sick wife. While there was nothing actually new about this combination of ingredients to most Italians, it was the celebrity of two American movie actors who made the

A 1940s **ITALIAN-AMERICAN** coffee shop in New York's Little Italy where men could congregate to talk and socialize much as they did in the Old Country. Note the ornate espresso coffee machine behind the bar.

dish's reputation in the United States and made Alfredo himself a very famous and wealthy restaurateur. Douglas Fairbanks and Mary Pickford sampled the dish on a honeymoon visit to Rome in 1927, after which they presented Di Lelio with a golden fork and spoon with which to mix the noodles. Within a year a recipe for the dish was published in *The Rector Cook Book*.

At the same time these Southern Italians enriched American English with new words—*calamari, prosciutto, salami, espresso, cappuccino, zabaglione*—often pronounced, and even spelled, according to a regional Southern dialect. "The Neapolitan working class dialect lopped off the final vowel from many words, sometimes transposing it to the front of the word," explains Tom Maresca, co-author of *La Tavola Italiana*. As a result, *ricotta* was pronounced "ah-ri-GAWT," *manicotti* became "mani-GAWT," *scungilli* became "ah-skoon-ZHEEL," *pasta e fagioli* became "pasta Fah-ZOOL," *broccoli di rape* became "broak-la-rob," and *pizza* was sounded as "ah-PEETZ," and often spelled "Apizz" on signs advertising the item.

Chicago's first Italian restaurant was Madame Galli's, opened around 1883, where the Rotary Club was founded in 1905. It was a favorite of artists and opera singers, including Enrico Caruso, who once drew a caricature of Mrs. Galli, whose sauce was so famous the H. J. Heinz Company tried to purchase the recipe, to no avail.

Many of San Francisco's Italian restaurants began as speakeasies during Prohibition, with the father of the family making wine in the basement and his wife cooking in the kitchen. Others established themselves in the North Beach neighborhood as bohemian hangouts like the Blue Moon Café. San Francisco had attracted more Northern Italian immigrants who went into the seafood industry and opened up Italian seafood restaurants, adding cioppino, a seafood stew based on a Genoese dish, to the Italian-American menu.

During the Depression, Lucca's, which opened in 1930, was one of the most popular restaurants in the Bay Area. Owner Pierino Gavello advertised, "All You Can Eat for Fifty Cents," and every night a line of customers would snake down Francisco Street around the corner of Powell. Once inside they would be greeted with an antipasto platter, then minestrone soup, then spaghetti or ravioli, then a meat main course, a speciality called "fried cream," and a tray of pastries and ice cream. The wine was very probably from the Napa or Sonoma Valley with the name "Chianti" written on the label.

The rich and varied traditions of Louisiana Creole cookery had a decided effect on the numbers of Sicilians who settled in and around New Orleans during the immigrant era. A place like Mosca's, which opened in 1946 in Waggaman, was very much a second-generation restaurant, offering Creole-influenced Italian food that was very heavy, spicy, and dependent on the seafood of the Gulf for its unique flavors.

But by and large the Italian-American menu as Americans know it developed in New York and is still firmly entrenched in most cities in this country. One 1939 New York dining guide remarked that the city was "full of Italian restaurants—good, bad, and indifferent—all serving the same courses of minestrone, spaghetti, ravioli, scallopine and tortoni." One could

TELEPHONE: GArfield 9711

THE VENETO RESTAURANT — 389 BAY ST. — SAN FRANCISCO, CALIF.   SA-H1712

find regional delicacies in some of New York's better Italian restaurants, which usually were still cheaper than the food at other deluxe dining rooms. In 1939 "Veal Chop Parmigiana" with two vegetables at Barbetta went for 60 cents, a full bottle of Chianti for $1.90. At Jack Dempsey's restaurant on West Fiftieth Street a lamb steak with baked potato would set you back $1.75, while the "splendid French wines" at Le Café Chambord on Third Avenue went for an exorbitant $3.50.

Most Americans would have felt ill at ease in an Italian restaurant that did not have the requisite checkered tablecloths, straw-covered bottles with candles in them, and a strolling accordionist—an image touchingly brought into Technicolor focus in a scene in the Walt Disney animated feature *Lady and the Tramp* (1955), when an Italian restaurateur named Tony and his chef cook up a plate of spaghetti and meatballs and serenade two stray dogs to the tune of "Bella Notte."

By the 1950s Italian-American food, in all its modifications, elaborations, and excrescences, was all but unrecognizable to visitors from Italy. A businessman from Turin might peruse a menu in an Italian restaurant in Chicago and not be able to decipher a single item.

You can still find the old dishes, the peasant dishes, the *contadino*'s dishes at places like Mario's on Arthur Avenue. And the pizza there is made the way it's still made in Naples. And the Migliucci family is always there. Always. All of which makes Mario's a vital link to an Italian-American heritage that began in hunger and moved inexorably toward abundance.

While no other ethnic cookery has come close to the all-conquering success of Italian-American food, each wave of immigrants brought to the United States a diversity of foods and food service that radically and delectably altered the way Americans eat. "Ethnic food" in the United States is a convenient term used to describe the foods the post–Civil War immigrants brought with them, from German sauerkraut to Greek baklava, from Hun-

THE VENETO WAS TYPICAL of Italian-American restaurants in San Francisco's North Beach neighborhood. This 1935 postcard shows the attempt to re-create the look of a Venetian kitchen, complete with murals of Italian landscape.

garian goulash to Jewish pastrami. That French cuisine has never been termed an "ethnic food" is due as much to the fact that Americans thought of it as an already entrenched "restaurant cuisine" as it does to the small number of French who emigrated here in the late nineteenth and early twentieth centuries.

Few of the early ethnic eateries were owned by immigrants who had any restaurant experience in Europe or Asia. Indeed, while Europe had its share of deluxe restaurants catering to the wealthy and cafés and taverns to the lower classes, there were few restaurants of any kind catering to the general public in Italy, France, Germany, Greece, and other countries. Thus, the food in the new immigrant eateries less resembled restaurant cuisine than it did home cooking—stomach-filling, heavy, spicy, and cheap.

More often than not an immigrant family simply fell into the restaurant business, starting off, perhaps, by running a grocery, a café, or a bar and gradually expanding it into a full-service restaurant. As one family or generation succeeded in the business, others joined or went into that line of work without any previous experience. What Theodore Saloutos wrote in the *Harvard Encyclopedia of American Ethnic Groups* (1980) of the Greek experience was generally true of most of the immigrant groups:

> *The restaurant business . . . was the favorite route for Greeks. No one knows why so many Greeks became prominent as restaurant owners and cooks, activities for which they brought no special talent from their homeland. . . . Since many restaurants were—and still are—family enterprises, they could afford to stay open long hours. The Greeks did not necessarily excel in cooking, but the quality of their food was adequate, their prices low, and the bill of fare imaginative.*

The coffee shop and diner in particular have long been monopolized by Greek-Americans, the former an obvious outgrowth of Greeks' cherished love of coffee, the latter perhaps associated with the fact that so many Greeks worked the American railroads that inspired the first diners. The Greek diner was immortalized in the late 1970s when it became a featured segment on the comedy television show *Saturday Night Live,* which affectionately lampooned such an eatery (supposedly based on Chicago's Billy Goat), where the only thing they served was "chiz-burgers—Pepsi," no matter what anyone ordered.

Today souvlaki, baklava, moussakas, and the Greek equivalent to the Italian hero—the gyro—are standard dishes sold from pushcarts and corner luncheonettes in most major cities in the United States, although among non-Greeks such items would rarely be made at home and almost always purchased in a restaurant.

In no instances, however, did ethnic cookeries remain "pure" or unchanged. The differences in meats, vegetables, fruits, and dairy—as well as the discovery of ingredients brand new to the immigrants—modified the old dishes in both subtle and distinct ways, helping to create new dishes like chow mein, chop suey, chili, chimichangas, lox, Liederkranz, and London broil, all in restaurant kitchens. Home cooking was a far different thing from restaurant cooking, and immigrants who opened eateries to the general public found it easier to sell a modified form of an old dish to Americans who regarded such establish-

ments as quaint, picturesque, and rather adventuresome places to eat.

Before the popularity of Italian restaurants took hold in the twentieth century, the most important immigrant cuisine in America was German. Although the earliest German settlements in America date to 1683, the first great wave of Germans came in 1816–17, followed by another in the 1850s and 1860s, when they made up a third of all the immigrants in the United States. German immigration reached a peak in the 1880s of 1,445,481 people, then gradually slowed down. One of their most important contributions was in beermaking, especially the bottom-fermented, light lager first made by John Wagner of Philadelphia about 1840. This became America's favorite style of beer, leading to an increased thirst for the beverage, which, after the Civil War, began to outstrip hard liquor in consumption.

In imitation of their beloved *Bierhalles* in Germany, the immigrants constructed lavish urban beer halls of Wagnerian dimensions, some holding up to 1,200 people. The food at such places was abundant, robust, and rich—bratwurst, weisswurst, sauerkraut, Bismarckhering, Ochsenmaul, rollmops, Sülze, and sauerbraten—all enhanced with hot mustard and washed down with lager served in decorated beer steins.

In 1854 Franz Joseph Uhrig brought the novelty of the outdoor restaurant to St. Louis, Missouri. At Uhrig's Cave, beer and wine were cooled and served as people enjoyed the new Gilbert and Sullivan operettas just then coming to the United States. Uhrig's Cave ushered in an era of outdoor beer gardens, whose popularity might be gauged by the local legislature's attempt to prohibit beer gardens from being open on Sundays. The size of these beer gardens grew and grew; some, like the Forest Park Highlands Amusement Park, eventually combined the beer garden with rides, shows, and other attractions.

As German immigrants grew more prosperous, German restaurants grew grander. In cities like Chicago, German food came close to being an indigenous cuisine. One of the city's oldest restaurants, Schogl's (opened in 1879), was famous for its wine room and its murals of free-drinking Bavarian

YORKVILLE WAS NEW YORK CITY's German-American neighborhood, once lined with restaurants like Maxl's, Old München, and the 86th Street Brauhaus, which offered up generous portions of German food, beer, and *gemütlichkeit*.

monks. Here congregated all the literary lights of the day—Carl Sandburg, Edgar Lee Masters, Charles MacArthur, W.A.S. Douglass, Heywood Broun, Sinclair Lewis, and others—along with the correspondents from most of the nation's newspapers. Chef Paul Weber was known for his Wienerschnitzel and Hasenpfeffer, and, although he did not invent it, for a German-sounding item that would become the most famous of all American foods: "Millionaires who can afford sirloins and tenderloins come here for Hamburger steak," exulted one of Schogl's admirers.

There was Kau's, opened just before World War I, designed by architect Peter J. Weber, who had done the Ravinia Opera Pavilion at the 1893 Chicago Columbian Exposition; the Red Star Inn was a replica of a Bavarian rathskeller. Old Heidelberg, on South Clark Street, was done up like a baronial medieval hall (complete with a seated plaster cast of Emperor Frederick Barbarossa), a fit setting for the tycoons and industrialists who ate and drank here. Less affluent customers might be found at the Lincoln Turner Hall Café, where German and non-German families gathered to dine while being serenaded by an orchestra playing popular favorites by Strauss, Mozart, and Wagner.

New York's most famous German restaurant was Lüchow's, a flamboyant, multi-storied edifice on Fourteenth Street featuring an eight-piece Viennese orchestra and imported Würzburger and Pilsener beers, of which twenty-four thousand seidels were drunk on an average night (thirty-six being the record for one person at one sitting, set by a fellow named Baron Ferdinand Sinzig). In fact, Lüchow's theme song—"Down Where the Würzburger Flows"—became a kind of anthem in German restaurants around the country.

August Guido Lüchow, who started out by running a brew hall in 1882, knew how to attract the crowds. He opened a menagerie next door, from which a lion escaped one night, shuffling into the dining room and causing instant panic among the customers in his way and loud guffaws among others more distantly seated.

One of Lüchow's most illustrious patrons, gastronome Ludwig Bemelmans, recalled of the restaurant's glory days:

> *A fragrance, delicate but not weak, and slightly male, rides in the air. It composes itself of the aromas of solid cooking, of roast geese and ducks, of game and Huhn im Topf, of various things, sour and spicy, and tender cutlets simmering among* Steinpilze. . . .
> *The food is supported by music equally enduring. The orchestra plays such aids to digestion as "Die Forelle" von Schubert,* The Tales of Hoffman, William Tell, *and "Sylvia," and such romantic fare as "The Evening Star." . . . I find it one of those places in which the mind hums in harmony with its surroundings. . . . There are large parties who call themselves "Our Bunch" and from whom most of the belly laughs issue.*
>
> *At other tables sit priests, students, national figures . . . diplomats, politicians with Italian friends in race-track suits with pearl stickpins in their neckties, theatrical folk with broad-shouldered blondes who have brought along Mama and Papa. It is alive with*

children and with dogs. It is the most kaleidoscopic restaurant in New York. Its waiters are the last of their kind, upstanding citizens, with a trace of servility in their make-up.

Lüchow was known as a tough employer but a fair one, allowing his staff to drink as much domestic beer as they wished as long as they kept their hands off the imports, and he'd check on what was going in any corner of the restaurant via mirrors mounted in his upstairs office. He fed his staff well, but regarded stealing and waste as betrayal. Having once found his longtime cellarmaster trying to discard the evidence of some purloined strawberry shortcake, Lüchow told the man it would cost five thousand dollars, an amount later deducted from the generous legacy left to the employee.

A good deal of anti-German feeling in pre–World War I America tainted the image and popularity of German restaurants, forcing the Hofbrau in Chicago to change its name to The States just before the outbreak of hostilities. Those restaurants that stayed in business when war broke out became stereotypical. "All waiters in these [New York] German restaurants wear short corduroy pants, Alpine hats, socks that cover only the calves of their legs, and funny suspenders," noted a 1934 guidebook entitled *Dining in New York, an Intimate Guide.* And anti-German feeling erupted during World War II, affecting the survival of many of the smaller German restaurants in large cities. Some survived by offering sentimental entertainment and a good dose of schmaltz to tourists, but as time went on second- and third-generation German-Americans were more absorbed into the mainstream of American life, retreating from the original immigrant neighborhoods into other parts of the city and suburbs, resulting in the closing of the smaller German restaurants while the larger ones struggled to stay open. German neighborhoods like New York's Yorkville, once home to many celebrated German restaurants like Maxl's, the Platzl, Old München, Rudi & Maxl's, and others, lost their German populations and with them their steady customers. By the 1970s German and Eastern European food fell into a heavy-handed sameness. There was no attempt to refine the food any further, as did French and Italian restaurateurs under the influence of *nouvelle cuisine* and new nutritional guidelines, and German food languished under an image of heaviness and fat.

Today few of the historic German restaurants are still in business—The Berghoff in Chicago, Karl Ratzsch's in Milwaukee, Haussner's in Baltimore, Grammer's in Cincinnati, Schroeder's Café in San Francisco, and Jacoby's in Detroit are nearly all that are left of those grand dining halls. The beautiful landmark building that was once Lüchow's now stands empty and boarded up. The only real imprint German-American food has left on this country is in two items derived from German antecedents and named after German cities—the hamburger and the frankfurter—which have since become synonymous worldwide with American food.

Other Germanic immigrants set up their own style of restaurants in America. The Pennsylvania-Dutch established themselves gastronomically by setting up large "family-style" restaurants cannily designed to appeal to tourists who sought to enter briefly into an old-fashioned farm atmosphere.

Sitting at communal tables, ladling out endless helpings of chicken and dumplings, Schnitz und Knepp, and shoofly pie, diners partake of a microcosmic cookery developed out of the American farmlands according to traditions set long ago in the German Palatinate.

Oddly enough many of the same rich, fatty foods beloved by the Jewish immigrants entered the American diet with far less flamboyance but much greater impact than did German food. The majority of the 2.3 million Jews who came to America between 1882 and 1924 were from Eastern Europe, and their food derived from German, Polish, Rumanian, Hungarian, and Russian roots, modified by the strictures of kosher dietary laws. Thus, many of the foods that came to be Jewish-American staples would be unfamiliar to Jews whose origins were French, Italian, Spanish, or Middle Eastern. Bagels, lox, pastrami, knishes, gefilte fish, cheesecake, latkes, and bialys were simply not part of their culinary heritage. Yet these foods have come to define Jewish cookery in this country, and many of the items have become tremendously popular with non-Jewish Americans.

Mostly this was due to the success of the delicatessen. Jewish immigrants did not at first open restaurants, but they took the concept of the *schlacht,* or grocery, store to far more delectable and diverse levels than Americans had ever before experienced. And, in most cases, one could eat on the premises. The word *delicatessen* comes from the German word, *Deli-*

NATHAN HANDWERKER, owner of Nathan's at New York's Coney Island amusement park, did more than anyone else to popularize the hot dog (also called a "Coney Island"), so much so that the local Chamber of Commerce for a time banned the use of the term lest people think the hot dogs actually contained dog meat.

katesse, for delicacy, although many New York Jews preferred the non-German word "appetizing." The deli counter's display of breads, smoked salmon, dried fish, noodle pudding, cured meats, pickles, and oddities like cream soda and celery tonic represented American bounty in its most voluptuous and self-indulgent form, and the experience of going to a deli—"Jewish deli" would have been a redundancy—became the stuff comedy and heartburn were made of. Americans took to the overstuffed sandwiches and fried potatoes with the same relish they would to ham-and-cheese sandwiches and French fries, and "deli counters" became as much a fixture in American supermarkets as a butcher or dairy case. The frantic, fast-paced urban setting of the deli, with its good-natured give-and-take between customers and countermen all punctuated with Yiddish epithets, offered customers a cornucopia of foods that fit quite easily into the established American diet and was a feast for the senses.

RAPHIL'S DELICATESSEN, opened in 1948 in Miami Beach, was typical of Jewish immigrants' eateries, featuring adaptions of Eastern European delicacies like pastrami, smoked fish, and kosher meats.

In his book *When Brooklyn Was the World: 1920–1957*, Elliot Willensky writes of the predictable form these delicatessens took in Jewish neighborhoods:

> First, in the window, under the mandatory neon sign with Hebrew lettering and the brand of cold cuts sold, was the frankfurter grill, with ranks of red franks enjoying peaceful coexistence with rows of yellow knishes, a kind of potato patty.... Adjacent were the obligatory mustard bowl and canister of steaming sauerkraut, awaiting the waiter's ritual summons, "Ordering two franks—with!"
>
> Inside the door you found a small, dark-stained, shiny, wooden serving bar. Sometimes it even had a beer spigot, and, to recall the character of a real bar, a short length of brass rail. And, of course, the cash register.
>
> Next in line came ... the sloped glass cases behind which lay delectable, tantalizing, mouth-watering displays of various kinds of cold cuts, all cut on the bias, the better to show off their stuff. Hard salami, soft salami, chicken salami. Roast beef, rolled beef, corned beef. Bologna, brisket, tongue.... Atop the meat case stood a teaser, an open display of small knobs of a thickly sliced knublvoorsht—garlic wurst ornamented by a hand-lettered sign, A NICKEL A SHTICKL—a nickel apiece. They were sachets of the delicatessen, redolent of garlic, and placed at adult nose level; gravity took care of us shorter kids. The owners really knew how to get your juices flowing.

Most delis were in the Jewish neighborhoods of East Coast cities, especially New York, where delis dimpled the streets of Brooklyn, the Bronx, East Harlem, and the Lower East Side, although some of the most famous—Reuben's, the Stage Deli, and the Carnegie Deli—were uptown attractions, as much for their celebrity clientele as for their food, and sandwiches were often named after Jewish comedians like Henny Youngman and Eddie Cantor.

The less stringent deli owners became about keeping kosher, the more appeal they had to Gentiles, and non-kosher delis began expanding their offerings and premises to bring in more customers. Gold's restaurant, located in Chicago's Jewish quarter, was called "The Rector's of the Ghetto," and played host to most every Jewish celebrity who passed through town, from Irving Berlin to Al Jolson and Georgie Jessel. In Miami, where large numbers of Jews relocated after 1920, delis like Raphil's and Wolfie's were the principal alternatives to the resort hotel restaurants, most of which kept kosher kitchens for their large Jewish clientele. On any given night during the season, 1,200 people might be fed at The Famous restaurant, which opened in 1945 on Miami Beach, and most people ordered the lavish coconut cake made from fresh coconuts gathered after storms knocked them down from the palm trees along Washington Avenue.

As did the Italians, the Jews adapted their cooking to the New World way of life and larder, and most culinary distinctions among European Jews were dissolved in the American stewpot. So, too, Chinese-American food came to be a modified form of the peasant cooking of Kwangtung Province, of which Canton is the capital city, because that is where the majority of Chinese immigrants came from. Between 1850 and 1882 (when the first Chinese Exclusion Act was passed) more than 320,000 Chinese immigrants entered the United States, 99 percent of them settling on the West Coast. They were poor people fleeing warfare, famine, and oppressive regimes (before 1860 emigrants leaving or returning to China risked execution). They took on the hardest, most menial labor on the railroads, in the mines, and on fishing boats. Wherever they went, owing to whites' enforced exclusionism and their own reluctance to enter fully into American culture, the Chinese settled their own Chinatowns within major United States cities, where they opened "chow chow" eateries, identified by their triangular yellow flags. At first these small, cramped eateries catered to their own people,

CHINATOWNS SPRANG UP on both coasts in cities that attracted immigrants from Chinese port cities like Canton. One of the easiest businesses for these immigrants to open was a restaurant, as shown in this postcard of Los Angeles's Chinatown in the 1930s.

then expanded their menus to attract curious Americans who dared cross into those mysterious cities-within-cities where the odors of garlic, ginger, and soy sauce mixed with thick, pungent pipe smoke.

The cookery in these new Chinatowns was basically stir-fried, rice-based Cantonese, which efficiently utilized every part of the animal, some as delicacies, some simply as a way not to waste any scrap of food. Americans not used to such economy were often dismayed by what they found in their rice bowl, and jokes as to the whereabouts of a stray cat or dog in the kitchen did little to sublimate the image of Chinese culture. Of his fifty-cent meal in San Francisco's Chinatown, Benjamin Taylor in his book *Between the Gates* (1878) wrote, "Pale cakes with a waxen look, full of meats, are brought out. They are sausages in disguise. Then more cakes full of seeds as a fig. Then giblets of you-never-know-what, maybe gizzards, possibly livers, perhaps toes."

"GOING FOR CHINESE" was considered adventurous eating for most white Americans at the turn of the century, as indicated by the sole Caucasian customer at this New York Chinatown restaurant in 1896.

Most of these eateries were primitive in design and atmosphere—"as uninviting as a pig-sty," generalized one observer of New York's Chinatown restaurants—although many Chinese prided themselves on their cleanliness, encouraging American patrons to walk through the kitchen on their way to the dining room, in order to assuage fears over unsanitary conditions.

Before long, however, Chinese cooks learned how to modify their dishes to make them more palatable to a wider American audience. In fact, most of the Chinese restaurants outside of Chinatown proclaimed in their windows that they were CHINESE-AMERICAN, lest Occidental customers shy away for fear of being served duck feet and bird's nests.

No one knows for sure how chop suey and chow mein became staples of Chinese-American menus. One story concerns the visit of the first Chinese statesman to America, in 1896, Viceroy Li Hung-chang, who, on being in-

terviewed by American newspapermen about his food, used a Chinese phrase that sounded something like "chop suey" and meant "a little of this and that." But the dish's name is found in print as early as 1888, eight years before the Viceroy's visit. "Chow mein," on the other hand, resembles a Mandarin dialect word for "fried noodles." Commenting upon the food in San Francisco's Chinatown in 1914, Clarence E. Edwards wrote that chop suey and chow mein were served in every Chinese restaurant, but that "neither is considered among the fine dishes served to Chinese epicures."

Egg foo yung is derived from a Guangdong word for "egg white," but it, too, is not a classic Chinese dish.

The fortune cookie probably came a bit later: Its introduction has been ascribed to one George Jung, founder of the Hong Kong Noodle Company in Los Angeles, who in 1916 gave them to his guests in imitation of the message-bearing cakes used in Chinese parlor games.

By the 1920s Chinese restaurants dotted the American landscape, and one was as likely to find a "chop suey parlor" in Kansas City as in New York or San Francisco, even though the typical menu in such places bore small resemblance to the foods the Chinese themselves ate. Many dishes were cloyingly sweetened with caramel and sugar, inundated with pineapple chunks and maraschino cherries, and fried in thick batters, while the ubiquitous flaming appetizer platter called "pu pu" (derived from a Hawaiian word for appetizer) was first served as a gimmick by Victor Bergeron at his Trader Vic's Polynesian-American restaurants in Oakland and San Francisco. Won ton soup, egg rolls, barbecued spareribs, sweet-and-sour pork, and beef with lobster sauce were all concocted to whet Americans' appetites, and to this day, it is standard procedure for an American in a Chinese restaurant to be handed a two-columned menu written in English, while a completely different menu printed in Chinese will be given to a Chinese patron, who, in any case, would probably disregard it and order from the specials written in pictographs on the walls.

"Going for Chinese" became very much an American expression, and when Americans began moving to the suburbs in the 1950s and 1960s, Chinese restaurants followed on their heels, particularly in suburban shopping malls. The opening of China to the West in the 1970s brought a whole new image of more authentic Chinese cooking, and the explosion of interest in the fiery flavors of Szechuan and Hunan dishes was enhanced by a new breed of far more elegant, considerably more expensive restaurants with modern decor, lighting, and service personnel. Restaurants like New York's Shun Lee Palace, Los Angeles's Madame Wu, and San Francisco's Mandarin mounted fantastic banquets for business travelers on expense accounts, and Chinatown *dim sum* parlors, like New York's Silver Palace and San Francisco's Grand Palace, became popular destinations for Sunday brunch. Then, as more Hong Kong and Taiwan money poured into American Chinatowns in the 1980s, the pendulum swung back to Cantonese cooking, although of a much more authentic form.

THE JAPANESE STEAKHOUSE was a 1964 creation of immigrant Rocky Aioki, shown at far right in this photo of his chefs honing their skills at a teppanyaki table in one of Aioki's highly successful Benihana of Tokyo restaurants; the branch in Tokyo was called Benihana of New York.

Perhaps more important to the success of the Chinese-American restaurant was its readiness to serve food at any and all hours and to pack it up and deliver it with dispatch, all at prices no other ethnic group could match. Chinese take-out went hand in hand with Americans' historic penchant for gobbling up lots of cheap food in as little time and with as little fuss as possible.

Japanese restaurants were almost unknown in the United States until well after World War II. New York had a few in the 1930s—Toyo-Kwan, Daruma, and Miyako, for instance—all serving a simple menu of sukiyaki, teriyaki, and tempura dishes, which even squeamish Americans could enjoy. Sushi bars did not make an appearance until 1957 when Moto Saito opened Saito restaurant in Manhattan. Dressed in traditional Japanese garb, Saito would instruct her customers on the correct way to eat raw fish—something completely foreign to most Americans—and sushi and sashimi restaurants grew in number in the 1970s, cresting in popularity a decade later. Other Japanese restaurants invented dishes especially for the American palate: New York's Nippon introduced negikami, rolls of beef wrapped around scallions in soy sauce. In California, the "Carifonia roll"—Japanese pidgin English for a morsel of sushi made with vinegared rice, avocadoes, and cucumbers—was a hit.

By far the most impressive gimmick to come out of the immigrant experience was the Japanese steakhouse, opened with thirty thousand dollars by immigrant Rocky Aioki in New York in 1964. He called his twenty-eight-seat restaurant Benihana of Tokyo, based on the idea of the Japanese teppan-yaki steel griddle. But Aioki took the concept to a far more theatrical level. Customers would be seated family style around an enormous griddle in the center of a wooden counter. A specially trained chef would arrive, bow to the customers, then, with the dexterity of a circus juggler, begin a dazzling display of knife-sharpening, slicing, dicing, and flipping and arranging steak, shrimp, lobster, and vegetables. The food would sizzle and flame up. The chef would flick a discarded shrimp tail into his pocket, then slide his *hocho* knife into its scabbard with the speed of a samurai. It was great fun, Americans had no gustatory aversions to the food because it was what they liked to eat anyway, and for the price of dinner customers got quite a show.

By the mid-1980s Aioki's Benihana restaurants were located in every major American city, grossing sixty million dollars annually. Ironically, Aioki's father, Yunosuke Aioki, opened a branch in Tokyo in 1958, which he called Benihana of New York.

Mexican restaurants, whose popularity coincided with the arrival of large numbers of Mexican immigrants after 1950, have for the most part followed the form and style of what is called "Tex-Mex" food, an amalgam of Northern Mexican peasant food with Texas farm and cowboy fare. Chili, which some consider Texas's state dish, was unknown in Mexico and derived from the ample use of beef in Texan cooking. "Refried beans" are a mis-translation of the Mexican dish *frijoles refritos,* which actually means "well-fried beans." The first taco stands, found mostly in the South and West, served up cheap, belly-filling food made without much finesse from readily available ingredients, and the proverbial term "hole-in-the-wall" connotes the image of the Mexican-American restaurant probably more than it does any other ethnic eatery.

The combination platter of enchiladas, tacos, and tortillas became the unvarying standards of the Tex-Mex menu, while new dishes like chimichangas (supposedly invented in the 1950s at El Charro restaurant in Tucson, Arizona) and nachos (supposedly first served at a concession at Dallas's State Fair of Texas in 1964 and since then become a staple at American ball parks) were concocted to please the American palate. The salt-rimmed Margarita cocktail, about which there are several stories as to its origin, was developed as a perfect way to set the appetite roaring.

One Tex-Mex item that may someday rival the pizza as an extraordinarily successful ethnic dish is the fajita, a dish of marinated grilled beef in a wheat tortilla, introduced at Ninfa's in Houston on July 13, 1973, as "tacos al carbon." No one knows when or where it acquired the name *fajita*, which means "girdle" or "strip" in Spanish and refers to the skirt steak originally used in the preparation, but the item took off with Americans and was almost immediately extrapolated to mean any kind of meat, fish, or fowl grilled and served in a wheat tortilla.

OPENING DAY IN 1927 for Los Angeles's El Cholo restaurant (across the street from its present location on Western Avenue), a Mexican-American restaurant that has always drawn a non-Latin crowd for dishes like enchiladas, tacos, and burritos. Chef Joe Reina stands at far right.

Only in the last decade has refined, regional Mexican food taken a foothold in American cities, reflecting not only the tenets of Tex-Mex cookery but the cuisines of Mexico City, the Yucatán, and other regions with long-standing culinary traditions.

It would seem that the more an immigrant cook was willing to adapt his traditional foods to the American palate—even creating new dishes when necessary—the more successful he might become. Those cuisines that did not adapt well did not succeed outside of the ethnic neighborhoods nor gain much popularity among American diners.

Despite the influx of Puerto Ricans to the United States from the 1950s onward, no restaurants featuring that island's cookery have made it into the American mainstream, and those that have opened have been largely confined to the Puerto Rican enclaves of the Eastern cities. The same has thus far been true of the Cubans, who started coming to the United States in significant numbers in the 1960s and 1970s to Florida, particularly in the Miami area, where they opened up coffee shops and large-scale restaurants in what came to be called "Little Havana" along "Calle Ocho" (Eighth Street). In terms of ethnic purity, these restaurants, with names like El Bodégon de Castilla, La Esquina de Téjas, and Malaga, served rich, very sweet Cuban coffee, Cuban sandwiches, and Spanish-derived dishes like arroz con pollo, which deviated little from their origins in Cuba.

Traditional Spanish food, on the other hand, has yet to make much headway in American cities, although the oldest and one of the most famous restaurants in Florida is the Columbia in Tampa, opened in 1905. So renowned was chef Francisco Pijuan at the Columbia in the 1920s that when the U.S. government threatened to deport his family for illegally entering the country, local politicians petitioned Congress to pass Private Law 225 to allow them to stay in the United States.

Afro-American food has not had a significant impact on the restaurant industry of America, but it is one of the most interesting examples of adaptive ethnic cooking in the United States. Clearly the slave history of American blacks precluded any opportunities for restaurant ownership in the South before the Civil War, and blacks' food culture was almost entirely based on what they were *allowed* to cook on the farm plantations. A diet rich in vegetables, particularly starches, and chicken and pork led naturally to an affinity for barbecued ribs, fried chicken, chitterlings, collard greens, sweet potato pie, and other deeply flavored foods. But it was not until the 1960s that this basic Southern farm food, though widely eaten by urban blacks, became known as "soul food," to distinguish it from other forms of food eaten in the South.

After the Civil War blacks did open primitive roadhouses, sometimes selling food and drink out of their own homes. In contrast to the white-owned "honky-tonks," blacks opened "juke joints" or "juke houses," where they would have entertainment, liquor, and some form of food service, usually fried chicken. The word "juke" means "disorderly," which pretty much characterized the atmosphere in such places, and generally refers to black-run enterprises, although in Georgia and Florida a juke joint may well denote a white tavern.

Segregation obviously cut off a black restaurant owner from a sizable segment of the population, leading some blacks to cater exclusively to an all-white clientele. In his book *Southern Food* (1987), John Egerton remarks about a once-segregated restaurant called Colonel Hawks run by Louis "Hawks" Rogers in Bardstown, Kentucky:

For almost twenty-five years, the restaurant was prohibited by law from serving both black and white customers, and during that time it stood as a classic example of the nonsensical contradictions of segregation. It was a black-owned public accommodation with an all-white clientele, and the ultimate irony was that America Rogers, Hawks's wife, could cook on the wood stove in the kitchen and Hawk could wait tables, but they could not legally sit down in their own dining room and eat.

In New Orleans, where the African influences on Creole cooking had long been evident in their rich gumbos, after the Civil War blacks opened oyster houses, cafés, and barbecue shacks. In turn, black cooking there absorbed the flavors of Spanish, French, and American Indian ingredients. Today one might dine at a black-owned restaurant like Dooky Chase or Chez Helene and savor the differences between their renditions of jambalaya, fried oysters, and shrimp étouffée and those at white-owned Creole restaurants like Galatoire's, Antoine's, or Arnaud's, despite the presence of black cooks in the kitchen.

In many ways Afro-American food, though itself a jumble of African, Caribbean, and American influences, has remained relatively pure over the

ONE OF THE ODDEST BLENDS of ethnic cuisines is Chinese and Spanish food, as served in several New York eateries like Chinita Restaurant, that are commonly run by immigrants from Puerto Rico.

THE TRADITIONAL ITEMS of African-American food culture—barbecued chicken and ribs—began on southern plantations, but have proliferated in black neighborhoods like New York's Harlem, as shown in this photo of a black barbecue cook in the late 1940s.

last three hundred years, and to eat in a black-owned restaurant today is to eat much as one might have on a Southern plantation in the eighteenth century.

Those dishes that would be as familiar to most white Americans as they would be to blacks—fried chicken, biscuits, ham, and fruit pies—formed the basis of a small menu featured with little variety in some of the more celebrated Harlem nightclubs of the 1920s, 1930s, and 1940s that catered largely to whites and were known more for their entertainments than for the high quality of their food. The famous Cotton Club on Lenox Avenue was exclusively for whites and featured bands led by Cab Calloway and Duke Ellington, but Small's Paradise (where a split of White Rock Ginger Ale cost $1.50) on 135th Street and Seventh Avenue was a mixed "black and tan" club that only opened after 10:00 P.M. The Radium Club was notorious for its "breakfast dances," which lasted from late Saturday night through Sunday morning. At Connie's Inn you could get anything from chow mein to lobster à la newburg.

Where blacks have best succeeded has been in barbecuing, which for centuries in the South has been an important part of public and private entertaining. During slavery days it was the job of black cooks to tend the hot, smoky fires while the whites ate, and the skill of cooking meats over hardwoods was honed over decades and passed down from one black family member to another.

In contrast to the predominance of beef barbecue in the West, Eastern barbecues are based on pork, with ribs and shoulder the preferred cuts. The shoulder meat might be "stripped" or "pulled" or diced with a hatchet or cleaver, then served on a hamburger bun. Slowly tended over a hardwood fire, slathered with a reduction of ingredients commonly containing hot peppers, tomatoes, sugar, and vinegar, or rubbed with nothing but dry spices, barbecue is taken very seriously by both those who cook it and those who eat it, and endless arguments can result over the question of just what makes one person's barbecue "authentic" and another's "commercial."

Barbecue restaurants began popping up around the turn of the century and proliferated throughout the South. Memphis has proclaimed itself the unofficial capital of barbecue in America, with more than three score commercial "pits" in operation, many of them black owned.

Possibly because restaurant work in the South has traditionally been considered menial labor, many modern-day blacks have chosen not to go into the restaurant business nor to maintain the traditions of Afro-American cookery. Too often overlooked is the predominance of blacks in food service, both in kitchens and dining rooms owned by whites. Restaurant food in the South is still largely cooked by blacks, as it was on the railroad dining cars, and as it still is in urban restaurants ranging from short-order luncheonettes to deluxe dining rooms. The unsung black chefs who often just went by their first names—Henry, Thomas, Arthur, Norma, Mary, Esther, and others—may have cooked at the behest of white employers, but it was a cookery often refined by blacks over decades of working in the same kitchen. It was these black chefs who shucked the oysters, turned the spit, basted the turkeys, cut the biscuits, whipped the cream, and set the berries on tables they themselves were forbidden to eat at for most of this century. They formed the backbone of the waitering industry for decades, and today their grandsons and granddaughters have chosen other routes in life.

As Edna Lewis, a chef and authority on African-American cooking, puts it, "The young black girls and boys would just as soon work at McDonald's for minimum wage. They can't make much more in other restaurants in the South, and they just don't seem to show much interest in learning the old-fashioned foods their parents ate."

Perhaps distancing oneself from the foods of the past is one way of being assimilated into a national culture, which took much longer for some ethnic groups than others. For many ethnic cuisines have never fully entered the American food culture, despite a sizable population of immigrants from the countries of origin. The foods of the Armenians, Poles, Czechs, Basques, Hungarians, Irish, Arabs, Puerto Ricans, Spanish, Cubans, Norwegians, Turks, Swiss, and Swedes have all given American cookery extraordinary breadth and depth, but except within those urban neighborhoods where the

THE COOKING OF THE MIDWEST has been much influenced by black food culture as evidenced at Stroud's, which opened in 1933 in Kansas City, Missouri, and today still serves fried chicken dinners, mashed potatoes, and fried chicken gizzards.

NEW YORK'S FAMOUS Russian Tea Room, located "just to the left of Carnegie Hall," was opened in 1926 by expatriate members of the Russian Imperial Ballet and has ever since been a mecca for artists, dancers, and musicians.

immigrants settled, their effect on restaurant-going has been small and their grandsons and granddaughters are more likely to eat "American" dishes rather than go out to a restaurant serving their own ancestors' foods.

Yet for each successive wave of immigrants to this country, from the Germans to the Italians, from the Mexicans to the Cambodians, there has always been a further enrichment of American cooking, all the while based on the idea of abundance, of unlimited access to meats, fruits, and vegetables. In this context, it is easy to understand why recently arrived Russian immigrants, many of them Jews who have settled in Brooklyn, New York, find all notions of modern nutrition and diet completely foreign to their attitude toward food.

The first Russian restaurants in America were attempts to maintain a nostalgic link to a vanished tsarist era. In 1910 there were only ninety thousand Russians in the entire United States, but the Bolshevik Revolution caused many White Russians to flee to New York, where some opened restaurants as gathering places for dislocated émigrés. "New York is rich in Russian haunts," observed Charles G. Shaw in a 1931 guide to Gotham's nightlife. "Certain of these nooks are run by impoverished nobles, so don't be surprised to learn that your waitress was once a princess." Indeed, New York's famous Russian Tea Room was opened in 1926 by members of the Russian Imperial Ballet on the site of a former girls' school and began almost immediately to attract Russian artists, writers, and musicians. To this day the Russian Tea Room, which is, as its ads say, "slightly to the left of Carnegie Hall," has functioned as a worldly evocation of pre-Revolutionary Russia, where the caviar and vodka flow amid a festive atmosphere of bright silver samovars and Expressionist paintings.

But the new wave of Russian immigrants has only arrived on these shores in the last decade—fifty thousand in 1990. Forced from a multinational society into a multiethnic urban swirl of races, colors, and creeds, it is only natural for these people to close ranks and congregate together in restaurants of their own devising, places exemplifying all that America has ever represented to immigrants. The Russian community in Brooklyn's Brighton Beach is called "Little Odessa," where twenty thousand Russians settled in 1990, and on weekends the immigrant families pile into club restaurants like the National, the Zodiac, and the Primorski for an exercise in overconsumption that would amaze the average American. The people dress up in the most colorful, ostentatious clothes. A band plays sentimental Russian songs. Waiters deliver trays of rich *zakuski* (appetizers), platters of sausage, skewers of lamb, bowls of *pelmeny* dumplings, pots of red cabbage, and all manner of pastries. All of it, along with gallons of vodka, is consumed with unbridled gusto, as the people desport themselves in age-old dances and roar out folk songs late into the night. There is no let-up, no pulling back, no desire to turn down the volume or stop eating.

They are people who in their own country may never have been to a restaurant, never had more than a few pounds of meat per month to eat, and took no joy in the prospect of waiting on another line for whatever was left on the shelves of a dreary supermarket. "Russians suffered from a lack of food for years," a reporter for the Russian-language newspaper *Novoye Ruskoye Slovo,* told *The New York Times,* "and so the notion of dieting is alien to our culture. Every calorie is prized, even if it is all fat. Russians often had trouble getting clothes, so now many dress in these garish outfits and expensive shoes that look like wedding cake designs of Stalinist architecture. The clubs let them show off and eat and drink to excess, all signs of success in the immigrant country."

It was not so different for most of the immigrants who came to this country, beginning with the Pilgrims, who almost starved that first winter at Plymouth. For these Russians, and for the Germans and Jews, the Italians and the Chinese, the Cambodians and the Mexicans who came before them, America was a land of milk and honey, all served up on silver platters in restaurants they themselves crafted to replicate some fantastic restaurant of their imagination, places they might only have dreamed of being part of before coming to America.

The imposing iron gates of New York's "21" Club

Chapter 6

Joe Sent Me

Eating Out During the Noble Experiment

IT WAS AN IRONY of the late nineteenth century that while Americans' consumption of alcohol had dropped precipitously after the Civil War, the movement to wipe out alcohol abuse gained its greatest potency. In 1830 Americans drank an astonishing seven gallons of spirits per person per year—and little of that was wine or beer. Twenty years later annual consumption had dropped to only about two gallons per person and has never gone higher than three, yet the call for temperance grew louder and more vociferous as the century turned over, culminating in the passage of the Eighteenth Amendment on January 16, 1919, which prohibited the manufacture, sale, and distribution of intoxicating liquors in the United States.

If the principal goal of the Temperance Movement was to stop drunkenness, the direct object of its wrath was the saloon. The movement's most notorious crusader was Carry Nation, a Kansas woman who, beginning in 1899, tore into saloons with her hatchet (she called herself a "hatchetarian"), showing the ends to which zealots would go to destroy what they believed to be the satanic crucibles of so much wickedness. Her favorite synonym for a saloon was "hellhole." Carry Nation's radical tactics may have set back the movement more than it helped, but the more reasonable Anti-Saloon League, founded in Washington, D.C., in 1893, lobbied not so much against the drunkard as against the source of his drinking.

THE PASSAGE OF THE EIGHTEENTH Amendment on January 16, 1919, set the stage for the opening of illicit saloons called "speakeasies," whose proliferation outpaced law officers' resources to close them down in any significant numbers.

From the beginning, temperance leaders had inveighed against saloons as the instigators of a moral decay that threatened to destroy family, community, and nation through alcohol abuse. And where they found saloons, they invariably found evidence of other forms of sin, particularly prostitution. In Philadelphia alone in 1876 a census found that of the more than eight thousand legal and illegal drinking establishments, nearly half of them were associated with brothels.

Concern over drunkenness in American taverns dates back to the earliest of the colonies. In the nineteenth century problems of alcohol abuse were exacerbated by the rigors, stresses, and inequities forced upon workers in the industrial cities. Social workers of the post–Civil War era estimated that at least 20 percent of urban poverty cases were in some way caused by alcohol, and "skid rows" (derived from Seattle lumberjacks' term for the track down which they slid logs) became rampant from coast to coast, although, as Mark Edward Lender and James Kirby Martin point out in *Drinking in America* (1982), most skid row inhabitants have never been alcoholics. Mostly they were the urban poor, driven out of work by the immigrants who flocked to the cities and took their jobs at lower wages, a fact of economic life that served to fuel a national antipathy toward foreigners.

Temperance leaders picked up on and used this hatred for their own purposes. Even though the Italians and Jews had the lowest rate of alcoholism in the United States, Prohibitionists blamed the immigrants for spreading the "free-and-easy drinking customs of Europe," corrupting American values, and, noted the vitriolic Reverend Daniel Dorchester, the names above the doors of liquor shops, saloons, and beer gardens were immigrant names, while the liquor trade itself was clearly seen to be "in the hands of a low class of foreigners." And World War I further stirred up anti-German resentment against brewery owners in the United States.

Finally, the Temperance Movement fit impeccably into the ideals of progressive Americans who feared factories would fill up with unproductive, foreign drunkards with no real stake in the nation's future. As a result, men like Henry Ford, John D. Rockefeller, Andrew Carnegie, and other tycoons of big business were drawn into the Prohibitionist fold, and Carnegie's first dictum to a young man bent on achieving success in this world was "never enter a bar-room, nor let the contents of a bar-room enter you."

In some ways the fears were justified. For although Americans were drinking less alcohol than many Europeans, too much of what we did drink was hard liquor, and much of it was consumed with the sole object of getting drunk. Wine with meals has never been a part of the average American's lifestyle; in fact, the most wine Americans ever drank before World War I was less than half a gallon per person per year, whereas in France and Italy annual consumption was nearly thirty gallons per person.

The popularity of saloons—from the skid row drinking houses to the marble-and-mahogany gentlemen's bars—was abetted by the concept of the "free lunch," a gimmick designed to attract customers who would run up a bar bill while indulging themselves with the complimentary food. Some believe the idea of the free lunch began in New Orleans, possibly at the St. Louis Hotel, while others contend it was contrived in San Francisco in the 1880s along what was known as "the Cocktail Route." At the Palace of Art restaurant in that city the free lunch menu listed crab salad, clam juice, head cheese, pig's head, sausages, chili con carne, corned beef, pork and beans, beef stew, popcorn, apples, and other items intended to make the customer stick around and order more beer or liquor.

Cocktails were very much an American invention and were in many ways as typical of American life as baseball, marching bands, and motorcars. Cocktails were mixed drinks that married Americans' love of spirits with their genius for invention, so that an array of new cocktail recipes may be found in almost every decade since the 1860s, when the cocktail shaker was invented. The first mention of the word "cocktail" in print was in 1806, though no one knows for sure where the term came from. The most famous recipe book of the nineteenth century was *The Bon-Vivant's Companion, or*

How to Mix Drinks (1862), compiled by "Professor" Jerry Thomas, bartender in San Francisco's Occidental Hotel, but even the ladies' books of the era sometimes included a few recipes for sours, fizzes, smashes, and flips.

Cocktails were introduced to Europe at the turn of the century, and the "American bar" became popular in cities like London and Paris before World War I and fixtures after the onset of Prohibition. But cocktails were not nearly so much a part of European social life as they were in the United States. Evelyn Waugh said that the idea of a cocktail before a dinner party had little cachet in England until after World War I.

At first the cocktail was regarded as a morning tonic, which is really not so difficult to understand once one realizes that originally alcoholic distillations were the product of apothecaries, and the American cocktail began, like Coca-Cola, in the pharmacies as a medicinal aid full of aromatics and herbs like gentian, orange, quinine, and ginger. Wormwood, used for centuries as an elixir, was popularized in 1792 by French physician Pierre Ordinaire as absinthe. By the 1830s the drink was being served as a liqueur in New Orleans, where it was the featured drink at the Old Absinthe House and the basis of the Sazerac cocktail. After the turn of the century wormwood was discovered to have deleterious effects on the nervous system and was outlawed in the United States in 1912.

While the idea of a cocktail as a "pick-me-up" (a term used at least since 1867) persists to this day, the naming of cocktails in the late nineteenth and early twentieth centuries shows that they had long since lost their original purpose. Cocktails were named after people (Tom and Jerry, Gibson, Ramos gin fizz), places (Daiquiri, Bronx, Manhattan), heroes (Rob Roy), even military weapons (French 75, after a French gun of World War I), but none ever took on the iconography of the Martini, the origins of which, ironically, have never been certified. "Professor" Thomas has been credited with concocting a similar, though somewhat sweet, drink called the "Martinez," but, despite the best efforts of the most indefatigable scholars, like Lowell Edmunds, who devoted an entire book to the "The Martini in American Civilization" entitled *The Silver Bullet* (1981), the cocktail's birthplace and progenitor remain a mystery.

The Martini's symbolic importance can hardly be underestimated, however, for it was a drink that helped define a segment of American society at the turn of the century, associated not with the coarse laborer drinking beer in a workingman's saloon or the immigrant gulping down rough red wine or whiskey in a city tavern, but with a more worldly, urbane sophisticate who drank in grand gin palaces fitted out with potted ferns, tile floors, brass railings, and paintings of voluptuous nudes.

When the hero of Hemingway's *A Farewell to Arms* (1929), Frederic Henry, joins his lover, Catherine Barkley, at a hotel bar on Lake Maggiore to eat sandwiches and drink Martinis, he remembers, "I had never tasted anything so cool and clean. They made me feel civilized." H. L. Mencken called the Martini "the only American invention as perfect as a sonnet," and American writer Bernard De Voto pronounced it the "supreme American gift to world culture."

The thought that such a "gift" could possibly be interpreted as a contributor to depravity was laughed at by those who regarded temperance

DESPITE THE EFFORTS of federal agents to locate and destroy stocks of illegal alcohol, as shown in this attempt to burn a store of Chicago beer and wine kegs, finding a drink anywhere in the United States during Prohibition was fairly easy to accomplish.

advocates as ridiculously out of step with the Gilded Age. Mencken scoffed at the idea of teetotalers, saying, "A prohibitionist is the sort of man one wouldn't care to drink with—even if he drank." But the march toward national Prohibition was relentless, claiming victories even before the Civil War. Maine had gone dry as early as 1841, most of the South followed after the war, and by 1913 more than half the population of the United States lived in regions where some form of prohibition was in force. The Webb-Kenyon Act of 1913 stopped liquor distributors from shipping their goods from wet states into dry ones, and by World War I, a majority of Americans seemed ready to give enforced abstinence from alcohol a try.

Easily ratified by Congress on December 5, 1917, the Eighteenth Amendment was rushed to state ratification. The Amendment was passed on January 16, 1919, and the law went into effect one year later, over Woodrow Wilson's veto. Herbert Hoover proclaimed it "a great social and economic experiment, noble in motive and far-reaching in purpose."

The enforcement of the amendment was provided for under the Volstead Act (formally called the National Prohibition Act, but named after its sponsor, Representative Andrew Volstead of Minnesota), and the enforcers started off the mark with zeal, sending agents after as many mountain moonshiners as they did bar keepers, so that the reformers' long-sought goal of closing down saloons was immediately (if temporarily) achieved. But in shuttering the saloons, Prohibition also severely restricted the business of all restaurants where alcohol was sold, whether it was a deluxe hotel dining room with a fine wine list, a German beer hall, or a storefront eatery in Little Italy. Indeed, the more conspicuous the eating place, the more difficult it was to conceal illicit liquor service. And, more troubling still to the honest restaurateur, the more illicit an entrepreneur was willing to be, the more chance he had of making a very good profit from the sale of booze.

"Prohibition has taken away the incentive for leisure at the table," wrote James Remington McCarthy in his history of the Waldorf-Astoria, *Peacock Alley* (1931). "One does not sit long over a demi-tasse; it is apt to become cold. After-dinner discussion (once the accepted final course in the meal) has languished and vanished because it lacks fuel. . . . The unhappy result of all this is reflected in some first-class restaurants and hotels, where chefs, *maîtres d'hôtel,* managers and proprietors are making a stand to maintain the old traditions of dining. They respect and obey the law—and at what a price their thinning numbers testify. They are soon to be extinct, it seems."

Prohibition crippled fine dining (as well as a wine industry in its infancy) in this country for longer than the decade in which it was the law of the land. At the same time it gave rise to a new species of food service operations—the speakeasy—whose short but notorious history had an enormous impact on the way many Americans dined out after World War I, not least in bringing gangsterism into the restaurant business and corruption to municipal government. This intrusion, of course, played right into the hands of those who had always regarded even the most decorous of restaurants as occasions of sin and dens of iniquity, where gluttony was but a facet of dissolution.

Ironically, even before Prohibition some connoisseurs were complaining that too much alcohol was ruining fine dining. Music critic James Huneker observed in 1914 that "cocktails and the common consumption of spirits have banished all sense of taste values." In fact, the ratio of beer versus hard spirits consumption was dramatically altered during Prohibition: Before the Volstead Act, Americans consumed 55 percent of their alcohol as beer and 37 percent as liquor; afterward, the figures changed to 15 percent beer and 75 percent spirits.

The grand restaurants like Delmonico's and Louis Sherry's struggled to survive but were squeezed into insolvency by Prohibitionist strictures. Hotels like the Ritz-Carlton, the Plaza, and the Waldorf-Astoria, which depended on their room rentals for profits, were forced to keep their restaurants open but lost much of the gaiety—and most of the free-spending customers—of the past. The bar at the Hotel Jerome in Aspen, Colorado, was turned into a soda fountain. And the famous Wine Rooms at Boston's Locke-Ober Café had to be shuttered and the wine cellar sealed up. The Depression made it difficult for hotels to stay open at all. The lavish Pierre Hotel in New York opened in 1930 and filed for bankruptcy two years later. By 1930 paying guests at the Broadmoor in Colorado Springs totaled sixty for the entire season; the kitchen staff was commensurately reduced to seven. And The Homestead resort in Hot Springs, Virginia, which had been around since 1846, was only rescued from closure by World War II, when 363 Japanese diplomats, newspapermen, and businessmen were interned there.

The Roaring Twenties did not roar in fine restaurants, where flappers and their boyfriends could not get a drink, but in speakeasies. The term

THE NOTORIOUS Mary Louise Cecilia "Texas" Guinan seems little fazed by being arrested for running a series of New York speakeasies she called "Portable Night Clubs," knowing she will probably be released on bail within hours and running her establishments again by the next evening. Guinan taunted authorities by wearing a gold police whistle around her neck, and greeted her customers with the phrase "Hello, sucker."

"Café Society" predated the onset of Prohibition by a year, when New York columnist "Cholly Knickerbocker" (Maury Paul) used it to describe a chic young crowd that spent most of their free time in saloons. When Prohibition came, these people turned away from the fine restaurants and cafés and headed straight for the speakeasies, which, in addition to serving liquor, had the intoxicating allure of being more than a little risqué and, therefore, glamorous.

The term "speakeasy" dates back to the early nineteenth century, to the English "speak-softly-shop," an underworld term for a smuggler's house where one could purchase cheap liquor. The word was picked up in the 1920s to describe the new saloons springing up first in the cities, then in rural areas, usually hidden away in the scruffier parts of town.

THE "21" CLUB was the last and most successful of speakeasies run by Jack Kriendler and Charlie Berns, who catered to "Café Society" throughout Prohibition and afterward. In this photo, Kriendler is third from the left.

In fact, most of the early speakeasies were rough, unsavory places, where a knock at the door brought a grunted response from a bouncer behind a sliding panel who asked the visitor for some form of reference. As time went on, the demands for secrecy loosened and a simple "Joe sent me" was usually sufficient to gain access. Journalist Waverley Root wrote of that period, "I do not recall that we were overly conscious of the fact that we were breaking the law, though of course we were not ignorant of it. There was probably more pleasure to be derived from a sense of superiority at being able to gain admission to a closed circle that did not admit everybody (though it is difficult to imagine anyone too uncouth to get into *some* establishment)."

French diplomat Paul Morand, visiting New York for the first time in 1925, described his experience at a speakeasy, sparing little in his ethnic slurs:

There is a truly New York atmosphere of humbug in the whole thing. The interior is that of a criminal house; shutters are closed in full daylight, and one is caught in the smell of a cremation furnace. Italians with a too familiar manner, or plump, blue jowled pseudo-bullfighters, carrying bunches of monastic keys, guide you through the deserted rooms of the abandoned house. Facetious inscriptions grimace from the walls. There are a few very flushed diners. At one table some habitués are asleep, their heads sunk on their arms; behind a screen somebody is trying to restore a young woman who has had an attack of hysteria. . . . The food is almost always, poor, the service deplorable.

As enforcement authorities lessened their vigilance or were corrupted into unofficial negligence, the image of the speakeasy became a lot more risqué than the reality. The so-called "cocktail hour" began when a restaurant named Tony's on East Fifty-third Street began promoting the hours from four P.M. to six, when, according to an understanding with the police, speakeasies were allowed to open for business. Thanks to a thoroughly entrenched system of graft and police corruption, New York's speakeasies flourished, so that after a while, no one paid much attention to their illegality. P. J. Clarke's, an Irish saloon that opened in 1904, never closed its doors for a moment during Prohibition. They sold "3.2 beer" (the legal limit for alcohol was 3.2 percent), but stocked the real beer in kegs in the basement, and only brought up one bottle of liquor at a time, kept in a locked cabinet called the "coop."

Nationally, the Volstead Act had teeth: The federal government arrested half a million people during Prohibition and convicted three hundred thousand of them. But, as Lender and Martin note, "New York . . . repealed its enforcement act in 1923, claiming it was ineffective, which was true enough—juries in wet areas often flatly refused to convict even the most blatant violators. Of some seven thousand New York arrests between 1921 and 1923, only twenty-seven resulted in convictions." Maryland never even bothered to pass an enforcement act and other states put up only a ridiculously small amount of money—one thousand dollars a year in Nevada, Utah, and Missouri—to support the new law. As a result, New York had more than thirty-two thousand speakeasies within its boroughs—twice the number of saloons closed down by the Volstead enforcers.

Prices at these establishments were absurdly high, even though the liquor itself was generally of poor—if not toxic—quality. Lender and Martin show that cocktails that sold for 15 cents in 1918 were going for 75 cents after the onset of Prohibition. And a barrel of beer that once cost $10.50 soared to $160. Imported liquor was even more outrageously priced, and bootlegging became established as a profession during the 1920s.

Not all the speakeasies lived up to their opponents' dire descriptions. By far the most celebrated of all the New York operations was a place that drew the toniest of crowds almost from the day it opened. This was the infamous—now famous—"21" Club, opened by John Carl Kriendler and Charles A. Berns, the sons of Austrian immigrant families.

Back in 1922 Jack Kriendler had no thought of making his life as New York's premier saloonkeeper; he simply wanted to make a little money one summer before returning to Fordham University. Borrowing $1,000 from relatives, he opened a "tea room" he called the "Red Head" at Sixth between Fourth and Washington Place under the elevated subway. Whether or not tea was ever served there is doubtful, for with its curtained-off kitchen and covered windows, the Red Head's customers were after harder stuff, and the place immediately drew a college crowd, musicians, artists, and newspapermen. "It wasn't the usual speak where people silently packed down the hooch," said Pete Kriendler, Jack's younger brother, who came in to help out. "Jack ran the Red Head like a fraternity room . . . a jivey, jazzy place, good clean fun—everyone danced the Charleston, played practical jokes, and shouting 'Nerts to you.' When the band took a break, the customers themselves picked up the beat on the club's piano, banjoes, and drums. It was nondescript, a room to pack into and to smoke, dance, talk and drink in."

Berns came aboard first as accountant for the bustling little speakeasy, then as full partner, while continuing his studies. He even got his law degree, which eventually helped in fending off the authorities. The booze was supplied by Kriendler's uncle Sam Brenner and packaged by his own mother. The two boys prospered, but it was not a success without a few setbacks, as on the night a drunken fireman slashed Berns's throat from ear to ear with a razor. After that incident, the boys sought the protection of the local politicians and police, who were only too happy to help out—for a regular fee—two enterprising young fellows who ran a clean speakeasy, with no drugs, gambling, or prostitutes.

The boys' next venture was a far more attractive spot across the street called the Fronton, which seated sixty people at banquettes and tables, had tablecloths, and a bar whose liquor could easily be poured down a drain underneath the floor boards. Before long an Italian chef was brought in to cook up a simple menu of steaks, chops, and sandwiches, which was considerably more than most speakeasies of the time bothered to offer their patrons.

In addition to attracting Greenwich Village artists and writers, the Fronton lured many of New York's powerbrokers, none more so than the ebullient, unrepentant mayor himself, Jimmy Walker. To their amazement, Kriendler and Berns were fast becoming arbiters of New York society, so that getting past the peephole at the Fronton was considered a downtown rite of passage. No revenue agent ever set foot in the Fronton—at least not with any intent of closing the place down—but a new subway forced the property to be condemned, so Kriendler and Berns decided to move their business uptown to the carriage trade district of West Forty-ninth Street.

Their new club was named, quite flagrantly, the "Puncheon Grotto," but everyone called it "No. 42," after its address, 42 West Forty-ninth Street, or just plain "Jack and Charlie's." It was an instantaneous, overnight success. Soon it was a magnet for a new, even more celebrated clientele than the Fronton had enjoyed, including Robert Benchley, Alexander Woollcott, Edna Ferber, Dorothy Parker, and other members of The Algonquin Round Table.

Far more important to its longevity than its momentary celebrity, however, was the novelty of a speakeasy serving its customers very good food and excellent wines, while keeping out the riffraff, prostitutes, and the merely curious by charging outrageous prices—twenty dollars for lunch. But Jack and Charlie's largesse was constant, through good times and bad. When the Stock Market crashed in October 1929, Kriendler and Berns granted faithful patrons a great deal of long-term credit and lent them money to get them back on their feet, even issuing "21" Club scrip.

But progress once again forced them to move: The Puncheon Grotto unfortunately stood in the way of plans for Rockefeller Center. So, on its last night in operation, New Year's Eve, 1929, Kriendler and Berns held a "demolition party," which began with a lavish dinner and ended with Berns handing out crowbars, axes, and hammers to his staff and customers, inviting them to tear the place apart in preparation for the move to 21 West Fifty-second Street.

"What we didn't want to take with us we chopped to splinters," recalled one reveler, "and a friendly cop on the beat, *riding his horse,* came inside and helped trample the rubble. A famous banker . . . tore apart the men's room and wore the toilet seat around his neck while he did the hula. [Film star] Doris Kenyon personally demolished the ladies' room, wearing *that* toilet seat around her neck as if it were a lavaliere. During the party, everyone tried to think of a name for the new place. Charlie simply figured that since No. 21 is half of 42, and No. 42 brought them luck, then why not just call it Jack & Charlie's '21.'" The next day Kriendler and Berns were serving lunch at their new place with the new name.

ALWAYS ONE OF THE MOST DAPPER dressers in New York, Jack Kriendler (*opposite*) epitomized the swagger of the Roaring Twenties and set the style for "21" Club habitués. Jack's younger brother, Pete (*this page, on the left*), oversaw one of the finest wine cellars in the world, to this day sequestered behind a massive, two-ton brick door opened by a piece of wire.

The "21" Club was set in a beautiful Manhattan townhouse (today three times its original size). Upstairs were lavish dining rooms, but downstairs was the small, preferred bar area more in keeping with the raffish spirit of the place. The Club was raided during Prohibition, but no agent ever turned up a drop of booze. When the raiders banged at the door of "21," a buzzer sounded throughout the building, and within minutes all liquor bottles were swept down bins by tilting the shelves. A cache of thousands of cases of rare wines—many the private stock of customers—lay hidden (as it still is) behind a massive two-ton door that was a masterpiece of obfuscation and security, opened by a thin piece of wire inserted into one of many holes in its surface and swung open so smoothly that it would not wake an infant in a nursery. In June 1932, ten agents scoured "21" for twelve hours and came away empty-handed, only to find tickets on their car windows, courtesy of the New York Police Department, which good citizen Berns had called to complain of the agents' illegally parked vehicles.

"21" was easily the most sophisticated watering hole in the United States, not just for its clientele but for its food, which rivaled that at the finest hotel dining rooms of the day. Captains flamed dishes tableside and went through the dramatic ritual of pressed duck. Caviar was plentiful, the *foie gras* was from Strasbourg, and, of course, the best wines and liquors were always available. The "21" Club's wholesale food bills ran fifty thousand dollars in 1933, and they charged accordingly. Broadway writer Howard Dietz once said of "21" Club's clientele, "It is the New York that can afford the price but is afraid to go where it's too fancy." And Damon Runyon once wrote that Kriendler and Burns had a secret room where they met to laugh hysterically after presenting checks to their customers.

Kriendler and Berns were master restaurateurs for a new age, not the supercilious, swooping maître d's like Oscar of the Waldorf, but men who felt very much on the same proletarian plane as their illustrious customers and who sometimes functioned as much like father figures as they did members of a secret society whose only rules were to have a good time and to outwit the feds. They instructed their doorman, the notorious Jimmie Coslove, to turn away all who did not fit the "21" image, no matter how much money or fame had accrued to them. As a young Jewish immigrant child from the Lower East Side, Jack Kriendler could not possibly have hoped to become part of the uptown social world, yet he did. He golfed, motored, and rode horses with the most celebrated people of his day—all of them customers wanting a downstairs table at "21." He was called by one wag, "an impenetrable iceberg of defense against elements undesirable."

Yet the majority of speakeasies during Prohibition were run by undesirables, and organized crime flourished throughout the period by producing, shipping, distributing, and serving booze, usually in speakeasies run by mobsters like Big Jim Colosimo in Chicago, who was himself gunned down in 1920 by an upstart Al Capone.

When police moved in on a speakeasy, more often than not the owner simply moved elsewhere, and customers faithfully followed. At San Francisco's Hotel d'Oloron in North Beach, federal agents would repeatedly hold raids, then ask the court to shut down the premises at that address. The resourceful hotel owner would thereupon have a carpenter cut out a new front door into the alley, declare a new address, and go back in business. The feds would raid the new address, and the cycle began again.

Strange as it may seem, the citizens of Los Angeles and Hollywood staunchly supported temperance even before the onset of Prohibition, with

HOLLYWOOD'S COCOANUT GROVE, opened in 1921, attracted the movie star community for dining and dancing. Though not a speakeasy, liquor flowed freely throughout Prohibition, often dropped off in suitcases by private limousines.

most of the wet communities and bars lying beyond the city limits in Venice, Watts, and Vernon. When Prohibition came, a string of cabarets, gambling houses, and speakeasies opened in Culver City with names like the Kit Kat Club, Harlow's Cafe, Monkey Farm, Midnight Frolics, DooDoo Inn, and the Sneak Inn, most of them run by mobsters and all serviced by flotillas of rum-runners' boats plying the coast.

When the posh Ambassador Hotel opened on Wilshire Boulevard in 1921, the garish Cocoanut Grove nightclub became the first of many lavish night spots Hollywood's movie colony hied to, where getting a drink was no problem. "On nights when a big shindig was planned," wrote Jim Heimann in *Out with the Stars: Hollywood Nightlife in the Golden Era* (1985),

"long lines of limousines would drive up to the Ambassador's porte cochere and deposit heavy suitcases. Later in the evening, guests who had made provisions ahead could find their beverages discreetly placed under their table."

Food was never a high priority at the Grove, floor shows took precedence over good taste, and the gimmickry of the faux-jungle decor spurred other entrepreneurs to come up with even more outrageous designs. At Coffee Dan's, customers would slide down a chute into a den where Apache dancers performed to jazz.

People went for the excitement, not the food. Burgers, chili, and fried chicken were pick-up items in places like Ptomaine Tommy's, the White Spot, and Pigs and Zeppelins. One restaurant that did try to upgrade food service and offer the Hollywood crowd a scintilla of sophistication got its name from an offhand remark of actress Gloria Swanson's ex-husband, Herbert Somborn, who said, "You could open a restaurant in an alley and call it anything. If the food and service were good, the patrons would just come flocking. It could even be called something as ridiculous as the Brown Derby." And so it was that a restaurant opened in 1926, opposite the Ambassador Hotel, named after and shaped like a hat.

THE ORIGINAL BROWN DERBY, opened in Los Angeles in 1926, was known for its ridiculous name, its quirky shape, its simple American fare, and its Hollywood clientele.

The Brown Derby soon became the favorite hangout for Hollywood. Three years later a second, larger version was opened off Hollywood Boulevard and Vine. The place was anything but sleazy, and management prided itself on the cleanliness of the premises and the spiffiness of the waitresses (who were dressed in hoopskirts starched to resemble derby hats) as well as on the food, which was simple and basically American—lobsters, corned beef hash, ham sandwiches, Cobb salads, and creamed chicken. Somborn even hired a public relations firm to get his restaurants into the celebrity pages as often as possible.

The twenties spent itself on extravagance, and the Depression that followed was to stunt still further fine dining in America. To be sure, there were good, wholesome eateries serving basic American food in every town in the United States, and family restaurants serving up menus full of clam chowder, shrimp cocktails, Virginia ham, leg of lamb, mashed potatoes, creamed spinach, pecan pie, and doughnuts suffered little from the deprivations of Prohibition. But it was unquestionably a time when fine dining was not something most Americans knew nor cared much about, as long as they were having a good time whooping it up or enjoying a simple meal with a glass of milk or cup of coffee on the side.

The Waldorf's chronicler, James Remington McCarthy, bemoaned the fact that "cultured, leisurely dining no longer is an important or vital part of their lives, at least so far as public dining-places are concerned. We do not live to eat. We sometimes eat to live. Sometimes—generally, in fact—we just eat."

Critics may have been too harsh, for they underestimated the savoriness of American regional cooking, which was being done quite nicely in small restaurants from Maine to San Diego. But there can be no doubt that fine dining had been severely limited by and took a long while to recover from Prohibition, even after it ended on December 5, 1933.

Although ultimately Prohibition was a failure, to a large extent it achieved many of the goals of its advocates. Mark Twain was only half right when he observed back in 1867, "Prohibition only drives drunkenness behind doors and into dark places, and does not cure it or even diminish it." For despite the persistent popular belief that the sale and consumption of alcohol increased during Prohibition, studies have shown that during Prohibition absolute alcohol consumption rates were one third to one half less than before it went into effect, and that after its repeal there was no dramatic increase in consumption. It took a decade for alcohol consumption to grow to pre-Prohibition levels—about two gallons per person per year—and rose upward by less than a gallon over the next thirty years. Also, hospital admissions of patients suffering from alcohol abuse did in fact drop sharply during Prohibition, as did the death rate from alcoholism.

By the time national Prohibition ended with the adoption of the Twenty-first Amendment (with many states and counties continuing to restrict the sale of alcohol), Americans had been sobered up by other, more devastating deprivations in their lives. The Depression, exacerbated by droughts in the mid-1930s, threw America into shock. The land of plenty was dry in a far more troubling sense than the temperance advocates would have had it. Food was scarce, but Americans still had to eat. And in an odd, almost innocent way, the most amazing chapter of eating out in America was set to begin.

Form and function architecture by the American roadside

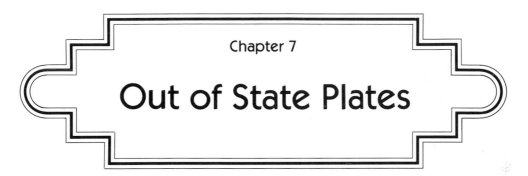

Chapter 7

Out of State Plates

Roadside Restaurants in the 1920s and 1930s

"THE VISION OF MILK AND HONEY, it comes and goes," wrote E. B. White, "but the odor of cooking goes on forever." In the 1920s the aroma of hamburgers and hash browns on the griddle, the sound of a milk-shake being whirred in a blender, and the sight of freshly baked pies coming out of the kitchen were as ubiquitous out on America's highways as they were in Americans' homes. Those who dreamed of the West as a land of milk and honey went out to find it, but found instead orange groves, tomato farms, potato fields, and vineyards. And along the route they found the land dotted with eateries of every shape and size, from a beanery in Oklahoma City to a taco stand in Santa Ana.

In 1930 the population of the United States stood at nearly 123 million—up 30 million in just ten years—with the most rapid growth occurring in the West and in the suburbs of Eastern cities. Americans were on the move, some displaced by the upheavals of the Depression, some seeking a new way of life in new industries, and others who just wanted to see the breadth of the United States, now grown to forty-eight states.

No other people on the face of the earth had the freedom to move or the inclination to leave their homesteads so readily. Every form of modern transport encouraged in the American mind mobility—faster steamships, streamlined trains, and airplanes that could carry passengers from coast to coast in hours rather than days. But no form of transportation molded the

American character or became more synonymous with it than the automobile, of which there were twenty-six million in 1930. Brand new highways crisscrossed plains, deserts, forests, and mountains, with thousands of miles added every year, even during the darkest days of the Depression.

With uncharacteristic insight and prescience Herbert Hoover observed in 1928, "The slogan of progress is changing from the full dinner pail to the full garage." And if Americans did not take the dinner pail (or, more likely, a picnic basket) with them in the car, they needed to find a place to eat alongside of the road. This new demand was met with dazzling ingenuity. Small-time entrepreneurs and big-time operators created an array of roadside eateries in many forms and at every level to feed a population that was expanding, literally and figuratively, across the highways of America.

These new restaurants created unique styles of populist architecture and invested the culture with an iconography that would feed off itself in countless paintings, dramas, motion pictures, books, and songs that would become as familiar to Americans as stories in the Bible. The sassy yet sentimental lunch-counter waitress, the screaming Greek diner owner, the jovial black short-order cook, the truck driver who knows where to get the best meal in the worst town, the drifter who gets a job as a dishwasher and becomes an object of intense scrutiny by townspeople—all became stereotypes of American culture, from potboilers and B-movies to Pulitzer Prize–winning plays and novels by America's finest writers. The works of Sherwood Anderson, Ernest Hemingway, Ring Lardner, James Farrell, John Dos Passos, John

THREE EXAMPLES of American **Programmatic restaurants**—(*above*) **Hood's Ice Cream stand, Boston, Massachusetts;** (*right*) **The Ice Cream Carton, Berlin, Connecticut; and** (*far right*) **Randy's Donuts, Inglewood, California**

Steinbeck, William Inge, William Saroyan, Carson McCullers, and Tennessee Williams are full of such characters, and a whole genre of "on-the-road" books, movies, and pop music has been built around diners and lunchrooms and the melodramas and tragedies played out in sad cafés.

The United States was saturated, almost overnight, with new kinds of eateries—diners, cafeterias, soda shops, luncheonettes, Automats, barbecue stands, drive-ins, refreshment stands, ice cream parlors, and the new chain restaurants that blossomed during the 1920s and 1930s. This rapid expansion was made possible by the highway system itself, while new technologies made the availability of a wide array of foods a common denominator of American life. The self-contained refrigerator, introduced in 1915 by the Frigidaire division of General Motors, gained immediate acceptance: Within five years there were more than two hundred refrigerator brands on the market. In 1931 the product was further improved when Frigidaire brought out a unit that used Freon, thereby reducing the risk from toxic fumes. At the same time Clarence Birdseye developed a successful method for freezing vegetables.

Other, less dramatic inventions like the bottlecap (invented in 1892), stainless-steel cutlery (1921) and cookware (1927), the automatic toaster (1924), the electric mixer (1931), the coffee percolator (1890), the milk bottle (1884), homogenized milk (1927), butter molded in one-pound packages (1922), and sliced bread (1928) gave rise to new forms of faster, more appealing, and more consistent food service. A durable plastic laminate called Formica made sanitation easier and decor colors brighter than ever before,

while the jukebox (1905) turned small restaurants into convivial meeting spots for all age groups at all hours of the day and night.

No longer did you go to a restaurant merely to eat. You went to see friends, play music, swap stories, and gossip. Romances were begun and ended over malted milks and cups of coffee. Families enjoyed Sunday dinner at the local cafeteria, men got away from their wives (and vice versa) at the corner coffee shop, business was conducted over ham and eggs, and deals clinched over steaks and baked potatoes. Thus, the American restaurant had become an opportunity for the small businessman to make a good buck by feeding a previously untapped mass market that had great mobility and an insatiable curiosity for new gadgets like electric mixers, soft ice cream dispensers, soda machines, deep fryers, percolators, and new decorative elements like stainless and porcelain-enameled steel, Naugahyde, glass blocks, and neon lights. Restaurant-going became a night out, an entertainment, an adventure, and everybody was welcome.

The evolution of the modern roadside restaurant began in 1872 in Providence, Rhode Island, when Walter Scott took the pushcart idea a step further by hooking a horse to his Pioneer Lunch wagon. Designed to serve workers who got out after 8:00 P.M., when most restaurants were closed, the Pioneer featured boiled eggs, pies, coffee, and what Scott called the "chewed sandwich," made from meat scraps, all served from the back of the wagon. Scott soon had competition: Retired policeman Ruel B. Jones built a series of snappy-looking, glass-topped, bright red wagons with open counters from which to serve customers.

The next advance came in 1887 at the New England Fair, where Samuel Messer Jones of Worcester, Massachusetts, introduced an eight-hundred-dollar sixteen- by seven-foot food wagon that customers could actually walk into, complete with stained glass and working kitchen. Entrepreneur Charles H. Palmer bought several of the new wagons and took out a patent on the idea September 1, 1891. Now the tiny food wagon industry began to gather speed. W. A. Bowes introduced the lunch wagon in the West by bringing one to Denver, Colorado. Ever resourceful in their attempts to wean drinkers away from saloons, the Church Temperance Society set up lunch wagons on the streets of New York City in 1893, which they called "Way Side Inns."

But the man who became known as the "Lunch Wagon King" for his expansion of the concept into national prominence was Thomas H. Buckley, whose New England Lunch Wagon Company had wagons in 275 towns across the United States by 1889. In 1897 he debuted a wagon with nickel-plated coffee urns, tile mosaics, and lamps set atop ebony pedestals. Buckley also built an immobile lunch stand in Worcester called the White House Café, complete with soda fountain and decorated with eighteen thousand square feet of Mexican onyx. But the idea flopped. Stationary food wagons only became popular after some New England communities, which regarded the wagons rolling through their streets with annoyance, insisted that the wagons close at 10:00 P.M., causing many wagon owners to detach their horses and set the wagons down on stationary sites, thereby transforming them into more conventional restaurants, which were allowed to stay open twenty-four hours a day if they so desired.

Still, the low-class, somewhat tawdry image of these eateries persisted, especially after owners began buying up and converting old, dilapidated electric trolleys. "Their effort was absolutely devastating," wrote Richard J. S. Gutman and Elliott Kaufman in *American Diner* (1979). "For the first time a stigma, growing out of the disreputable-looking trolley lunches began to be attached to the wagon lunch wagon," an image not helped by the prejudice leveled against an increasing number of Greek immigrants then entering the business.

Manufacturers, led by Patrick J. (Pop) Tierney of New Rochelle, New York, tried hard to modify the unsavory image by changing the look of their eateries to resemble the more respectable railroad dining cars (which were themselves rarely converted). He incorporated the latest amenities in his diners—booths, ventilators, exhaust fans, and toilet facilities, all of which helped make them fit establishments for women to dine in. Tierney took to calling these sleek new eateries "diners" and small, one-man units "dinettes." When he died in 1917 (of acute indigestion), Tierney was a millionaire, and by 1925 his company was manufacturing one diner per day.

Streamlining, which came in the mid-1930s for everything from refrigerators to locomotives, was perfectly adaptable to diner design, and the gleaming, stainless-steel Art Deco majesty of those 1930s and 1940s streamlined diners has come to represent a lost era of glamour and populist elegance, which Gutman and Kaufman call the "Golden Age of the Diner," a time when more than 6,700 diners fed one million people each day in America.

In the late 1940s at least thirteen manufacturers were building diners, at a rate of 250 per year. But the streamlined designs had begun to look dated, and diners were getting bigger, with larger windows, featuring space-

IF THE CUSTOMER couldn't come to the restaurant, the restaurant would go to the customer, as did this lunch wagon selling barbecue and ice cream to construction workers in Washington, D.C., in December 1941.

age motifs that echoed the glitzy ornamentation of 1950s automobiles. In the 1960s the Kullman Dining Car Company of Newark, New Jersey, made the first Colonial-style diner in Ocean City, New Jersey, a style that co-existed with a far more flamboyant style adapted from classical Greek architecture by Greek diner owners.

The diner went into a slow decline as fast food chains proliferated in the 1960s and 1970s, and today most of the older diners have been enlarged and converted into modern designs, with false brickwork, mansard roofs, and lavish interiors, often evoking classic Greek statues and pillars and reflecting the taste of the Greek immigrant owners. But there has been a modest renaissance of the diner in large cities where their nostalgic charm has been rediscovered by a generation of restaurateurs barely old enough to remember the classic designs of the past. Pawtucket Rhode Island's Modern Diner has even been placed on the National Register of Historic Places. Some new diners, like the Buckhead Diner in Atlanta, the Silver Diner in McLean, Virginia, and the Fog City Diner in San Francisco have been built from scratch to resemble the streamlined look of the 1930s, while others, like Ed Debevic's in Chicago and Phoenix, are send-ups of the more glittering, flamboyant California style of the 1950s.

One American artist, John Baeder, has devoted his entire oeuvre to painting diners, some in landscapes as bleak as purgatory, others seeming to prop up skyscrapers, some sitting like homeless puppies in winter's shadow, and some gleaming proudly in the California sunshine.

The diner concept is, in fact, more a question of design than of food service. Take away the look of the diner and you have the common coffee shop, the café, or luncheonette, all of which increased in number in the 1920s and 1930s. Many were outgrowths or expanded versions of the soda fountain, which itself germinated out of the nineteenth-century pharmacy.

The service of soda water in drugstores began in Philadelphia in 1825 when Elias Durand began selling the bubbly beverage as a remedy for dyspepsia. And Coca-Cola was the creation of an Atlanta pharmacist named Dr. John Styth Pemberton, who concocted the drink from the cola nut on May 8, 1886, and peddled it down the street at Jacob's Pharmacy.

There are conflicting claims as to who concocted the first ice cream soda—Texans claim it was a San Antonion named Herr Harnisch of the Harnisch & Baer Ice Cream Parlor in that city—but the man who popularized the idea was Robert M. Green, who featured ice cream sodas at the semicentennial exhibition at Philadelphia's Franklin Institute in October 1874, and was making six hundred dollars a day before the exhibition ended. By 1893 an American magazine called the ice cream soda "the national beverage."

The installation of the first soda fountain *behind* a counter (as opposed to the more traditional wall unit) at Philadelphia's Broad Street Pharmacy in 1903 redirected the center of the action and added immeasurably to the give-and-take rapport of customer and soda jerk (a term known at least since 1916). New concoctions like ice cream cones (first served at the St. Louis World's Fair of 1904), milk shakes, malteds, sundaes, frappés, parfaits, fizzes, egg creams, and banana splits were soon being whipped up in soda fountains with gilded mirrors, long marble counters, tiled floors, potted ferns, and

THE TYPICAL AMERICAN counter-man had to be adept at making everything from sandwiches to sundaes, while translating customers' requests into a lunch counter slang that turned poached eggs on toast into "Adam and Eve on a raft" and sausage and mashed potatoes into "zeppelins in a fog."

bent-metal chairs; the fountains' opulence grew commensurate with their popularity—by 1908 there were more than seventy-five thousand in the United States. Kaiser's, which is still extant in Oklahoma City, had stained-glass windows, an eighteen-foot-high tin ceiling, a twenty-five-foot-long mahogany display of ice cream, and a fifty-foot-long tiled counter. The Broadmoor fountain on New York's Madison Avenue could seat eight hundred people, while Chicago's Merchandise Mart fountain sat four hundred more. Movie stars would flock to C. C. Brown's in Hollywood to savor the novelty of hot fudge, introduced to Los Angeles in 1906. In New York debutantes began a tradition in the 1930s of ending their evenings with a visit to the swank Rumpelmayer's in the St. Moritz Hotel.

And when people could not get to the ice cream parlor, American ingenuity brought the ice cream parlor to them. Refrigeration techniques made unlimited quantities of ice cream available to the wholesaler and retailer, and ice cream was sold from urban pushcarts at the turn of the century. In 1923 a Youngstown, Ohio, ice cream parlor operator began selling his chocolate-covered ice cream bars from a white truck whose bells alerted children in the neighborhood to the arrival to the Good Humor Man. Before long the trucks were plying the streets of Detroit, Chicago, and many other cities, and the Good Humor Man became a harbinger of spring as eagerly anticipated as the first crocus.

In 1934 a Greek immigrant named Thomas Andreas Carvelas (later shortened to Tom Carvel) of Yonkers, New York, looking for a sideline to his job as a test driver for Studebaker, borrowed fifteen dollars from his future wife, bought a battered old truck, and started selling a new soft ice cream, which he called "frozen custard," from a machine he himself had invented. Carvel ice cream stores sprouted throughout the Northeast, while another soft ice cream company, Dairy Queen (which Sherwood [Sherb] Noble began in Joliet, Illinois, in 1940, with the slogan "All You Can Eat for 10 Cents"), proliferated throughout the Midwest.

THE STREAMLINED DINER (*below*) and the ice cream stand (*above*) became familiar icons to every American driving the extensive interstate highway system.

It was inevitable that soda fountains and ice cream parlors would serve a little food, a few sandwiches, and some hot meals, and some were transformed into lunch counters, or "luncheonettes" of more modest scale. Behind the counter was a soda jerk, whom *The New York Times* in 1939 described this way:

> *Ninety percent of them are native Americans for the simple reason that, aside from the ability to break and drain an egg with one hand, carve chicken, butter toast, remember orders, and pull the proper faucets, the prime requisite of their station is the ability to bandy words.*

Lunch counter slang was a patois all its own, a verbal shorthand that developed into a kind of baroque elaboration of shouted orders and instructions from waitress to cook and back again. "Gimme Adam and Eve on a raft, no axle grease, a bowl of red, a cuppa java, shoot one from the south and ice the rice!" translates as "Give me ham and eggs on toast with no butter, a bowl of chili, a cup of coffee, a Coca-Cola with lots of syrup, and rice pudding with ice cream." "The queer lingo used in transmitting orders from table to kitchen," wrote H. L. Mencken, "was first noted by a writer in the *Detroit Free Press* so long ago as Jan. 7, 1852, *e.q., fried bedpost, mashed tambourine* and *roasted stirrups.* . . . It was richly developed by the

BRAND NAMES LIKE HIRES Root Beer and Moxie soda pop were trusted trademarks that lent an assured consistency to lunch counters from Maine to Oregon.

colored waiters who flourished in the 1870s and 80s, but it is now [in 1948] pretty well confined to the waitresses and countermen who glorify third-rate eating houses."

Lunchrooms grew rapidly after World War I: Thompson's of Chicago numbered 104 units by 1920, as did the Baltimore Dairy Lunch out of Baltimore. In 1904 Harry S. Kelsey named his first lunchroom in Springfield, Massachusetts, Waldorf Lunch, after New York's lavish Waldorf-Astoria Hotel, and built seventy-four more up and down the Northeast by 1920. In 1915 he designed a combination one-armed table and one-person booth called a "settle," which provided a modicum of privacy for the patron and ease of cleaning for the staff.

The atmosphere of these lunchrooms, at first purely utilitarian, later quite lavish, evolved into a look of antiseptic cleanliness. While some urban lunchrooms like Schrafft's, which was begun as a candy factory by William F. Schrafft in Boston before the Civil War and became a chain of stores and restaurants in New York, starting in 1898, maintained an old-fashioned, genteel mahogany-and-polished-silver decor, the introduction to the industry in 1905 of a white metal alloy called Monel Metal, whose surface was bright, shiny, easy to scrub clean, and resistant to rust and corrosion, radically changed the look of lunch counters, which were enlivened still further by another new invention, neon lighting, introduced in Paris in 1910 but not much in usage in the United States until the 1930s.

STRIKING GRAPHICS and clean, sleek lines provided a shiny glamour to diners of the 1930s and 1940s, as in the Shore Post in Chicago, Illinois, circa 1941.

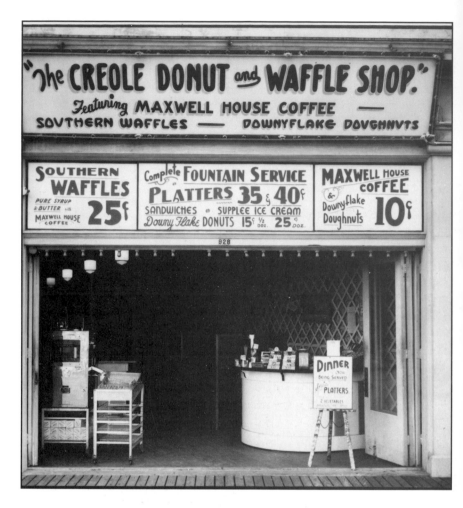

Regional, rural, and urban distinctions in the kind of food served at lunch counters were considerable. A breakfast in a Northern coffee shop might consist of bacon and eggs, hashed browns, a Danish pastry or an English muffin, and a cup of black coffee. In the South the plate would more likely be heaped with flapjacks and country ham, grits, biscuits and red-eye gravy, and sweetened coffee with cream. In the West, the day might begin with huevos rancheros and tortillas. Lunch in a Georgia restaurant might include collard greens, corn bread, and pot likker on the menu, items virtually unknown in the North and West, except to blacks who moved from the South.

The sandwich typified both a quintessential American lunch item and a study in regional diversity. Sandwiches made from a loaf of French or Italian bread and any number of ingredients took on various names, meats, and seasonings in different parts of the country. In the Northeast such an item might be called a "hero," a "wedge," or a "grinder." During World War II, the commissary of the United States Navy's submarine base in Groton, Connecticut, ordered five hundred hero sandwiches a day from Benedetto Capaldo's Italian deli in New London, where the name "sub" was soon applied to the item. In the early 1900s in New Orleans such an item

FOOD OUTLETS MIGHT POP UP any-where and in any guise, as in this Creole Donut and Waffle Shop off an amusement park boardwalk or enclosed in a tent like Earl's Café.

was called a "push" sandwich, because it was made with a meager slice of meat pushed through a length of French bread so that the eater could savor the meat last. In 1927 two enterprising New Orleanians named Clovis and Benny Martin took the idea, added some ingredients, put them on a long, specially made French loaf, and called it a "po' boy." Place salami, cheese, and pickled vegetables on a round sesame seeded loaf, and you have a "muffuletta," created in 1910 by Salvatore Lupa at Central Grocery in the French Quarter. In 1930 two Philadelphia brothers, Pat and Harry Olivieri, started making a grilled steak sandwich with hot sauce on an Italian loaf, added cheese in 1948, and called it a "Philadelphia cheese steak." The "Cuban sandwich" or "Cuban mix" of ham, sour pickle, and mustard on a slender loaf was featured first in Tampa, Florida, at the Columbia Café in 1905, while Miami's Cuban community called a sandwich eaten as a midnight snack sandwich a "medianoche" (Spanish for "middle of the night").

There are two claimants in the 1930s as creator of the Reuben sandwich—two slices of rye bread, corned beef, sauerkraut, Swiss cheese, and Russian dressing—Reuben's delicatessen in New York City and Reuben Kulakofsky of the Blackstone Hotel in Omaha, Nebraska. But the Hot Brown sandwich—sliced turkey with Mornay sauce and sliced bacon—could only have come from one place, The Brown Hotel in Louisville, Kentucky, where it was created in the early 1930s.

If the diner has taken on mythic associations in the popular consciousness, the cafeteria has come to represent a gentler strain of American food service, associated more with school lunches and family vacations. The idea of the

THE POPULARITY DURING WARTIME of cafeterias like Scholl's in Washington, D.C., which served one customer per minute, cut across all class lines when it came to good, honest food, clean, well-appointed dining rooms, and cheap prices.

cafeteria is based on a sense of community and wholesomeness. The food is arrayed to dazzle the eye and to tempt the passerby into transient, unbridled gluttony. The bounty of offerings, the anxiety of having too many choices, the urgency of moving down the line, and the giddiness of piling one's tray full of good food at a cheap price constitutes American eating in its most fundamental, democratic form. Cafeterias also made enormous sense at a time when workers had short lunch hours and needed to get a good midday meal fast and without fuss.

The first self-service restaurant was the Exchange Buffet in New York, opened September 4, 1885, but it catered to an exclusively male clientele who bought their food at a counter and consumed it standing up. The 1893 World's Columbian Exposition in Chicago was the site of the first nondiscriminatory self-service eatery, run by John Kruger, who'd based the idea on the Swedish smorgasbord but who chose to call it a "cafeteria," from the Spanish word for a coffee shop. (Kruger's eateries were also nicknamed "conscience joints," because customers tallied their own bill.) Within a year several competitors opened cafeterias in Chicago.

About 1898 the Childs brothers introduced the tray to the self-service line in New York City, where such establishments were being called "grab joints." Customers would move along the line, pile up their trays, then eat their food at wooden chairs with one-arm tables attached. Two years later New Yorker Bernarr Adolphus Macfadden came up with the idea for a "penny restaurant" (formally called the Macfadden Physical Culture Restaurant), at which most items cost only one cent.

An innovation far more in gear with the era's new technologies was the Automat, opened in Philadelphia on June 9, 1902, by Joseph Horn and Frank Hardart, who'd ordered the machinery from a German company that had bought the patents on a Swedish idea. The Automat offered self-service with a dispassionate precision: The customer simply walked up to a wall of gleaming boxes with windows that showcased the food inside, dropped a coin into the slot, and removed the pre-cooked, pre-sliced item without further ado. Most items cost only a nickel. On reviewing the new contraption, *The Evening Bulletin* proclaimed, "The horseless carriage, the wireless telephone and the playerless piano have been surpassed. . . . Artistically, it is a

HORN & HARDART'S AUTOMATS were an East Coast phenomenon that allowed people to purchase their food directly from little glass showcase windows. This 1940s example in New York fed everyone from bankers to blue-collar workers from morning till late at night.

CAFETERIAS adapted the architectural look of their surroundings, in the way the Dwyer Cafeteria in St. Petersburg, Florida, drew on the region's rich Art Deco heritage.

glittering, though effective, combination of plate glass, marble tiling, weathered oak wainscoting and hammered brass trimming. Practically, it is a boon to thousands of hungry business men and women."

Horn & Hardart, as the company was named, opened several more Automats in Philadelphia before bringing their concept to New York's Times Square, where, on July 2, 1912, they opened a gargantuan establishment decorated in meticulous Beaux Arts style with mosaic tile floors, marble-topped tables, and thousands of light bulbs strung in clusters on the ceiling. Horn & Hardart designers were always very much in step with modern architecture, as shown in the gorgeously sleek Automat they opened in 1934 on New York's West Fifty-seventh Street, done in pink terra-cotta and up-to-the-moment Art Deco motifs.

By 1939 there were forty Automats in New York. Oddly enough, the Automats did not fare well outside of New York and Philadelphia, and, after Horn & Hardart's ventures in Chicago and Boston failed, none was established anywhere else in the United States. But the basic cafeteria concept was ideal for the American market: The food was plentiful, good, and wholesome, the prices more than fair, and the gregariousness of the enterprise made going to one an event for many families. Cafeterias proliferated on the West Coast after Helen Mosher introduced the concept—and female cooks—to Los Angeles in 1905, and Easterners even took to calling cafeterias "California-style restaurants."

But cafeterias found full flourish in the South, where they offered access to a bright, spotlessly clean, modern, mechanized world of abundance, espe-

cially at a time when the South was in severe economic distress. Large, fancy restaurants in the South were few, far between, and really unnecessary. As of 1920 only nine Southern cities had populations over one hundred thousand. Except in New Orleans, most restaurants in the South were either located in the large city hotels, tea rooms, diners, or in boarding houses, all segregated. There had long been roadside barbecue pits, honky-tonks, catfish shacks, and places to get boiled crawfish, but these were bare-bone establishments, hardly fit for a Sunday family dinner.

The first cafeteria in the South was Britling's, opened in 1918 atop a Birmingham, Alabama, department store by A.W.B. Johnson I, who cribbed the name of the restaurant from one of his favorite books, H. G. Wells's *Mr. Britling Sees It Through.* The cafeteria's success was immediate and overwhelming, causing him to open a separate facility across the street. The Morrison cafeteria chain began in Mobile, Alabama. The S & W Cafeteria chain started out of Asheville, North Carolina. The Piccadilly chain was headquartered in Baton Rouge, Furr's was in Lubbock, Texas, Wyatt's out of Dallas, and Luby's from San Antonio.

The cafeteria concept struck just the proper balance of formality and traditionalism, serving a solid, old-fashioned Southern cooking—hot biscuits and gravy, fried chicken, turkey with corn-bread dressing, fried catfish, mashed potatoes, numerous vegetables, and congealed salads. Tea was served iced and presweetened, and you could have as much as you could drink without paying another penny. The great tradition of Southern baking was always maintained—from sweet potato, pecan, and Key lime pies to fruit cobblers and Lady Baltimore cake.

INSIDE ANOTHER St. Petersburg cafeteria—the Tramor—Spanish decor and airplanes painted on the ceiling gave the room a mood of sophisticated internationalism.

KEEP 'EM FLYING!

TRAMOR CAFETERIA   The Finest Cafeteria in the South   ST. PETERSBURG, FLA.

THE ORIGINAL HOWARD JOHN-SON'S soda shop (*right*) opened in Wollaston, Massachusetts, in 1925. Within a decade the Howard Johnson's name had been franchised and the trademark orange roofs and diversity of ice cream flavors made it a symbol of quality and consistency for Americans on the road.

However devoted cafeterias were to serving the masses, they were also genteel examples of Southern hospitality, at least if you were white. Women would wear their nicest clothes and white gloves to dine at the cafeteria, and pushing and shoving in line was frowned upon. As Jane and Michael Stern pointed out in their study of the American cafeteria, "J. A. Morrison, a restaurateur in Mobile, Alabama, opening his first cafeteria, in September of 1920, overcame what he believed to be Southerners' objections to serving themselves by providing waiters to carry trays from the service counter to the table—an amenity that still prevails in the South."

In many Southern towns the cafeterias were not just the least expensive places to eat, they were also the most luxurious. Many were decorated in a contrived antebellum style of Greek pillars and Georgian wainscoting, flowered carpets, and, often, chandeliers, and poor people marveled at the spick-and-span look of the flatware, the china, and the glasses hot from the dishwasher.

The quality of food offered at such chains was consistent, and the prices always kept low by careful monitoring of ingredients, with nothing ever wasted: Leftover roast beef became tomorrow's beef hash; carrot and celery peelings would be thrown in a pot to make a rich stock; and fresh food was made throughout the day, used up, and replenished before the customers' eyes. The fidelity of employees, many of them black, was legendary, and hardworking dishwashers could graduate to positions as cooks and waitresses, so workers stayed in place for ten, fifteen, or twenty years, and cooks learned to refine their recipes over decades.

When the cafeteria began to lose ground to newer forms of restaurants in the 1960s, they still thrived in the South, particularly in suburban shopping centers, where one is quite likely to find a Morrison's or Piccadilly's or Furr's serving up much the same food as they did fifty years ago.

Crucial to their success was the chain concept that allowed for volume buying and cost cutting. Indeed, it was the dual concepts of the chain and the franchise that made the explosion of new restaurants possible in the first half of this century. "The 1920s and 1930s saw the restaurant evolve from a luxury to a necessity," wrote Richard Pillsbury in *From Boarding House to Bistro* (1990). "The chain restaurant began to be transformed from a group of two or three stores under the same management to a complete organism of interchangeable parts which could be and were duplicated by the hundreds."

No one did it better than Howard Dearing Johnson of Wollaston, Massachusetts, who, in 1925, at the age of twenty-seven, borrowed five hundred dollars, and took over a patent medicine store in Quincy, which he turned into a soda fountain serving three flavors of his own, very rich ice cream. Before long he'd added hot dogs and hamburgers. Within four years he opened another store. When he received an offer, but insufficient capital, to expand into Cape Cod in 1935, Johnson franchised his name and concept to a yacht captain named Reginald Sprague. By 1940 Johnson had franchised 130 restaurants, including all the food service facilities along the brand-new Pennsylvania Turnpike.

Johnson's success was not due to the quality of his food, which was good and of consistent quality but not markedly different from his competi-

tors'; it was in his decision to sell his name and his particular style of restaurant. Franchisees had to use architects (primarily Joseph G. Morgan) chosen by Johnson and follow Johnson's recipes to the letter, so that the fried clams, brown bread, and twenty-eight flavors of ice cream tasted exactly the same in Massachusetts as they did in Florida. His logo drew on a beloved nursery rhyme, "Simple Simon and the Pie Man," and his orange-roofed structures looked like a cottage out of a children's book.

The distinctive design and placement of the Howard Johnson's restaurants was very carefully thought out. "These were conspicuous restaurants," notes Philip Langdon in *Orange Roofs, Golden Arches* (1986). "Johnson had a knack for selecting sites that would be visible from a great distance. They stood at major intersections, at traffic circles, along gradual curves—wherever they were sure to be noticed. There had been public outcries in the twenties and early thirties against billboards and other roadside signs, and Johnson was reluctant to resort to such crude advertising devices. He set out to make the building his own advertisement—complemented, however, by a big sign out front."

There had been chain restaurants earlier than Howard Johnson's—John R. Thompson in Chicago, Childs' in New York, and White House Lunch in Washington, for instance—but Johnson's acumen in franchising became a model for others to follow. That Howard Johnson's itself would suffer bad times in the 1960s was due to overexpansion and neglect of Johnson's original formula, while the rise in gasoline prices in the 1970s kept many Americans off the highways and out of Howard Johnson's restaurants.

Two events occurred in the same year—1921—that had an indelible effect on the American restaurant industry: the opening of the first drive-in and the start-up of the first successful hamburger chain. The combination of the two ideas would eventually come to dominate and define American food service in the eyes of the world, which at first dismissed, then embraced it as an example of guileless, American exuberance.

The drive-in idea came about because its creator, J. G. Kirby, a Dallas tobacco and candy wholesaler, had come to the conclusion that "People with cars are so lazy they don't want to get out of them to eat." With the help of Dr. Reuben Wright Jackson, Kirby designed and opened a drive-in pork barbecue eatery he called the Pig Stand in September 1921 on the Dallas–Fort Worth Highway. Within a decade Kirby and his franchisees had Pig Stands all over the Midwest and as far away as New York and California.

The waiters and waitresses at drive-ins were called "carhops" (because they'd hop up onto the running board of the car to take a customer's order) and were chosen for their youth, attractiveness, and pep. Their uniforms combined the crisp look of the military with the coy sexiness of a Hollywood chorus line, and a balance of hospitality and sass became part of the job description.

The drive-in was a direct expression of the appetite of an automobile-obsessed culture for basic food and social interaction. In his disquisition on the sociology of the drive-in, Langdon explains its success as a uniquely American phenomenon:

The drive-in was a gathering place, and one that embodied deeply engrained American attitudes about proper spatial relationships. Americans enjoy opportunities to be outgoing, to congregate in a friendly setting, and this the drive-in enabled them to do. But Americans also prefer to keep a certain distance between themselves and others—and this, too, the drive-in made possible. Just as the preferred American housing pattern of single-family dwellings serves to offset the tensions of coexisting with neighbors of different religions, ethnic, and class backgrounds, the drive-in's assemblage of individual vehicles ensured a similar physical buffer zone, allowing the person to keep his or her privacy essentially intact. Inside the movable capsule of space that was an automobile, protected by a shell of metal and glass, an individual or family could act gregarious without risking too great an involvement with other people. Customers were free from being bumped, jostled, or pressed too closely, vexations that occurred all too frequently in indoor restaurants.

The second event of 1921 that forever changed the way Americans ate out was the opening of a hamburger stand in Wichita, Kansas, by fry cook Walter Anderson and real estate and insurance man Edgar Waldo "Billy" Ingram. Anderson had already perfected a method of slow-cooking (really steaming) a ground beef pattie with onions, which he sold from a streetcar eatery he'd opened in 1916. Four years later he joined with Ingram to open three unexceptional hamburger stands that did well enough to justify a very exceptional fourth. This was a fifteen- by ten-foot cement (later stuccoed) building with nothing more than a griddle and five counter stools inside.

CUSTOMERS WHO ATE at any of the company-owned White Castles, like this 1950 example in St. Louis, Missouri, knew exactly what to expect in terms of decor, service, and food, which never varied from unit to unit.

The unusual thing about it was its shape: The structure had a vaguely medieval-looking turret and crenelated walls, which served no purpose other than to catch the eye and to give visual support to Ingram's notion to call the stand "White Castle." "'White' signifies purity and cleanliness," he said, "and 'Castle' represents strength, permanence and stability."

The quirky-looking building drew customers in droves, and business soared. Within ten years the partners had 115 units. Ingram (who bought the company from Anderson in 1933) was a man with a fertile sense of marketing and before anyone else in the industry, saw the value of advertising his product. Since White Castle's five-cent burgers were fairly small, Anderson had come up with the registered slogan, "Buy 'em by the Sack," in 1921 and, in June 1932, was the first hamburger-stand owner to advertise in newspapers by putting coupons in the St. Louis newspapers that offered five free burgers to anyone who showed up by the end of the day. By 2:00 P.M., there were lines around the block. Within an hour the store had run out of meat and buns.

In an effort to bolster the squeaky-clean image of the White Castles, Ingram hired a prim, attractive woman he named "Julia Joyce" to invite women to inspect the sanitary conditions of the operation, which included new under-the-counter electric dishwashers. He created a mug with a slotted rim so that water would drain from it. In 1925 the first folded paper napkins came on the market; Ingram took the idea further by developing a folding paper hat that could be changed frequently and discarded after use. His staff was trained according to strict company guidelines of behavior and dress, which precluded the wearing of wristwatches or "flashy jewelry." And Ingram worked hard to guarantee that there was no variation in the quality or taste of his food, whether it was served in Wichita, Kansas, or New York City. The hamburger meat was frozen and dented with five holes that made for even cooking throughout. He developed a heat-resistant paper carton in 1931 for carry-out orders. "When you sit in a White Castle," Ingram proclaimed in a brochure given out to customers, "remember that you are one of several thousands; you are sitting on the same kind of stool; you are being served on the same kind of counter; the coffee you drink is made in accordance with a certain formula; the hamburger you eat is prepared in exactly the same way over a gas flame of the same intensity; the cups you drink from are identical with thousands of cups that thousands of other people are using at the same moment; the same standard of cleanliness protects your food."

Ingram was guaranteeing what Fred Harvey had promised in the nineteenth century and what every chain restaurant operator sought to provide ever afterward—no surprises, no variations, no deviations, no unfamiliar tastes, nothing to disturb one's peace of mind or palate. In so doing, Ingram deliberately challenged the notion that success in the restaurant business depended on offering food quite distinct from the next fellow's and that good-tasting food could only be made by an experienced chef who kept his recipe secrets to himself. White Castle cooks had to follow the corporate recipe book to the letter in an effort to produce food that tasted precisely like that from every other White Castle kitchen.

WALT ANDERSON and Billy Ingram (*above*) originated the idea of the White Castle system and built their fourth Wichita, Kansas, unit (*below*) to look like a "strong" and "pure" castle, meant to draw customers to its unique design. Strict rules of appearance and cleanliness (*opposite*) had to be scrupulously maintained by White Castle workers.

LOOK YOURSELF OVER

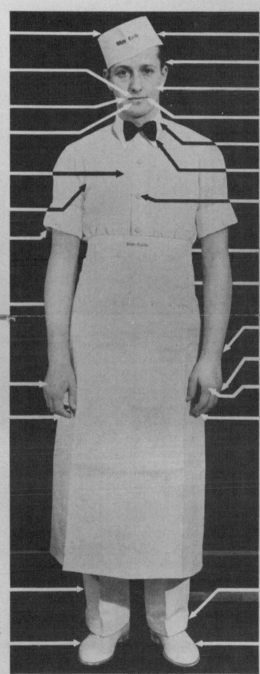

3. Be ready to make suggestions.

5. Be prepared to speak pleasantly.

7. Correct bad breath.

8. Get rid of chewing gum.

11. Wear clean shirt.

13. No body odor.

14. Fold shirt sleeves neatly.

17. No patches in trousers' seat.

20. Wash Hands.

21. Clean fingernails.

22. Wear clean trousers.

24. Wear comfortable shoes.

1. Cap should cover hair

2. Keep hair trimmed.

4. Have clean shave.

6. Brush teeth.

9. Wear clean collar.

10. Be sure tie is no frayed or dirty.

12. Button all shir buttons.

15. Fasten apron neatly.

16. Have shirt neatl tucked in trousers.

18. No wrist watch.

19. No flashy jewelry.

20. Wash hands.

21. Clean fingernails.

23. Turn up trousers if too long.

25. Wear clean shoes.

Ingram labored hard to build customer loyalty, and those who loved the little steamy burgers (affectionately known as "sliders") would go to great lengths to satisfy their cravings. One customer in Joliet, Illinois, waited fifteen hours in the cold for a new White Castle to open so that he could place his order—1,550 hamburgers. And in 1982 the company perfected a technique of freezing their hamburgers so that they could send them to American soldiers and Marines overseas. Five years later the frozen sliders could be purchased in American supermarkets.

Ingram's other significant contribution was architectural. He abandoned the stucco exterior of his restaurants in favor of the new porcelain-enamel steel paneling that not only served better as a fire shield but was also extremely easy to maintain and keep clean.

White Castle's immediate competitors—White Tower in Milwaukee (1926), Little Tavern in Louisville (1927), White Taverne Shoppes in Shelbyville, Kentucky (1929), Toddle House in Houston (1929), Krystal in Chattanooga (1932), White Hut in Toledo (1935), and Royal Castle in Miami Beach (1938)—were direct imitations of Ingram's original concepts, and White Castle spent years in court trying—successfully—to get White Tower to alter its look-alike architecture so as not to be confused with White Castle's. As Langdon points out, "nearly every aspect of [White Castle] and its buildings served as inspiration for other restaurateurs. Throughout almost the entire United States, local or regional chains took as their model one or more attributes of White Castle—the name, the menu, operating procedures, construction techniques, materials, and design."

The naïve, almost childlike architecture of White Castle had evolved out of an American fondness for startling designs in public buildings. American architecture has always been mimetic, and the image a restaurant wished to project was usually built around an inherited style. Thus, the restaurants of the Gilded Age took Parisian elegance to opulent extremes, German-American restaurants expanded on the traditional look of the Bavarian beer hall, and White Castle reduced the solidity of a medieval fortress to the enameled walls of a hamburger stand. White Castle was but one of scores of examples of what architect Robert Venturi would later characterize as "vernacular architecture" and what Jim Heimann and Rip Georges, in their book *California Crazy* (1980), called "Programmatic architecture."

One of the earliest instances of using an animal form for a building was the Elephant Hotel (nicknamed "Lucy"), built in Margate City, New Jersey, in 1881, a sixty-five-foot-tall structure shaped like a pachyderm with twenty-foot legs. Designed by William Fee of Philadelphia, Lucy and her descendants were meant to awe, or at least to get a kick out of, the common man. "All of the Programmatic structures, whether a tamale stand built in the form of a tamale, or an airplane built as a service station, were created to be eye-catchers," observed Heimann and Georges. "They were meant to startle, shock and amuse. Humor was an essential element in the audience's response to these structures."

Most Programmatic architecture was even more literal than White Castle's design, often taking the form of a grotesquely oversized food item featured at the restaurant housed within. The need to be noticed by a fast-

BY THE 1940s, roadside restaurants like The Coffee Pot in Bedford, Pennsylvania, were designed both to attract attention from people driving by and to serve as a literal advertisement for what was served.

126

speeding automobile made the construction of a gigantic upside down ice cream cone like that built in 1928 in Santa Ana, California, a design as pragmatic as it was Programmatic.

There were no bounds to the imagination and no rules to follow for these outrageous monuments to public taste, especially in Southern California, where one will still find the Brown Derby, the Chili Bowl, The Teapot, The Big Donut, and the Tail o' the Pup (shaped like a gigantic hot dog). Others, like The Igloo ice cream parlor, The Dog Café, and the Hoot Hoot Ice Cream (shaped like a fifteen-foot-high owl whose head revolves), are long gone. Such oddities helped break up the flat, numbing Western landscapes with unexpected, cartoonlike shapes, and were, no matter how tastelessly rendered, irresistible beacons to the motorist on the wearying leg of a long journey across the desert.

Such designs were hardly exclusive to Southern California. One of the most extravagant was The Ice Cream Carton, built in 1939, in Berlin, Connecticut, with three towering, open ice cream cartons built into the design. The Popcorn Ball, built around 1931 in Canton, Ohio, the Noah's Ark Motor Inn and Restaurant built in the 1940s in Natchez, Mississippi, the Cranberry Bottle built around 1931 in Onset, Massachusetts, the Bedford Coffee Pot in Bedford, Pennsylvania, and The Coffee Pot in Tacoma, Washington, were all outrageous, outlandish, hilarious, and quite lovable restaurants that made the American roadway into an extension of the amusement park. The MGM Studio theme park, opened in 1989, that is part of Disney World in Lake Buena Vista, Florida, has a replica of the Brown Derby restaurant, as well as a snack shop built like a sailing ship, and an ice cream stand shaped like a dinosaur.

Even in their heyday, such restaurant designs were unusual, but, together with the more conventional diners, lunchrooms, tearooms, ice cream parlors, family restaurants, drive-ins, and cafeterias, they came to form an eccentric array of eateries spread out across the Interstate highways of the 1930s and 1940s and dotting the corners of every neighborhood in every town and city, offering Americans not just a choice of food but a choice of atmosphere no other people on earth could even imagine, much less afford.

Innovations followed inspiration, and imitations created whole sub-categories—"refreshment stands" like Carvel and Dairy Queen that sold only soft ice cream, restaurants like the International House of Pancakes that served breakfasts (all day long), and doughnut shops, milk bars, and all sorts of hamburger stands—all duly reported on by a growing number of industry magazines with names like *American Restaurant, Restaurant Business, Fountain Service, Restaurants & Institutions, Restaurant Hospitality, Nation's Restaurant News, Drive-In Restaurant,* and *Diner & Counter Restaurant.*

The public, however, depended for guidance on where to eat on travel guides that too often were in the service of the very restaurants they reported on. Most dining-out guides of the 1930s and 1940s read like advertisements rather than critical opinions. Few guides, if any, went out of their way to recommend lunchrooms or cafeterias—the very places most American would tend to frequent on the road. Which is, perhaps, why a little book entitled *Adventures in Good Eating* by a Chicago traveling salesman named Duncan Hines became a nationwide bestseller within three years of publication of its first edition in 1936. Hines, a salesman for a printing and advertising company, never intended to become America's gastronomic navigator and tastemaker. By the age of fifty-six, he had crisscrossed the United States numerous times, fifty thousand miles a year, and like all salesmen, relished a good meal at the end of the day. So, in 1935, for his own use and as a favor to friends and colleagues, he compiled a list of 167 favorite places to eat in 30 states, and sent off 1,000 copies as Christmas cards.

A Chicago newspaper reporter saw a story in the novelty of a local salesman writing up restaurant recommendations and published an article about Hines that caused a deluge of readers' requests for the list, so, in 1936, Hines published an expanded version as a booklet entitled *Adventures in Good Eating.* He sold five thousand copies, but took a loss on expenses until an article in the *Saturday Evening Post* brought the book national publicity. By 1939 he was selling one hundred thousand copies a year (the book had grown to include two thousand listings), enabling him to quit his job, move back to his native Bowling Green, Kentucky, and begin a profitable new career as the man who ate on behalf of millions of Americans who'd came to trust him for his good taste and unassailable honesty.

Hines certainly did earn his reputation. He was scrupulous in maintaining his anonymity (his perennial photo in successive editions of *Adventures in Good Eating* was one taken when he was in his thirties), thorough (he'd visit and eat at three, four, or more restaurants per day), ethical (he accepted neither free meals nor advertising), and dedicated to regional American cooking (he'd inquire of a New England restaurateur, "Why don't you people in Maine serve fiddlehead ferns?").

PROGRAMMATIC ROADSIDE EATERIES like this 1920s lemonade stand (its location is unknown) were much admired as examples of folk art by photographers sent out by federal agencies to chronicle the American landscape during the Depression years.

DUNCAN HINES had been a traveling salesman who accidentally became America's first national restaurant critic after drawing up a list for friends of his favorite places to dine while on the road. They were eventually published in a guidebook entitled *Adventures in Good Eating* (*opposite*), which by 1939 was selling 100,000 copies each year.

Perhaps Hines's most valuable virtue was his common-man attitude toward eating out. He was little impressed by finery, once saying that he steered clear of "dishes disguised with French names that don't mean anything in a Midwest hotel," and pronounced "plain American cooking is the best in the world," adding, "and it can also be the worst." Nor was he impressed with expensive dining rooms. "The finest lemon pie I ever had was in a town of 50 people," he recalled. "It cost 10 cents. One of the poorest was in a large New York hotel. That cost 40 cents."

Earning the "Recommended by Duncan Hines" seal of approval could mean a fortune in business for a restaurateur, and Hines worked hard, later with assistants (including opera singer Laurence Tibbett), to make sure restaurants met his high standards—which for decades were the standards for eating out in America.

"This directory is compiled solely from the viewpoint and in the interests of patrons," he wrote in the preface to his 1939 guide. "The inn that makes the grade and qualifies for this honor roll receives a rating—a distinguished service decoration of substantial value which has not cost the beneficiary a cent. Entirely welcome! And they can't do anything about it, either, except to maintain or improve the quality of their food and service. My interest lies wholly with a discriminating public; you, their guests."

Hines would alert readers to innovations like air conditioning and give regional notes like "No gasoline sold on Sunday in Nashville." His descriptions of restaurants were brief, to the point, and never highfalutin. Indeed, Hines was no prose stylist. His entire review of the Hotel Richmond in Augusta, Georgia, read, "I enjoyed their T-bone steak plate for $1. The steak was very good and tender." Rarely was he as effusive as in his description of Billy the Oysterman in New York City: "I don't know what an oysterman (and what a one he is!) could be doing with serving corned beef and cabbage and pigs' knuckles. But he does and gets away with it in a large way. What you should order here, however, are Cape Cod oysters, broiled, or lobsters, or pompano, or broiled eels—or anything else you can think of in the fish or sea food line. He's known all over the country."

Hines was a pragmatic man, and did not, as he once noted, have a "gourmand's appetite for fine foods." And he knew from experience that hunger can cause a critic to drop his guard. "Remember," he cautioned, "we all have to eat no matter in what locality we happen to be. Therefore a few places are listed more as a matter of convenience rather than as serving outstanding food worth driving a distance to reach."

While Hines never compromised the standards of his guides, he did, in the late 1940s, together with Roy H. Park of Ithaca, New York, lend his name to a line of food items and cookware, and, three years before his death on March 15, 1959, sold exclusive rights to his name and guides to Procter & Gamble, which put the Duncan Hines logo on their cake mixes.

Hines's greatest contribution was to show Americans that there was a decent meal to be had at the end of the road—good food, wholesome food, food without pomp or pretension, regional American food that ranged from broiled lobsters to candied yams, from chicken pot pie to homemade ice cream. Although he much preferred the country inn to the hash house, Hines appreciated the breadth and depth of American restaurants, from posh society haunt like The Colony in New York to the modest charm of the Milam Cafeteria in San Antonio, Texas. In his flat, unexceptional style, Hines did something quite exceptional indeed. He bolstered the expectations and options for the man on the move, and in so doing helped improve food service in America at a time when too many restaurants had drifted into mediocrity.

In the 1920s and 1930s the American restaurant had evolved into something centipedal, generous, and wonderfully adaptable. Style often triumphed over substance, and sometimes restaurateurs seemed to favor adornment over nourishment. But it grew naturally and happily at a time when there was not much to be happy about in American life. Its exuberance was catching, its optimism beneficial. For a few hours people escaped into a more exciting, if contrived, place and came away feeling they'd got their money's worth. And yet, after a few visits, those restaurants became quaintly familiar, a part of the landscape, and expressive of the region's character.

As Jane and Michael Stern have written in their guide to America's roadside restaurants entitled *Roadfood and Goodfood* (1986), "Regional restaurants outside their own regions remind us of dioramas in a natural history museum: interesting, educational . . . but you cannot smell the mountain air. The joy of eating regional food is not just what's on the plate. It is sitting shoulder to shoulder with Amish farmers in Indiana, beach bunnies in Corona del Mar, and cowboys in Amarillo. It is seeing the sun set over Puget Sound and listening to the strident honk of the waitresses at Durgin-Park in Boston. There is no seasoning as pungent as authenticity."

ADVENTURES IN GOOD EATING

1937

FOURTH EDITION

A Directory of Good Eating Places along the Highways and in Villages and Cities of America.

By DUNCAN HINES

Price $1.50

Published by
ADVENTURES IN GOOD EATING, Inc.
856 W. Adams St.
Chicago, Ill.
Telephone MONroe 0006

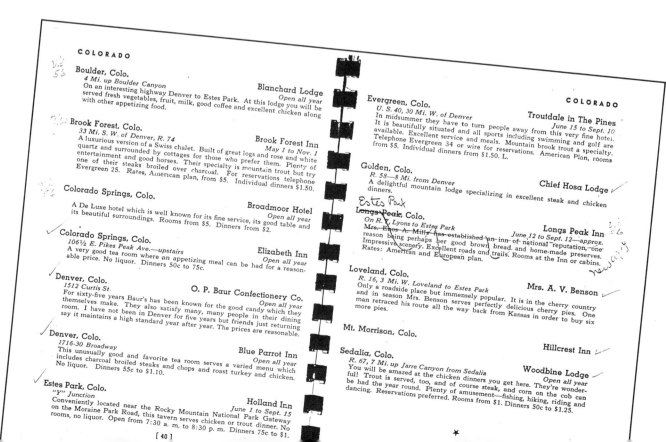

COLORADO

Boulder, Colo.
4 Mi. up Boulder Canyon
On an interesting highway Denver to Estes Park. At this lodge you will be served fresh vegetables, fruit, milk, good coffee and excellent chicken along with other appetizing food.
Blanchard Lodge
Open all year

Brook Forest, Colo.
33 Mi. S. W. of Denver, R. 74
A luxurious version of a Swiss chalet. Built of great logs and rose and white quartz and surrounded by cottages for those who prefer them. Plenty of entertainment and good horses. Their specialty is mountain trout but try one of their steaks broiled over charcoal. For reservations telephone Evergreen 25. Rates, American plan, from $5. Individual dinners $1.50.
Brook Forest Inn
May 1 to Nov. 1

Colorado Springs, Colo.
A De Luxe hotel which is well known for its fine service, its good table and its beautiful surroundings. Rooms from $5. Dinners from $2.
Broadmoor Hotel
Open all year

Colorado Springs, Colo.
106½ E. Pikes Peak Ave.—upstairs
A very good tea room where an appetizing meal can be had for a reasonable price. No liquor. Dinners 50c to 75c.
Elizabeth Inn
Open all year

Denver, Colo.
1512 Curtis St.
For sixty-five years Baur's has been known for the good candy which they themselves make. They also satisfy many, many people in their dining room. I have not been in Denver for five years but friends just returning say it maintains a high standard year after year. The prices are reasonable.
O. P. Baur Confectionery Co.
Open all year

Denver, Colo.
1716-30 Broadway
This unusually good and favorite tea room serves a varied menu which includes charcoal broiled steaks and chops and roast turkey and chicken. No liquor. Dinners 55c to $1.10.
Blue Parrot Inn
Open all year

Estes Park, Colo.
"Y" Junction
Conveniently located near the Rocky Mountain National Park Gateway on the Moraine Park Road, this tavern serves chicken or trout dinner. No rooms, no liquor. Open from 7:30 a. m. to 8:30 p. m. Dinners 75c to $1.
Holland Inn
June 1 to Sept. 15

Evergreen, Colo.
U. S. 40, 30 Mi. W. of Denver
In midsummer they have to turn people away from this very fine hotel. It is beautifully situated and all sports including swimming and golf are available. Excellent service and meals. Mountain brook trout a specialty. Telephone Evergreen 34 or wire for reservations. American Plan, rooms from $5. Individual dinners from $1.50. L.
Troutdale in The Pines
June 15 to Sept. 10

Golden, Colo.
R. 58—8 Mi. from Denver
A delightful mountain lodge specializing in excellent steak and chicken dinners.
Chief Hosa Lodge

Longs Peak, Colo.
On R. Lyons to Estes Park
Mrs. Enos A. Mills has established an inn of national reputation, one reason being perhaps her good brown bread and home-made preserves. Impressive scenery. Excellent roads and trails. Rooms at the Inn or cabins. Rates: American and European plan.
Longs Peak Inn
June 12 to Sept. 12—approx.

Loveland, Colo.
R. 16, 3 Mi. W. Loveland to Estes Park
Only a roadside place but immensely popular. It is in the cherry country and in season Mrs. Benson serves perfectly delicious cherry pies. One man retraced his route all the way back from Kansas in order to buy six more pies.
Mrs. A. V. Benson

Mt. Morrison, Colo.
Hillcrest Inn

Sedalia, Colo.
R. 67, 7 Mi. up Jarre Canyon from Sedalia
You will be amazed at the chicken dinners you get here. They're wonderful! Trout is served, too, and of course steak, and corn on the cob can be had the year round. Plenty of amusement—fishing, hiking, riding and dancing. Reservations preferred. Rooms from $1. Dinners 50c to $1.25.
Woodbine Lodge
Open all year

[40]

New York's dazzlingly elegant Rainbow Room in the thirties

Chapter 8

Flaming Swords and French Dressing

The Return of Deluxe Dining in the 1930s

THE OPENING OF THE NEW Waldorf-Astoria Hotel on Park Avenue on October 1, 1931, was heralded as a rather courageous—some said foolhardy—occasion at a time when America was being dragged deep into the Depression. So momentous was the event that President Herbert Hoover announced it to the nation by radio from the White House—the first time a President had ever dedicated a hotel:

> *Our hotels have become community institutions. They are the center points of civic hospitality. They are the meeting place of a thousand community and national activities. They have come to be conducted in far larger vision than mere profit earning. If we considered them solely from an economic point of view we should find them among the nine leaders of American industry. The opening of the Waldorf-Astoria is an event in the advancement of hotels, even in New York City. It carries on a great tradition in national hospitality. . . . The erection of this great structure at this time has been a contribution to the maintenance of employment and is an exhibition of courage and confidence to the whole nation.*

That evening in New York the Depression was far from everyone's minds. Marching bands played throughout the day, people thronged the lobby to be the first to check in, the King and Queen of Siam were served the first dinner, and Oscar of the Waldorf was there to greet his old and new clientele with the beneficence of a cardinal receiving homage.

Oscar had been at the Waldorf since December 1892. He had known every important personage of his era and, merely by showing deference to some and not to others, elevated many quite a few notches in New York society. He recalled the day French engineer Philippe Bunau-Varilla and politico Mark Hanna mapped out the idea for the Panama Canal at a table in the Palm Room. Oscar organized a series of Musical Mornings, which featured the most illustrious singers of the day, like Australian soprano Nellie Melba, who sang at the Waldorf shortly after her American debut. Oscar, whose full-length portrait by Paul Trebilcock looked down on all who entered the portals of Peacock Alley, had served all the Presidents of the United States, the tycoons, the European royalty, and the stars of Broadway. And he had no intention of stopping, no matter what the condition of the American economy in 1931.

Yet things had changed, and the unbridled gluttony of the past had become a thing of the past. The rich sauces were being passed over in favor of simpler reductions that preserved the flavor of the main ingredient. Indeed, Oscar himself had helped simplify menus and cut down on courses. He noted that, after the war, banquets became "less sumptuous—more, shall, I say, utilitarian?" The difference between a menu served in March 1904 to then-Secretary of War William Howard Taft and one served to President Calvin Coolidge in February 1924 was ten courses versus five. Also, there was not a drop of wine at the latter, nor at a dinner served to the Prince of Wales in 1919, which included turtle soup, oysters à la newburg, breast of guinea fowl with sauce diable, and rice pudding "à l'americaine." Apollinaris mineral water and White Rock club soda were the accompanying beverages. In fact, there had been no provision made for a wine cellar in the new Waldorf.

In his memoirs Oscar recalled with sadness, "I glance into menus, from 1921 on . . . to honor such figures as [steel magnate] Charles M. Schwab (on November 10, 1921); a rising young bandmaster, Paul Whiteman (August 14, 1923); Presidents Harding, Coolidge, and Hoover—and I find one thing strangely missing: a wine list. It was a pitiful blow to the art of public banqueting."

The significance of the new Waldorf-Astoria (the old one had been torn down to make way for the Empire State Building) was that it was designed to appeal to a much broader market than the old Waldorf had attracted. As a result, the epicurean meals of the past were modified to reflect the more plebian tastes of a larger public. Oscar once said about Americans' love of chicken and turkey dishes, "We broil them, we roast them, we boil them, we fry them. . . . Heaven knows what we don't do to them. But it doesn't matter. In the very simplicity of the food and its treatment is our right to acclaim ourselves a nation of good eaters."

Most Americans wanted simple food of good quality in big portions, and that was most easily found in chophouses and ethnic restaurants. Two Italians, John Ganzi and Pio Bozzi, opened a restaurant on New York's Second Avenue in 1926 they called "The Parma," in honor of their native region in Italy. But a licensing clerk misspelled the unfamiliar name and it became "The Palm," which was the prototype for the "Italian steak-house"—a no-nonsense men's hangout that served one-pound sirloins, five-pound lobsters, and a little spaghetti amid an atmosphere that was as raffish as the hotel dining rooms were genteel.

The low-end restaurant in New York thrived despite Prohibition, and the end of Prohibition brought renewed life to the hotel and restaurant scene, despite the Depression. The hotels even fought to hold onto their image as fine restaurants by obtaining a legal ruling that prohibited drugstores from serving hot soups or "complicated dishes," leaving them with the options of only sandwiches, cold dishes, and coffee.

One 1934 New York guidebook noted that there were 18,763 restaurants in Manhattan alone—somewhat *more* than there are in the borough today. Every kind of food could be found, from the hot tamales at the Mexican Garden to the shish kebabs at The Rajah. Up in Yorkville one could find hearty German food at Maxl's, the Platzl, and Old München. You could

go out to Brooklyn and enjoy a lavish "shore dinner" of fresh seafood at Lundy's on Sheepshead Bay, Feltman's at Coney Island, Joe's on Fulton Street, feast on the clam bellies at Gage & Tollner, or tuck into a massive sliced porterhouse at Peter Luger's, which opened in 1876 as a billiards room and bowling alley. There was a nightly smorgasbord at Stockholm on West Fifty-first Street; you could eat risotto at Enrico & Paglieri on West Eleventh Street; there was sukiyaki on the menu at Toyo-Kwan on East Nineteenth; and you'd go to Longchamps—which by 1939 had a dozen restaurants—for their special "sizzling platter" of meats, or to the White Turkey Town House in Greenwich Village, where you could get Thanksgiving dinner year round.

ROOM SERVICE AT THE WALDORF-Astoria in 1940 begins with breakfast (*left*) and continues throughout the night. Note the waiter placing food into a heated compartment (*right*).

Nightclubs abounded in the 1930s, from Harlem to Greenwich Village. Right after the end of Prohibition, Billy Rose opened his Casino de Paree, which initiated what was dubbed "The Music Hall Influence." The Casino had two orchestras, cheap food, and a supposedly naked girl who swam in a oversized goldfish bowl. Other music halls included the Hollywood Restaurant, the Paradise, and the Palais Royal. The sports figures got the best tables at Jack Dempsey's and Gallagher's, the literari still dined at The Algonquin's Rose Room, the theater crowd flocked to Sardi's, high society was to be found nightly at El Morocco, the Stork Club, and the Rainbow Room, which opened in October 1934 atop the new RCA Building in Rockefeller Center. The Rainbow Room was one of the most gorgeous restaurant-nightclubs ever built, taking full advantage of the New York sky-line as seen through twenty-four floor-to-ceiling windows. An organ converted music notes into colors reflected onto the domed ceiling, and the dance floor revolved to the music of everyone from Duke Ellington to Bea Lillie.

The menu at the Rainbow Room of 1934 was an amalgam of European dishes and American favorites, all of which came to be known as "continental fare." You might begin your meal with "Sliced Eggs Czarina" (75 cents) or "Gumbo Creole" (45 cents), then move on to "Filet Mignon Maréchale" ($2) and "Suprême of Guinea Hen and Virginia Ham Eugénie" ($1.50), get a side order of "Spaghetti Italienne" (50 cents), "Potatoes O'Brien" (50 cents), or corn on the cob (45 cents; 60 cents if served in a chafing dish). Dessert might be strawberry shortcake (75 cents), Peach Melba (60 cents), or "Cherries Jubilee" (75 cents). A bottle of Pommard 1929 went for a rather pricey $3.50.

But the most celebrated and imitated high-society restaurant of the 1930s was the Colony, which held considerable sway as Manhattan's premier supper club until well into the 1950s. Like the "21" Club, the Colony, began in the shadows of the Volstead Act. The front room of the original Colony, located at 667 Madison Avenue, functioned as a non-profit-making bistro, while to the rear gamblers and prostitutes plied their professions with considerably more success. Owner Joe Pani, headwaiter Ernest Cerutti, captain Gene Cavallero, and chef Alfred Hartman went through the motions of serving meals until certain members of New York society began frequenting the place at the end of 1921. The three employees bought out Pani for twenty-five thousand dollars, modernized the kitchen, and before long attracted the doyenne of New York society, Mrs. William K. Vanderbilt, whose mere presence caused the little bistro to be stormed the next day by the cream of New York's haut monde. Reginald Vanderbilt even took his sixteen-year-old daughter there for ice cream.

In 1926 the three owners moved the Colony around the corner to Sixty-second Street, and within two years had netted $500,000. Eventually Cavallero, together with George Fiorentino, bought out his partners and turned the Colony into one of the most famous and fairly notorious restaurants in America. *Vogue* magazine warned aspiring debutantes, "It is harder to get a good table at the Colony than to join the Junior League."

Nothing was too good for Cavallero's clientele. When Alfred Lord Tennyson's grandson inquired as to why the Colony had no bidet in the men's room, Cavallero had one installed immediately. When Bernard Baruch dined at the Colony in the heat of a New York summer, Cavallero would turn off the air conditioning because Baruch hated it. When Admiral Lord Louis Mountbatten arrived during the war with little pocket money, Cavallero told him, "My Lord, please honor us as many times as you wish, and never mind paying until the war is over, even if it be another Thirty Years' War."

The Colony was not the first restaurant to serve as a showcase for its clientele, but the layout of the three rooms—called the "Royal Box," "Midship," and "Quartier Latin" (or "Doghouse")—dictated the importance of the individual occupying a seat at one of the banquettes. Territoriality took precedence over the dining experience itself, even though Cavallero took great pains to offer the best food he could to an often undemanding clientele.

The cooking at the Colony was certainly impressive enough in terms of its menu, which included dishes like eel ragoût, pompano en papillote, roast baby lamb, pheasant Souvaroff, tripe à la mode de Caen, suckling pig, Irish stew, bagna cauda, pirojki, osso buco, chicken curry, kidneys à la Vichy, and crêpes Suzettes. The wine list carried eighty-five different champagnes. Far ahead of his time, Cavallero consulted with physicians and dieticians to come up with a "4-Day Reducing Diet" for customers who ate too well and too often at his restaurant. Even gastronome Lucius Beebe wrote in 1938 that "no other city in the world offers such a variety of restaurants as New York, or such a wide range of quality, for that matter" and ranked the Colony as the best in the city. And drama critic George Jean Nathan pronounced the Colony as one of five restaurants in the world that represented "civilization's last strongholds in the department of cuisine."

In their appeal to wealthy clients from whatever origins, restaurants like the Colony, the Rainbow Room, and others helped create a new high society in America, which included strata once held in low esteem by the self-proclaimed American aristocracy who'd made its wealth in the previous century. Artists, musicians, actors, and writers were the new aristocracy who made restaurants' reputations. When the board of directors of New York's Hotel des Artistes commissioned Howard Chandler Christy to paint murals in the downstairs restaurant, the Café des Artistes, in 1932, the result was a series of thirty-six young American girls cavorting nude in an idyllic forest. "The Café is a happier place for the relish with which he carried out the commission of the board of directors," wrote social chronicler Brendan Gill. "His pinkly silken hamadryads instruct us by their wanton rompings in how far [New Yorkers] have come from those dour Dutch burghers and buttoned-up Britishers of the seventeenth century."

The glamour that surrounded such restaurants opened during and just after Prohibition was buoyed by theater, music, and movie stars who frequented such places, all duly reported on by the new gossip columnists with whom restaurateurs established a synergetic relationship that provided the former with unchecked power to make or break a celebrity or a restaurant. Of course, a little scandal now and then never hurt anybody. A major scandal could mean a boost in business that could carry a restaurant for a decade.

In Chicago the equivalent of the Colony was The Pump Room, opened on October 1, 1938, by hotelier Ernest Lessing Byfield on the premises of the

Ambassador East Hotel. Until then deluxe dining rooms had fared poorly in Chicago under Prohibition, and the owner of the defunct Richelieu Restaurant once cried, "I lost a million dollars trying to make Chicago eat with a fork."

Byfield sought to break the mold of the funereal hotel dining room, taking instead the model of The Pump Room spa in Bath, England, where, wrote Byfield, "Commoners, authors, poets and painters were encouraged to come . . . to hobnob with titled folk." While others remained shocked at Byfield's choice of a name for his new restaurant, the hotelier persisted with his concept, echoing the architecture of the original and decorating the room with a mural of actress Sarah Siddons and a portrait of Bath's social arbiter, "Beau" Richard Nash. He even dressed his waiters in red swallow-tail livery, white stockings, hats with ostrich feathers, and turbans.

Byfield also wanted his Pump Room to be a meeting place for all levels of society, but was well aware of the value of discriminating between the lofty and the low. He knew about how the best barroom tables at the "21"

Club were saved for celebrities, was aware of El Morocco's "Siberia" section (so-called after socialite Peggy Hopkins Joyce scoffed at being escorted to a less-than-desirable table at the New York nightclub by saying, "Where are you taking me, Siberia?"), and had himself once been shunted to the "penal colony" section of Boston's Ritz-Carlton by its notorious headwaiter, Theodore. Byfield gave his best tables to celebrities, and the next best to high-society types. Sometimes the best table of all—Booth One—would go empty all night, if no one was deemed worthy of sitting there. "The old families were out of the social limelight," wrote Rick Kogan in his history of the Ambassador East, *Sabers & Suites* (1983). "Hollywood stars and bathing beauties were in. And if they weren't [Byfield would] provide a little push."

They didn't need much of a shove. John Barrymore was a frequent

ENTERTAINMENT rather than food was the high point of a night out at Chicago's Palmer House (*right*), while food served on flaming swords was one of the attractions at The Pump Room in the Ambassador East Hotel (*opposite*).

guest, putting away so much liquor that the house ordered his drinks watered. And Marilyn Monroe, Humphrey Bogart, Ronald Reagan, Elizabeth Taylor, Bette Davis, Betty Grable, and Clark Gable all sat at Booth One.

The food at The Pump Room had to match the swagger of the decor, and Byfield was not above naming dishes after his guests, or even after himself. Waiters pushed wagons of hors d'oeuvres, roasts, soups, and ice sculptures through the dining room, but the most flamboyant tradition at the restaurant was a display of culinary pyrotechnics by which waiters would bring out food skewered on flaming swords. One party even got hot dogs served to them on flaming swords, and another received an order of twelve ripe olives brought in on long brochettes by twelve individual waiters. "We serve almost anything flambé in that room," Byfield was fond of repeating. "It doesn't hurt the food much." Robert Benchley observed such proceedings at The Pump Room and quipped, "Any minute now they'll be bringing in the manager on a flaming sword."

Other cities had similar restaurants that doted on a celebrity clientele. Detroit's London Bar (later called the London Chop House) was opened in 1938 by Lester Gruber, who effectively made this subterranean, wood-paneled restaurant famous for "table number one" and "table number two," whose occupants Gruber chose from among the city's most important auto industry executives or visiting celebrities. The London Chop House was also significant for its commitment to basic American fare rather than "continental cuisine," and was one of the first restaurants in the United States to promote the better American wines.

But nowhere were the merits of glamour more evident than in Hollywood, a town within a city that fed off its publicity mills dependent upon restaurateurs, maître d's, captains, and busboys for their daily fodder. In fact, most Los Angeles restaurants reflected the importance of the motion picture industry in the city's culture, whether in the form of a hot dog stand shaped like a cartoon dog or an extravagant place like the Cocoanut Grove (where the Academy Awards festivities were held from 1930 to 1936). Many of the most famous Hollywood restaurants were private, like the Embassy Club, which had Charlie Chaplin, Gloria Swanson, and Marion Davies as club officers, and La Bohème, a grand gambling den on the fast-developing Sunset Boulevard.

With the repeal of Prohibition restaurants grew larger and more theatrical, with show girls and dance bands clearly more of an attraction than *haute cuisine.* The Biltmore Bowl, which opened in 1934, was 140 feet long and sat 1,200 customers, including most movie stars of the era as well as students for their Friday Collegian Nights, which broadcast the music of Jimmy Grier's orchestra throughout the nation. Omar's Dome, located downtown, had gold damask walls, murals of Persian luxury, gold mesh curtains, and a fifty-two-foot mahogany bar set with stainless steel and coral glass. The Circus Café on Hollywood Boulevard was done up like a circus tent. The Crystal Marine Room in the Club Seville, opened at the end of 1935, had a see-through dance floor under which fish swam.

Entrance to these nightclubs came remarkably cheap—usually a five-dollar charge that might well have included dinner or a bottle of champagne—but as the night spots became more established, the idea of serving food took on distinct marketing possibilities. A gourmet delicacy shop called The Vendome became the city's most famous luncheonette after it began serving imported European foods to celebrities like Mae West, Clark Gable and Carole Lombard, and Louella Parsons. So, owner Billy Wilkerson opened a lavish restaurant called Café Trocadero in September 1934, with the "West's first genuine Paris sidewalk café" and a menu full of French dishes like "tenderloin of beef *forestière*" and "vol au vent of sweetbreads Toulousaine." The restaurant was an overnight success, inspiring more elegant, more sophisticated restaurants like the Victor Hugo in Beverly Hills and Ciro's on Sunset Strip, while at the same time causing less pretentious eateries like the Brown Derby to improve their food service.

Chasen's began when vaudevillian Dave Chasen borrowed three thousand dollars from Harold Ross, editor of *The New Yorker,* to open the Southern Pit Barbecue on Beverly Boulevard. Its six tables and eight counter stools attracted a high-profile crowd that included Jimmy Cagney, Frank Capra, and W. C. Fields, all of whom came for the bowl of chili, the barbecued ribs, and the cheap drinks. A year later Chasen expanded the eatery, and before long it was a full-service restaurant called Chasen's, which became, as Heimann noted, "a swanky hangout that rivalled even New York's 21 and Chicago's Pump Room." Customers like Humphrey Bogart and Errol Flynn would go to Chasen's after a rough night of drinking just to use the sauna in the rear.

But it was the theme restaurant that epitomized Hollywood night life, and no motif was too outrageous as long as it was fun, featured scantily clad women, and attracted movie stars. A fellow named Don the Beachcomber featured exotic rum cocktails with names like the "zombie" and the "vicious virgin" at his namesake restaurant done up in imaginary Polynesian decor with palm trees, rooms with names like The Black Hole of Calcutta, and a tin roof on which water was sprayed to create the illusion of a tropical rain forest. The food was a concoction of Chinese, Hawaiian, and make-believe that was widely copied by other restaurants with names like Ken's Hula Hut, the Seven Seas, and Hawaiian Paradise, which housed live parrots, tropical fish, and two waterfalls.

There were African jungle restaurants like Zampoanga (which featured the "Tailless Monkey" cocktail) and Latin American restaurants like La Conga, Club Zarape, Casa Mañana, Sebastian's Cubanola, and La Bamba.

One of the oddest theme restaurants was the Pirate's Den, whose investors included Bob Hope, Bing Crosby, Rudy Vallee, Errol Flynn, and Johnny Weissmuller, where mock pirate battles took place, female customers were "kidnapped" and thrown into the brig, and waiters who dropped trays were jokingly flogged or hanged. Obviously in such atmospheres good fun prevailed over good food, and Hollywood's reputation as Tinseltown largely derives from the manufactured fantasies at such night spots.

The average Los Angeleno went to such night spots infrequently, but everyone went to the Lucca Restaurant at Fifth and Western for the Italian food, to the Hofbrau Gardens on Sunset for the German food and oompah

ONE OF HOLLYWOOD'S more sophisticated dining rooms was **The Rendezvous Room at the Biltmore Bowl, where continuous live entertainment was always part of an evening.**

band, and to El Cholo on Western for the Mexican fare. Milwaukeean Law-rence L. Frank opened a restaurant in Beverly Hills in 1938 the gimmick of which was that it served only one signature item—Lawry's Prime Rib—along with large helpings of Yorkshire pudding, mashed potatoes, creamed corn, and sweet peas. Frank based his concept on the established Simpson's-in-the-Strand restaurant in London (which he'd never visited), utilizing the same kind of glistening silver serving cart from which trained carvers dispensed lavish portions of roast beef. He also introduced the nov-elty of the "spinning salad bowl," served *before* the main course, an idea that caught on in the rest of America. He provided fixings for his baked potatoes, like bacon and chives, another idea that took off. And it was Frank who first offered his patrons "doggie bags" in which to take home food they couldn't finish.

The theme concept was not lost on restaurateurs in other cities. Not long after Don the Beachcomber opened his restaurant, a one-legged grocer named Victor J. Bergeron opened a tiny "glorified beer parlor" in Oakland, California, called Hinky Dinks, which had as its main appeal meals for a quarter and the opportunity for customers to stick ice picks into his wooden leg (Bergeron had lost his leg to childhood tuberculosis). "I got the idea for the South Pacific decor from a couple of guys who said Don the Beachcomber was selling a lot of food and booze in Los Angeles," Bergeron said. "I looked over his place for a week and decided I could build a better mousetrap. Why the Pacific stuff? It intrigues everyone. You think of beaches and moonlight and pretty girls without any clothes on. It is complete escape and relaxation. Besides, I didn't

LAWRY'S PRIME RIB, opened in 1938 in Beverly Hills by Lawrence L. Frank, pioneered service of roast beef from a silver cart, serving salad before the main course, baked potatoes with various stuffings, and the "doggie bag" for customers to take home leftovers.

know a damn thing about that kind of food or booze, and I thought I'd like to learn."

Bergeron thereupon enlarged Hinky Dinks, decorated it with Polynesian artifacts, and renamed the place Trader Vic's (opening in 1937), where he too began concocting "Polynesian cocktails," including his own concoction, the Mai Tai. The place caught on locally and did booming business when servicemen adopted it as their favorite Bay Area bar. "They sure carried the message around the world," recalled Bergeron. "We helped them remember by smuggling booze on board supply carriers for random distribution in the South Pacific." In 1945 the United Nations appointed Trader Vic's as the "official entertainment center" for dignitaries visiting San Francisco that year. Bergeron went on to open a Trader Vic's in San Francisco in 1951, where it became that city's equivalent of New York's Colony, drawing San Francisco's social elite to its exclusive Captain's Cabin room, and it is said that Trader Vic's is the only public restaurant Queen Elizabeth II ever ate in. Still later Bergeron franchised the name and theme, setting up more than twenty Trader Vic's restaurants around the world, with branches in London, Hamburg, Singapore, Tokyo, and Bangkok.

By the end of the 1930s every major American city had a deluxe supper club/nightclub, like the Skyway and adjoining Plantation Roof set atop Memphis's Peabody Hotel, mecca for Southern society figures who came to dance to big bands like Tommy Dorsey's, Paul Whiteman's, and Harry James's. Nashville's Hermitage Hotel was quite in the same league and gave the Peabody competition with young singers like Dinah Shore.

Haute cuisine was slowly making headway, and French restaurants were doing better too, led by New York establishments like Voisin, Le Café

"TRADER VIC" BERGERON manufactured a Polynesian fantasy of totem poles, bamboo, and outrigger canoes to go along with concoctions like the Mai Tai cocktail at his Trader Vic's restaurant in San Francisco.

Chambord, L'Aiglon, Versailles, Marguery, Le Coq Rouge, Café Louis XIV, Belle Meunière, Café Saint Denis, Passy, Divan Parisien, and Lafayette, which was named by the man who put up the twenty-five thousand dollars for Lindbergh's flight across the Atlantic. There were wines in the cellars again, and there was a bit more money to be spent on them as America pulled slowly out of the Depression. World War II would interrupt the evolution of fine dining in America, but just before the United States entered into hostilities, an event occurred that would significantly alter the direction it would take.

With his usual bonhomie President Franklin D. Roosevelt opened the New York World's Fair on April 30, 1939, with the announcement, "All those who come to the World's Fair will find that the eyes of the United States are fixed on the future."

With the Old World crumbling, America seemed blushingly optimistic and open to all new ideas (3-D movies, Kodachrome film, television, and superhighways were among the thousands of exhibits), and that included a fervid curiosity about the sixty nations that had exported their culinary culture to Flushing Meadows in a dazzling array of international restaurants

THE SERVICE STAFF at Le Restaurant du Pavillon de France at the 1939 New York World's Fair, which brought a remarkable array of international foods to Americans' attention. Le Restaurant du Pavillon's maître d'hôtel, Henri Soulé, who later opened his own restaurant in New York called Le Pavillon, is the round-faced man in the center of the first row.

where American palates were awakened to everything from feijoada at the Brazilian Pavilion to vodka and borsht at the Soviet Pavilion.

There were nearly fifty places to eat at the Fair, and at any given moment, more than twenty thousand people could be fed. One could dine on Scottish woodcock at the four-hundred-seat British pavilion, sip Pilsener Urquell beer at the Czech beer garden, relax at a Formosan Tea Room, consume arroz con pollo, ajiaco criollo, and conqrejo crab at the Cuban Village, or sample two hundred different sausages at the Albanian Pavilion. At the Italian Pavilion's restaurant, which simulated the dining room of the oceanliner M. V. *Victoria,* you could feast on dishes never before seen in America—saltimbocca, Piedmontese agnolotti, and fonduta with shavings of white Alba truffles, all complemented by Barbera, Barolo, Valtellina, and Grignolino wines.

But no dining room at the Fair made so astounding an impression on the American public as did Le Restaurant du Pavillon de France, created by a Syndicat des Restaurateurs that included the Café de Paris, Drouant, Fouquet's, Meurice, Le Pavillon d'Armenonville, Pré Catalan, and the chefs of The French Line. The uniqueness of the cuisine, service, and decor in

the 350-seat, glass-walled dining room was immediately recognized, with *The New York Times* reporting, "Every gesture of the staff, from the august Jean Drouant, director of the establishment, down to the most unobtrusive waiter, signaled the pride of the employees in what was instantly signed, sealed and delivered to the fairgoing public as a retreat for epicures."

Americans had never imagined, much less tasted, food like this before—*double consommé de viveur* (duck consommé with celery and beet-root juice topped with cheese croutons), *homard Pavillon de France* (lobster in shellfish cream sauce with rice), *filet de sole à la Russe* (sole with a reduction of vegetables and cooking stock), *suprême turbotin Armenville* (turbot with a glaze of white wine, tomatoes, and mushrooms), and *noisettes de pré-sale aux laîtues royale* (medallions of lamb with braised lettuce and chicken mousseline). Le Restaurant du Pavillon de France introduced the silver *voiture* service of daily specials to America, which afterward became standard in French restaurants in this country.

Within a month of its opening, the restaurant was turning out five hundred lunches and a thousand dinners daily. The waiting list stretched for weeks, and by the end of the year it had served 132,261 meals to Americans who carried back stories of Lucullan feasts to every state in the union. Every pot and pan, fork and knife used at Le Restaurant was brought from France, along with thirty-five kitchen workers and sixty dining room staff, including an eighteen-year-old assistant *poissonier* from Restaurant Drouant named Pierre Franey. "Working at the fair was a great education for me," he says now. "I worked split shifts six days a week, at a salary of thirty-six dollars a week—not bad for a teenager then. Two years later, in 1941, my job as a *commis saucier* at the Waldorf-Astoria paid twenty-five dollars weekly."

The influence of Le Restaurant might have evanesced as quickly as a dream, had it not been for a diminutive, stout, pompadoured young man named Henri Soulé. Born on March 12, 1903, in Saubriges, near Bayonne, this son of a building contractor left home at fourteen to begin his career as a busboy in Biarritz. He then became a waiter in Paris, moved on to London and back to Paris to become a captain at Ciro's, where he was one day asked if he'd be interested in a two-season stint in New York as maître d'hôtel for the French Pavilion dining room. Within months Soulé was on his way to America and gastronomic history.

When war broke out in Europe in the fall of 1939, Soulé and many of the staff of the French Pavilion returned to France, but, as hostilities seemed to abate that spring, they returned to New York to reopen the French Restaurant for the second season. By summer, however, France had capitulated to the Germans, and the whole idea of a World's Fair disintegrated. The season, to put it mildly, was not a success. The occupation of France placed Soulé and his compatriots in political limbo. Safe on American soil, they were, nonetheless, men without a country. Most thereupon crossed into Canada, then quickly reentered the United States as refugees, some of whom were immediately drafted into the U.S. Army.

Soulé, at forty too old for military service but loathe to return to occupied France, managed to scrape together fourteen thousand dollars and, on October 15, 1941, opened a restaurant at 5 East Fifty-fifth Street. He called it Le Pavillon. To his surprise and delight, the place was jammed on opening night, mostly with customers who remembered him from the World's Fair. That evening they all feasted on caviar, *filet de sole bonne femme, poulet braisé* with Champagne sauce, cheese, and desserts.

Despite the war and the shortages it exacted, Le Pavillon prospered, so that within a year Soulé had grossed $263,714—this, at a time when his *table d'hôte* lunch was only $1.75. When the war ended, Soulé became a United States citizen and the fame of Le Pavillon spread, not only for its fine cuisine but for Soulé's attention to detail and for the high standards he set for everyone—including his customers. Soulé was not only a master restaurateur; he was a teacher, first of those young men who worked in his kitchen and dining room, and second, of those customers innocent of the intricacies and pleasures of dining in a great French restaurant. Dining at Le Pavillon became a rite of passage, a monumental step up in a world of increasing sophistication that marked the 1950s in America.

"New York had wonderful restaurants before Le Pavillon," recalls Elaine Whitelaw, who dined there often in the 1940s. "There was Voisin, and others, of course. But when I first ate at Le Pavillon I remember suddenly feeling that for the first time an unquestionably great restaurant had opened in America. The food was exquisite, the smoked salmon the finest, and the service as elegant as could be. You realized immediately that Soulé was a master and was educating the public as to what fine food was. You must remember that Americans were just starting to go abroad, and the national taste was still in its infancy for most people."

THE *KITCHEN BRIGADE* of Le Restaurant du Pavillon in 1939. A young assistant fish cook named Pierre Franey (*upper row, first on left*) rose to become the head chef at Henri Soulé's Le Pavillon restaurant, later worked as a consulting chef to Howard Johnson's, and went on to become a food writer for *The New York Times* and a chef on public television.

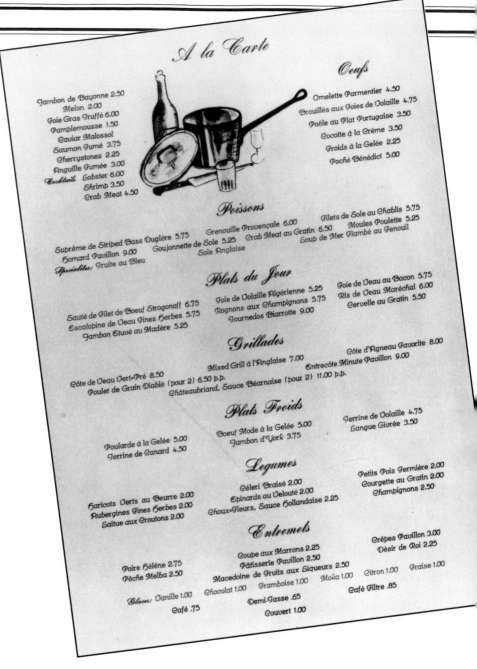

A la Carte

Oeufs

Omelette Parmentier 4.50
Brouillés aux Foies de Volaille 4.75
Poêle au Plat Portugaise 3.50
Cocotte à la Crème 3.50
Froids à la Gelée 2.25
Poché Bénédict 5.00

Jambon de Bayonne 2.50
Melon 2.00
Foie Gras Truffé 6.00
Pamplemousse 1.50
Caviar Malossol
Saumon Fumé 3.75
Cherrystones 2.25
Anguille Fumée 3.00
Cocktails Lobster 6.00
Shrimp 3.50
Crab Meat 4.50

Poissons

Filets de Sole au Chablis 5.75
Grenouille Provençale 6.00   Moules Poulette 5.25
Suprême de Striped Bass Duglère 5.75   Crab Meat au Gratin 6.50
Homard Pavillon 9.00   Goujonnette de Sole 5.25   Loup de Mer Flambé au Fenouil
Spécialités: Truite au Bleu   Sole Anglaise

Plats du Jour

Foie de Veau au Bacon 5.75
Foie de Volaille Algérienne 5.25   Ris de Veau Maréchal 6.00
Sauté de Filet de Boeuf Strogonoff 6.75   Rognons aux Champignons 5.75   Cervelle au Gratin 5.50
Escalopine de Veau Fines Herbes 5.75   Tournedos Biarrotte 9.00
Jambon Etuvé au Madère 5.25

Grillades

Côte d'Agneau Favorite 8.00
Mixed Grill à l'Anglaise 7.00   Entrecôte Minute Pavillon 9.00
Côte de Veau Vert-Pré 8.50
Poulet de Grain Diablé (pour 2) 6.50 p.p.
Châteaubriand, Sauce Béarnaise (pour 2) 11.00 p.p.

Plats Froids

Terrine de Volaille 4.75
Boeuf Mode à la Gelée 5.00   Langue Givrée 3.50
Jambon d'York 3.75
Poularde à la Gelée 5.00
Terrine de Canard 4.50

Légumes

Petits Pois Fermière 2.00
Céleri Braisé 2.00   Courgette au Gratin 2.00
Haricots Verts au Beurre 2.00   Epinards au Velouté 2.00   Champignons 2.50
Aubergines Fines Herbes 2.00   Choux-Fleurs, Sauce Hollandaise 2.25
Laitue aux Croutons 2.00

Entremets

Crêpes Pavillon 3.00
Désir de Roi 2.25
Coupe aux Marrons 2.25
Pâtisserie Pavillon 2.50
Poire Hélène 2.75   Macedoine de Fruits aux Liqueurs 2.50
Pêche Melba 2.50   Moka 1.00   Citron 1.00   Fraise 1.00
Chocolat 1.00   Framboise 1.00
Glaces: Vanille 1.00   Café Filtre .85
Demi-Tasse .65
Café .75   Couvert 1.00

Joe Baum, himself one of the great postwar restaurant innovators, once commented that a restaurant achieves greatness when it is able to "take the single act of eating and transform it into a civilized ritual." This is what Soulé set out to do from the beginning, suffering from that chronic French malady known as "the mission to civilize." It was a joke among Soulé's staff to say his angry stare could "curdle a béarnaise."

By the same token, Soulé was also a businessman—and a very good one—who knew the value of compromise and of adapting to one's native territory. The long, midday meal was not an American tradition as it was in France, so Soulé catered to the shorter lunch hour of his clientele. He fought, unsuccessfully, the tendency of customers to rush through their dinner in time to get make an eight o'clock theater curtain. And, much to his

THE A LA CARTE MENU at Le Pavillon, circa 1970

148

Le Pavillon

Dejeuner

Jambon Persillé, Dijonnaise   Pâté en Croûte Truffé
Terrine de Canard   Jambon de Bayonne   Saumon Fumé
Les Palourdes: Little Necks   Cherrystones   Fruits de Mer

Les Hors d'Oeuvre

Melon   Pamplemousse
Le Consommé Royale   Les Oeufs Pochés à l'Estragon
Le Potage du Jour

Les Entrees

Plats du Jour: Le Contre Filet Rôti Niçoise
Les Quenelles Nantua
Le Grain Grillé à l'Américaine
Le Délice de Sole Bonne Femme   L'Omelette Forestière
Les Foies de Volaille Sautés Algérienne   Le Jambon Etuvé au Xérès
L'Escalope de Veau Sauté Fines Herbes

Les Entremets

Les Tartes aux Fruits   Les Compotes de Fruits
La Mousse au Chocolat   Les Fromages de France
Glaces Tous Parfums
La Macedoine de Fruits aux Liqueurs   La Coupe St. Jacques
Les Pâtisseries Pavillon

Café   Demi-Tasse   Café Filtre

Prix Fixe Nine Dollars

distress, he watched his customers slurp down whiskey and soda with their meals, even though he stocked a tremendous cellar that included 161 different champagnes in 56 vintages.

His grace under pressure was enviable. One evening a party of six ordered a grand dinner with pheasant as the entrée. When the birds were brought out, a busboy knocked over the guéridon, sending the pheasant sliding across the floor, Soulé immediately announced to the guests, "Quick, tell the chef to send out the other pheasants!" The chef—Pierre Franey, who had taken over the kitchen in 1952—had no cooked pheasants in reserve, so the dropped birds were merely reassembled on a fresh platter and sent out, to be proclaimed by the customers as the best they'd ever eaten.

Soulé's own taste in food was indisputably classic (although he loved a

THE FIXED PRICE MENU at Le Pavillon, circa 1970

good American hot dog), and his chefs cannot be credited with much that was new in the Escoffier canon. He, like Escoffier, believed that a meal should be light on the stomach, although "light" was a relative term in those days: A half pound of butter for three pounds of fish went into Le Pavillon's *mousse de sole Pavillon.* Georges Briguet, now owner of New York's Le Périgord, defends those menus by saying, "In those days it was the right food for the right time—the lobster with the cream and sherry sauce, the medallions of beef with truffle sauce or bearnaise. Today everybody's on a diet, but we didn't cook that way then. It was the sauce that mattered, and saucemaking was an art in those days. Today you ask a young chef to make a classic sauce and he doesn't know how to do it."

Le Pavillon's printed menu rarely changed, but there were always two specials for lunch and two for dinner, served from a two-thousand-dollar Christofle silver *voiture.* There was also always the addition of a bourgeois dish like *tête de veau, daube de boeuf,* or *cassoulet,* made in very small portions and offered only to those Soulé knew would appreciate it. "Monsieur Soulé was the only one allowed to sell such specials," noted Franey. "Soulé was not a cook, and he never came down to the kitchen, but he knew what he wanted and how he wanted it made."

There was one dish Soulé did make himself, however. "I remember that every Good Friday a group of us would go to Le Pavillon for *brandade de morue,*" says Marion Gorman, now editor of *Gastronome.* "He would make it himself, and he told us it was his mother's recipe. He would stand there spooning it out to us, and there'd be tears in his eyes."

There were many dishes he introduced to French dining rooms in this country—quenelles of pike, *coulibiac* (done correctly with the sturgeon marrow called *viazega*), his trademark *oeufs à la neige,* and many other dishes, all made with the finest, freshest ingredients, when necessary flown in from France. Dishes cooked in wine were made with fine burgundies. The *foie gras* had to be from Strasbourg, and he got the best hothouse spring lamb he could find from Connecticut. It was this devotion to the best available that distinguished Le Pavillon from its predecessors and from most of its contemporaries.

Yet it was the *un*availability of certain foods that distinguished Le Pavillon from its models in France, a fact of the marketplace that caused Soulé to confide to his biographer, Joseph Wechsberg, "Some of the richest men in the world are dining here tonight. And for all the money on earth I couldn't give them the simple, good things that every middle-class Frenchman can afford from time to time. Six *Marennes.* A partridge—very, very young. Some *real* primeurs—the first spring vegetables. A piece of Brie that is just right. . . . And some *fraises des Bois.*"

In such a remark there is considerable sadness and not a little regret, the utterance of a perfectionist always sure to fall short of his goals. "He was not a happy man," recalls Franey. "He really had no life outside of his restaurant, and he didn't socialize with others very much. I don't think I ever saw the man relax." Indeed, Soulé once said his only hobby was "paying the bills promptly."

There's no question Soulé played the "table game," though he was hardly the first in New York to do so. "A" tables and "B" tables had never been a tradition in Parisian dining rooms, but in the United States the game of oneup-manship had been brought to tyrannical status by restaurateurs like Oscar of the Waldorf, Jack Kriendler and Charlie Berns of "21" Club, and Gene Caval-lero of the Colony long before Le Pavillon arrived on the New York scene.

Soulé disliked juggling tables, so that when he moved Le Pavillon to a larger space in 1957, he placed the front tables in a cramped, narrow pas-sageway leading to the rear dining room. Regulars nevertheless demanded to sit in that passageway, which Soulé joking christened *la salle royale,* a configuration many of his competitors would later imitate and which is still the design at New York restaurants like La Caravelle and Le Chantilly.

But Soulé would never allow the buying and selling of tables. Wechs-berg pointed out that being part of the "Inner Circle" was based on many factors, not simple wealth or position. From the beginning Le Pavillon was a magnet for the social elite, the international set, captains of industry, and the merely wealthy, but Soulé "decorated" his restaurant with those he felt brightened the room, whether it was a beautiful young American girl or a sitting President of the United States. Soulé might show deference—John F. Kennedy had his milk served in a silver champagne bucket—but was always aloof. "Soulé did not *accommodate* people as some restaurateurs do today by giving in to any whim," comments food writer James Villas. "If you were not behaving in a civilized manner, he would go to your table and tell you in no uncertain terms, 'There will be no bill tonight, but don't *ever* come to my restaurant again.'"

Soulé pushed himself hard and expected the best not only from his staff but from his customers. He could not be bullied by anyone, even if it cost him the lease on his restaurant, as it did in 1955 when his landlord (Harry Cohn, head of Columbia Pictures) raised the annual rent from $16,500 to $75,000 after Soulé refused to seat him at a good table. Soulé thereupon relocated to 111 East Fifty-seventh Street, off Park Avenue, where Le Pavil-lon reopened on October 9, 1957. (Ironically, in the end he got a good lease on the old premises, which in 1959 he made into a "bargain-priced" Le Pavillon he called La Côte Basque.)

Soulé labored on, fine tuning, maintaining standards, and watching his chefs and waiters go off on their own ventures. "Henri Soulé spawned through the former members of his staff, from chefs to busboys, nearly as many French restaurants as the face of Helen launched ships," wrote food historian Waverley Root. Charles Masson, who started with Soulé as a waiter at the World's Fair, went on to open La Grenouille. Willy Krause, chef at Le Pavillon as of 1960, opened Le Périgord and Le Périgord Park. Jean Fayet, *saucier* at Le Pavillon, was later owner of Lafayette, while La Caravelle's proprietors included Le Pavillon alumni Fred Decré and Robert Meyzen. For a quarter of a century Soulé's demanding culinary academy graduated scores of restaurateurs and chefs throughout the United States.

Throughout the 1950s and 1960s every deluxe French restaurant that opened in New York used Le Pavillon as its model, not just in decor but in their menus, so that one might have dined at Le Madrigal, Le Marmiton, La Grenouille, La Caravelle, Le Chambertin, Laurent, La Petite Marmite, or any number of other places and believed Soulé had been consultant to them all. And in a very distinct sense, he had. Yet rarely did the cuisine at any of those places come up to the level of Le Pavillon in its heyday, and by the 1960s many of those French restaurants that emerged from Le Pavillon's crucible had entered a period of mind-numbing copycat-cooking overlain with a veneer of snobbery that was a mindless corruption of Soulé's standards of behavior. The soup du jour was invariably cream of watercress, the special was always roast veal, and the soufflés were always cooked *au Grand Marnier. New York Times* food critic Craig Claiborne pinioned them all back in 1969 when he wrote, "There is too much sameness on the menu, and the food of one small establishment tastes uncommonly like that of another. You can recite the menu like responses to a catechism. Sole meunière, coq au vin, boeuf bourguignon, omelet with cheese, omelet with mushrooms, and on and on."

Even Le Pavillon had begun to coast by the mid-1960s as Soulé's health began to fail. The success of La Côte Basque had drawn customers away from Le Pavillon, and Soulé was forced to make cuts. "Monsieur Soulé asked me to cut the payroll at Le Pavillon," says Franey, who was chef for both restaurants, as well as at Soulé's East Hampton restaurant, The Hedges. "I did as much as I could. One day [in March 1960] he told me two cooks had to be gone by Monday, and I said, 'Monsieur Soulé, you cannot share an egg.' I got goddamn mad at him, packed up and left."

Such were the reputations of the two men that the story hit *The New York Times,* reporting that Franey called Soulé "stingy" and that Soulé labeled Franey "a fresh young man." Le Pavillon closed briefly, then reopened with a new chef, Clement René Grangier. "Le Pavillon is open again," wrote one observer at the time. "All's right with the world."

But all was not right at Le Pavillon. Soulé was growing old and even his friends saw a diminution in his once boundless energy. Finally, on January 27, 1966, he suffered a heart attack and died, just short of his sixty-third birthday. The news struck the food world as the death of a monarch might strike a nation. The *Times* obituary called him "the most dynamic force in the history of French cuisine in America."

Without Soulé, Le Pavillon was never to be the same again. *"Le restaurant, c'est moi,"* Soulé was fond of saying, and it was true.

La Côte Basque was taken over by a woman named Madame Henriette Spalter, a former coat-check attendant and manager of La Côte Basque to whom Soulé had, in fact, left half his East Hampton estate. Soulé did have a wife, Olga, who came briefly to the United States at one point but who returned to France to live out her life *sans* Soulé.

Chef Grangier took over the reins at Le Pavillon and immediately began altering the sacrosanct decor by removing the venerable Lamotte murals. Grangier could not keep Le Pavillon on its old keel, however, and the restaurant was bought by a group of former customers headed by restaurateur Stuart Levin. More changes were made—Soulé's beloved red roses were changed to carnations in a brandy snifter set on the tables. There was a new chef, Roland Chenus (later co-owner of Le Chantilly), followed by Michel Fortin. It was clear that Le Pavillon was no longer what it was under Soulé and had become as predictable as the other French restaurants in town.

"Now the ego and style is Stuart's," wrote *New York* magazine food critic Gael Greene. "Le Pavillon is no longer Le Pavillon. It is an American restaurant cast in the conventional Manhattan image of a French restaurant, serving very good French food with some lapses into mediocrity and some memorable triumphs." A 1971 *Forbes Magazine Restaurant Guide* review of the restaurant read like an irreverent obituary: "After that near-mythical great God of haute cuisine, Henri Soulé, died, so did the Soulé flavor of Pavillon, after what might be termed a long lingering illness. Along with his soul, Soulé's sole too departed." Still, perhaps out of reverence, the guide awarded Le Pavillon four stars—its highest rating.

By 1971 Le Pavillon had all but passed into gastronomic history when Craig Claiborne wrote, "Le Pavillon, long the foremost temple of fine French cooking and the standard by which all other French restaurants could be judged, has become something less than first-rate since [Soulé's death]."

Claiborne went on, awarding Le Pavillon a mere two stars: "In its days of glory Le Pavillon was the ultimate French restaurant on this continent. It was, in fact, the model and principal training ground for hundreds of chefs, waiters and the like, and the man responsible was the legendary Henri Soulé. . . . When he died in 1966 the spirit of the place went with him . . . and it remains a place of certain elegance and luxury. But however much one might devoutly wish it, Le Pavillon does not exist in all its former grandeur." Not long afterward, Le Pavillon was shuttered forever.

FIERCELY DEMANDING and dedicated to raising the standards of haute cuisine in America, Henri Soulé made New York's Le Pavillon the most famous French restaurant in the world this side of Paris.

Servicemen eating at a Fred Harvey restaurant in Chicago's Union Station

Chapter 9

Something for Everyone

Rations and the Restaurant Renaissance in the 1940s

IN MORE THAN ONE Hollywood movie of World War II, GI's in fox-holes fantasized about taking a pretty girl out to a restaurant where they could order an ice-cold beer and a two-inch-thick sirloin smothered in on-ions. For while the impact of Henri Soulé's Le Pavillon on the luxury dining market may be obvious in hindsight, *haute cuisine* was not much on the minds of most Americans during World War II. It is one of the ironies of the era that, despite shortages, rationing, and the loss of much of the male working force for four years, restaurants in the United States survived and many prospered.

There were still soup kitchens in 1940, and half of all men called up for conscription were turned down because of malnutrition. But most Americans still frequented drive-ins, luncheonettes, and restaurants when they could afford to do so, and there seemed little let-up in night life in the big cities. New Hollywood clubs like Romanoff's (run by a self-described "Prince" named Mike Romanoff and backed by movie stars like Cary Grant) and the Mocambo (which lured away the maître d' from New York's "21") were packed nightly. After Pearl Harbor they became central to fund-raising events for the war effort. In 1942 the movie studios bankrolled a place called the Hollywood Canteen, where enlisted men could come to eat, drink, and dance with movie stars who donated their time to serve coffee and sand-wiches as well as to entertain. (Jim Heimann reports that Betty Grable was said to dance with forty-two servicemen in eight minutes.)

ACTRESS BETTE DAVIS entertains the troops in the 1944 Warner Bros. film *Hollywood Canteen,* based on the actual studio-backed Hollywood Canteen where movie stars performed and hobnobbed with service personnel from 1942 through the war.

Other, less fanciful restaurants around the United States contributed to the war effort through special promotions, menus, and even "Victory Cocktails"—a glass of water and a ten-cent Defense Stamp—and change for true cocktails was given in the same fund-raising stamps.

Most Americans enjoyed plenty of fruits and vegetables during the war, and salads had become increasingly part of the meal. There was no shortage of seafood either. "I think we had a greater variety of seafood coming into the market during the war than after it," recalls Edmund Lillys, whose Gloucester House restaurant, opened in 1935 in New York City, did good business throughout. "Fish was not something they were putting into C-rations for the soldiers abroad."

Foreigners were amazed at the amount of foods—fresh and otherwise—available at restaurants in the United States. An English visitor investigating food service in the United States in March 1945 (two months before Germany surrendered) reported of the menu at the Waldorf-Astoria in New York, "It wasn't only that the variety of all the things we [British] have missed most that was so fantastic, but the general surroundings—beautiful linen, glass, and silver—beautiful women, well dressed, well groomed, and flowers and new shiny paint—in fact, luxury—all of which one has almost forgotten existed during the last few years." The report went on to note that the workers at the dining hall of a bomber factory even had fresh broccoli on the menu and that everyone was drinking "ice water."

There were some shortages, and rationing was put into effect early on in the war. Americans were limited to one pound of sugar per person per week, four ounces of butter, and four ounces of cheese, and there were cutbacks on coffee and flour as well. Sugar bowls disappeared from restaurant tables, while molasses, honey, and saccharin were substituted in desserts and pastries. Restaurants were allowed to use only one pound of coffee for every hundred meals and one pound of sugar for every thirty-three customers in 1943. Curiously, meat consumption rose, despite rationing, to only twenty-eight ounces per week. Chefs were reminded to conserve fats, oils, and shortenings, not only because they were energy foods but because they were ingredients in munitions. As one Wesson Oil advertisement put it, "It takes 1 lb. of fat to supply a machine gun with ammunition for 30 seconds!" A "butter extender" was added to butter or oleo to double its bulk for use in sandwich spreads.

Portions at restaurants were smaller, and even after the war, conservation became part of a crusade to feed the hungry in other parts of the world. A menu for May 6, 1946, from the Hotel Peabody in Memphis noted that "We, in cooperation with the Famine Emergency Committee Program for feeding the starving people of the world, are endeavoring to conserve on the use of oil and wheat. . . . Second slice of bread . . . and Extra helping of oil salad dressing and butter will be served you only if you request it."

Food prices rose 44 percent during the war, so chefs were forced to be more creative with a smaller larder from which to draw. There were shortages of tin cans, but frozen foods became more and more plentiful, and restaurants could buy pretty much anything they wanted on the black market. Except male employees. A *New York Times* article in 1943 entitled "Panic Prevails" warned that two thousand restaurants might have to close because of the labor shortage and that waitresses were being allowed to work until two A.M. to fill the gap, although at most restaurants operating hours were being cut to conserve fuel.

But there seemed no shortage of customers or money to spend in restaurants. Gross National Product and Disposable Income grew rapidly during the war, while inflation dropped. In 1944 Arnaud's restaurant in New Orleans grossed more than one million dollars. Railroad dining cars that grossed $22.5 million in 1939 did nearly $62 million in business three years later.

Airline food service was in its infancy (the first airline plane to have a galley was an American Airlines DC-3 in 1936; liquor on flights was not inaugurated until October 1949 by Northwest Airlines), but it would improve significantly after the war.

Restaurants offered an easy, convivial refuge for those trying to forget the deprivations of the war, whether it was a family out for Sunday dinner, workers getting together for sandwiches and coffee at a diner, or servicemen making the most of their time at home by going to a fancy restaurant with their loved ones. Restaurants were bright, gay, and offered the kinds of conveniences not yet part of most Americans' life-style. Advertisements for Toffenetti's restaurant in New York proudly extolled the modernity of its spotless stainless-steel surfaces, electric eye-operated–swinging doors, acoustic-paneled ceilings, and its controlled temperature. "In fact," read Toffenetti's promotional booklet, "we think our air-conditioning has added more delight to meals than any forward step in dining since the birth of Ham and Sweets."

With the end of the war, the restaurant industry in America was set for the biggest boom in its history, and it drew on the services of millions of returning GI's to man its kitchens and counters, improve its efficiency, and expand its possibilities as the population exploded: By 1950 there were more than 150 million Americans.

In 1948 the first serious cooking school, the New Haven Restaurant

IN THEIR BROCHURE "The Restaurant We Built for You" (1940), Toffenetti's in New York made much of all its modern amenities, like air conditioning, electric eye operated doors, stainless-steel kitchen surfaces, and acoustic paneling.

FRESH AIR ALWAYS —
NEVER TOO COLD —
PLEASANT AS THE
ADIRONDACKS . . .

● In fact, we think air-conditioning has added more delight to meals than any forward step in dining since the birth of Ham and Sweets.

THOUGH OUR WALLS
HAVE NO EARS, OUR DOORS
HAVE ELECTRIC EYES . . .

● The famed Toffenetti Spirit of Courtesy motivates our doors, as well . . . They wink their wise electric eyes the moment a waitress approaches, and open. A wonder direct from the New York World's Fair . . .

Institute (later called the Culinary Institute of America), opened in Connecticut, bringing true academic standards to the training of the nation's chefs. The federal government began the National School Lunch Program, which by the mid-1950s had radically changed the diet of many of America's schoolchildren for the better, helped along by new processes of freezing and dehydration of foods.

The food processing industry made cooking easier for everyone, both at home and in the restaurant. Mississipians could enjoy New England clam chowder whenever they wanted it. Arizonans could eat cherry pie every day of the year. Cranberry sauce was no longer just for Thanksgiving. Even completely prepared, cooked meals could be frozen and shipped out to restaurants anywhere in the world.

In 1951 a Hungarian chef named Louis Szathmary began experimenting with freezing meals while working in a roadside diner by day and a Jesuit seminary by night. His first success was with sixty portions of lasagne, but before long he was freezing all sorts of meals, and soon opened a food and catering company in Darien, Connecticut.

By the mid-1950s Midwesterners who'd never tasted ethnic dishes like manicotti or tortillas could order them at their neighborhood restaurants, and cooks with no formal training in sophisticated dishes like chicken Divan (created at New York's Divan Parisien restaurant), Swiss steak, sole floren-

GLEAMING STAINLESS STEELS — NEW PRECIOUS ALLOYS . . .

• Cleanliness rides on science' wings. Everywhere these singing ovens, ranges, grills, spice-filled cabinets and shined-bright utensils represent the most advanced designs in modern kitchen metallurgy . . .

ACOUSTICALLY PANELLED WALLS AND CEILINGS . . .

• No dining room diapason ringing in your ears while dining. Just the pleasant overtones of conversational contentment. And anything *you* want to say here you may say in confidence. Echoes of what you're discussing vanish in the muted walls . . .

tine, and tournedos Rossini suddenly found themselves serving such delicacies straight out of the warming oven.

At first glance, these technological breakthroughs would seem to have been a great enhancement to dining out in America. But in fact, with few exceptions, they had the reverse effect, halting the development of fine dining in this country with more damaging results than did Prohibition, the Depression, and World War II. By availing themselves of frozen, canned, and processed foods, many cooks no longer saw any useful reason to buy fresh ingredients or to support local producers, farmers, and fishermen. The young chefs coming into the restaurant industry were encouraged to economize by using processed foods, and many never learned to work with fresh fish or vegetables at all.

The temptation to buy frozen beans, canned corn, and powdered coffee became irresistible for the restaurant industry as a whole, and the public didn't seem to mind as long as they could eat whatever they wanted anywhere in the country at a fair price.

Processed food was a double-edge knife. On the one hand it made more food and more kinds of food available to more people than ever before. It prevented spoilage and deterioration. The food actually looked better, more uniform, and more appetizing. The industry could build a fatter animal and more abundant crops faster through the use of chemicals. It could reduce many of the variables that make a dish taste so different from one kitchen to the next, and cut food costs substantially. The ridiculous conceit about the ideal steak that can be "cut with a fork" was now easily accomplished by decomposing the steak under the assault of a meat tenderizer.

On the other hand, processing too often robbed foods of their natural taste and nutritional goodness. Sweeteners, binders, MSG, salt, preservatives, and other additives designed to enhance the flavor of a food, in fact, altered it. And, after a few years of familiarization, the taste of processed food became the taste of America, not so much a corruption of what it was before the war as it was a modification. It was a far cry from the days when Mark Twain insisted the only way to fix corn was to set a pot of boiling water up in the cornfield and shuck the ears right into it.

To be sure, not all Americans living before the war knew the flavor of a fresh vine-ripened tomato in season, but by the end of the 1950s there were many Americans who had never tasted one at all. In most restaurants it would be difficult to find freshly made fried potatoes, the boiled, mashed-up, uniformly shaped French fry having become ubiquitous. "Breaded shrimp, oysters, crab meat specialties, lobster Newburg and pompano are packed in attractive packages with four-color illustrations," gloated a report in *Quick Frozen Foods,* "and tend to make the chef proud of preparing a gourmet entrée."

As John and Karen Hess pointed out in their jeremiad against the United States food industry, *The Taste of America* (1977), tests showed that most Americans came to prefer the taste of frozen orange juice, disliked ketchup with a pronounced tomato flavor, believed strawberry ice cream made with real strawberries tastes artificial, and found the taste of fresh fish much too "fishy."

Whether they were eating at home, at a Howard Johnson's, or at a

deluxe hotel dining room, Americans came to expect all their fried chicken to be evenly "golden brown," their fish to be filleted, deboned, and breaded, their fruit salad to be swimming in syrup, their mashed potatoes to be lumpless, their tuna to be mashed up, their crab cakes to be largely filler, their bread to be white and fluffy, their spaghetti sauce to be sweetened, their tomato soup to taste like Campbell's, their ketchup like Heinz', their steak sauce like A-1, their cheese like Velveeta, and their mayonnaise like Hellmann's.

The phrase "just like Mom used to make" (superceded in the next generation by "just like Grandma used to make") still carried some marketing weight on a restaurant menu, but the American palate was becoming homogenized and regional distinctions were blurring fast in the 1950s, leading to what came to be regarded as the "bland American diet" full of tasteless meats, fish, vegetables, and fruits.

Something else happened after the war that would change Americans' attitude toward eating out as only an occasional indulgence. In 1949 a company named Diners Club offered a new gimmick called a credit charge card to two hundred New York subscribers for use in twenty-seven of the city's better restaurants. Suddenly traveling businessmen had enormous flexibility to dine out. No longer did they have to take their meals at dreary hotel dining rooms or carry cash to a restaurant. Once credit cards were widely accepted, a traveler could leave the hotel, eat anywhere, spend a little more, and not have to worry about the consequences for a month or more. And restaurateurs knew it too.

As ever, restaurateurs had to come up with new, enticing ideas in a postwar market that was rapidly expanding as Americans got back on the road with a passion. Six million cars came off Detroit assembly lines in 1949 alone, and passenger miles increased by more than 42 percent between 1950 and 1955. Train travel—and dining car service—declined badly, while airplane travel soared dramatically. Some of the old formulas, like the Harvey restaurants, weren't working as well any longer, while roadside restaurants were poised for another phenomenal leap forward into something called "fast food." The traditional urban restaurant was in for a remake, and Americans were hungering for something brand new again.

THE NEW HAVEN Restaurant Institute (later called The Culinary Institute of America) provided ex-servicemen with the training to enter a booming postwar job market that needed skilled workers for the expanding restaurant industry.

161

A carhop at a Southern fast food restaurant, circa 1942

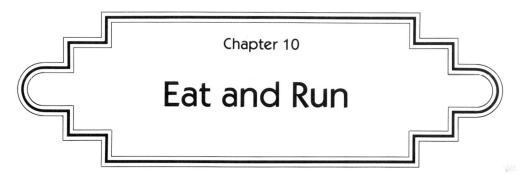

Chapter 10

Eat and Run

Fast Food in America

T HE MOST VIVID IMAGE Dutch-born painter Willem de Kooning remembered of his arrival in New York in 1926 was of watching a diner cook pour a continuous stream of coffee across a line of coffee cups, filling every one to exactly the same level. "Boom! Boom! Boom!" recalled de Kooning of the rapid-fire service. "The speed with which he served that coffee was amazing. And I said to myself, 'Ah! *This* is America!'"

One need not make too much of such an incident's effect upon an artist, but the image stayed with de Kooning, who went on to work on the Federal Arts Project in the 1930s and was to become one of America's greatest abstract expressionist painters, whose work embodied the same extraordinary degree of control over paint and canvas as did the counterman over his coffee and cups. Fast, seemingly furious, but done with both economy and precision, de Kooning's art and the counterman's skill are expressive of that quintessential American trait—speed wed to efficiency.

From the outset, American food service had manifested both those elements with gusto. The cooking, serving, and eating of food might be managed with some degree of savoriness, but, as we have seen, such activities were engaged in with dispatch at the colonial taverns and boardinghouses, the eating houses and oyster cellars of the early nineteenth century, the beer halls and pizzerias after the Civil War, and the diners, lunch counters, and cafeterias of the current century. Long, luxurious meals were foreign to the majority of Americans who did not dine out at Delmonico's, the Waldorf-Astoria, or Le Pavillon, and wolfing down one's food had always seemed part of the restless nature of Americans' eating habits away from home. The phrase "grab a sandwich" is as rooted in the American language as "time is money" or "two shakes of a lamb's tail."

But it was not until the 1960s that the term "fast food" gained currency in the United States, by then used to describe something quite specific—the preparation and service of a fairly short list of items like hamburgers, French fries, milk shakes, fried chicken, and pizza at a chain restaurant where people order their meals from a cashier who sets the prepackaged order on a tray with a regimented, almost robotic quickness that sends the customer on his way without further to-do. This was food as fuel. Boom! Boom! Boom!

On the surface, it doesn't sound like a process so different from the Automat, the cafeteria, or the roadside eateries like White Castle and Howard Johnson's. The hamburger stand had been a fixture on American highways for decades, and the drive-in was well established before World War II. But in the postwar period all of these began to fade in popularity as a new breed of restaurant evolved. Fast food establishments would, by the 1970s, come to dominate the restaurant industry, as cafeterias, diners, and family-style restaurants like Howard Johnson's went into decline.

The story of fast food begins with a name as recognizable around the world as Cadillac, IBM, Coca-Cola, or Elvis Presley: McDonald's. Indeed, within six years of airing its first national TV ad in 1965, the "Ronald McDonald" clown character was familiar to 96 percent of American children—far more than knew the name of the President of the United States.

The McDonald's story has been told so often it has become one of the classic examples of American entrepreneurism, while the man who eventually sowed McDonald's restaurants in every corner of the globe—Ray Kroc—has become a folk hero on the order of Johnny Appleseed. Case studies of the McDonald's managerial system have long been part of the business school curriculum, and social scientists from every discipline have tried to puzzle out the allure of the hamburger stand's mystique, sometimes stretching it into the most remarkably abstruse configurations. Anthropologist Conrad Phillip Rottak of the University of Michigan asks us to believe that "McDonald's has become nothing short of a secular religion, the shelter between the Golden Arches, a sacred place. One finds here spirituality without theological doctrine." And in his article "The Psychology of Food Happiness," Gregory Hall becomes positively ecstatic in pondering the teleology of McDonald's: "Like Faust before the Mater Gloriosa, an irresistible power draws us on and we may find ourselves in the sanctum of a McDonald's kitchen."

The origins of McDonald's are somewhat less sublime than those of the Garden of Eden. Actually they are prosaically grounded in the cook-'em-and-serve-'em world of the postwar drive-in. Just before the war two brothers named Richard and Maurice (";Mac") McDonald, originally from Manchester, New Hampshire, opened a small drive-in on E Street in San Bernardino, California. They had twenty employees and did pretty well for themselves, grossing more than two hundred thousand dollars a year. But as Philip Langdon points out, after World War II, "a fundamentally different labor market was shaking the restaurant industry. In 1940, restaurants had paid out 27 percent of their gross income as wages. This constituted the highest percentage for any sizable segment of retailing, and by 1947 the figure had climbed to the worrisome 35 to 40 percent range. Returning veterans could settle into more attractive jobs or use their service benefits to go to college; drive-ins were having a harder time attracting and holding reliable employees."

Having tired of "drunken fry cooks and dishwashers," the McDonald brothers took a step in December 1948 that would in time revolutionize food service throughout the world. They fired the carhops.

They also drastically cut their twenty-five-item menu to nine that could be handled easily by a minimum of employees, did away with china and metal flatware, and passed their savings on to their customers, who now had to get out of their cars, walk up to a service window, place their order, and go back to their cars (or somewhere else) to eat the low-priced fifteen-cent hamburgers (half what they'd previously cost), ten-cent French fries, and twenty-cent milk shakes. The McDonald brothers called their new concept the "Speedee System."

At six o'clock, employee Arthur C. Bender opened the window to the renovated hamburger stand and sold the first bag of food. It took six months for the idea to catch on, but before long they were attracting more and more families in addition to the local workers and teenagers who had always gone to McDonald's. Still, their self-service drive-in hamburger stand was no

ALTHOUGH HE DID NOT INVENT the McDonald's hamburger concept, entrepreneur Ray Kroc took the franchises to a level unmatched by any competitor and made famous the hamburger known around the world.

THE LIGHTED GOLDEN ARCHES of McDonald's (*right*) became an icon of Americana beloved by as many people as those who found them garish examples of American architectural kitsch.

HAMBURGER UNIVERSITY (*below*) was set up by the McDonald's Corporation in Elk Grove, Illinois, to ensure that all company workers adhered to the tenets of the McDonald's technique, routine, and philosophy, graduating students with a "Bachelorhood of Hamburgerology."

more than a local success and garnered little interest from the rest of the industry. Then, in the May 1952 issue of *American Restaurant* magazine, a shortening manufacturer named Primex took an ad that touted its product as a factor in the ability of McDonald's to turn out thirty thousand orders of French fries per month. When the same magazine two months later noted that McDonald's has also cut its labor costs to less than 17 percent, the industry sat up and took notice. "When this hit all over the country," recalled Richard McDonald, "that is when people really began to flock out, so we knew that we had something that was going to make us some money." In September the brothers took out their own ad in the magazines announcing that the McDonald's self-service system was "the most revolutionary development in the restaurant industry during the past fifty years!" The brothers McDonald could not possibly have known they were just being modest.

The ad went on to say that they were selling more than a million hamburgers a year, as well as half a million shakes, French fries, and soft drinks each. The accompanying drawing made their simple little octagonal-shaped stand in San Bernardino look like a glowing flying saucer had just landed atop a drive-in stand. And standing on the roof was the McDonalds' first cartoon character—Speedee—whose round, hamburger-shaped, winking face and energetic stride repeated the message that speed coupled with efficiency could lead to high profits.

The McDonalds decided it was time to make their mark. Bored with the conventional squat look of most hamburger stands, Richard McDonald wanted a design that would set his apart. Architect Stanley C. Meston came up with the idea of a tilted roof line, large windows, red-and-white horizontal tile, and McDonald added two golden yellow arches running from back to front of the building. Several architects scoffed at the arches, but Richard was persistent and finally got the none-too-enthusiastic Meston and neon sign supplier George Dexter to construct his dream drive-in. The final product fit in perfectly with the postwar airport look that gave the building lightness, solidity, and a sense of futurism. The brothers also planned out their ideal kitchen for maximum efficiency by drawing chalk marks on their nearby tennis court and having workers act out their movements around imaginary refrigerators, stoves, and counters. But before a draftsman got to the tennis court to transcribe the chalk marks, they'd been washed away by a middle-of-the-night rainstorm.

The first of these new McDonald's opened in Phoenix, Arizona, in May 1953 (the original arches of this store are now on permanent exhibit at the Henry Ford Museum in Dearborn, Michigan), followed by others in Downey, Los Angeles, Sacramento, and other California cities. All of these were franchised, but the McDonalds' first franchise agent, William Tansey, didn't work out, and the brothers did not want to do it by themselves.

The arrival of Raymond Albert Kroc, a former piano player and Chicago-based paper cup salesman and distributor of milk shake machines, at McDonald's San Bernardino drive-in in 1954 was therefore fortuitous. Kroc, who came out just to see how McDonald's was managing to turn out forty milk shakes at one time, was suddenly gripped by an entrepreneurial epiphany. "I can't pretend to know what it is," Kroc later explained, "certainly, it is not some divine vision. Perhaps it's a combination of your background and experience, your instincts, your dreams. Whatever it was, I saw it in the McDonald operation, and in that moment, I suppose, I became an entrepreneur. I decided to go for broke."

Just what exactly it was that Kroc saw in the McDonald's concept was certainly not clear to a lot of other restaurant industry people who knew the operation nor to the small number of franchisees who were simply doing pretty good business with the McDonald's idea. After all, McDonald's seemed almost a step backward in food service. As Joseph Monninger has pointed out in an article in *American Heritage* magazine (April 1988) on the history of fast food, McDonald's had done away with those amenities—indoor seating, plates, silverware, glasses, place mats, salt, pepper, and sugar shakers—that made eating out at a luncheonette or even in one's car a delightful experience

MCDONALD'S LATER REDESIGNED its structures by adapting a mansard-roof motif more in keeping with traditional American architecture.

for the American family. "The result was a meal that vaguely resembled dinner at a family table," he wrote. "The food might be poorly prepared or erratic in quality, but the goal of many restaurants, even down to their advertising, was to make the dinner seem 'home cooked.'"

Fast food, on the other hand, never tried to make such associations. Notes Monninger, "What we now perceive as a normal fast-food serving system—paper cups, styrofoam hamburger containers, even paper bags—were a unique experiment in the McDonald brothers' restaurant in 1948. Forty years later it is not even a matter of thought to eat french fries with our fingers, add ketchup from plastic capsules, pour milk shakes from quick-drawing machines."

If Ray Kroc did not create the gimmick, he had a good idea of how to promote it. He talked the McDonalds into making him franchise agent, and for a fee of $1,500 and 1.9 percent of the gross sold a franchise in Fresno, California. Kroc's next step was to run his own McDonald's, which he opened at 400 North Lee Street in Des Plaines, Illinois, on April 15, 1955 (the McDonalds already had an unopened Chicago store under franchise). Everyone seemed to prosper, new McDonald's franchises opened throughout the Midwest, and Kroc respected the McDonald brothers original concepts and designs.

Like White Castle's Billy Ingram, Kroc was determined to distance his hamburger stands as far as possible from the "greasy spoon" image of the past, and he was fanatical about cleanliness. According to Edward Schmitt, president of McDonald's in the 1970s, "What McDonald's did—what was really a stroke of genius on Ray's part—was to create a fishbowl type of atmosphere. You could see the cleanliness. How many restaurants do you know of in the United States where you look into their food facilities and preparation area. Man, very few."

ONE OF THE MCDONALD'S MEAT suppliers, shown here in a photo from 1982, could produce 540 beef patties per minute, which were inspected daily by a USDA inspector, then code dated, refrigerated at 0 degrees Fahrenheit, and then shipped out to various restaurant units.

But there was more to it than that. McDonald's had a design that seemed as expressive of its era as did tail fins on automobiles, bat wing lounge chairs, kidney-shaped swimming pools, and glass skyscrapers. Other chain restaurants copied the McDonald's design, most specifically by using the tilted roof line and, with variations, adapting the golden arches. Burger King's "arches" actually looked more like handlebars; Carrolls Hamburgers ("A Serving a Second" read their signs) were shaped more like sharp-edged boomerangs. This was the look of the 1950s and early 1960s, and the more outlandish the design—like Jack in the Box's gawking puppet—the more eye-catching it would be from the road.

In 1961—the year McDonald's sold its 500 millionth hamburger—Kroc bought out the McDonald brothers for $2.7 million and made plans to improve the basic concept and to make the company one of the most profitable and powerful in American history. One of the first things he did was to retire the character of Speedee in 1962, replacing him three years later with a clown figure named Ronald McDonald, who debuted on TV in 1965 and appeared at the Macy's Thanksgiving Day Parade the following year. He began adding new food items—the Filet-O-Fish in 1964, the Big Mac and apple pie in 1968, the Quarter Pounder in 1971, the Egg McMuffin in 1973, cookies in 1974, and the tremendously successful Chicken McNuggets in 1982.

On April 20, 1965, with 738 stores, Kroc took the company public; four years later, having sold one billion burgers, McDonald's established an international division, opening units in Canada and Puerto Rico in 1967. The first European unit opened in the Netherlands in August 1971, then in the Paris suburb of Creteil in July 1972 (it sold red wine), and by October had another on the Champs Elysées in Paris. Within ten years the five thousandth McDonald's opened (in Japan) and today half of the units opened each year are in foreign countries, including Great Britain, Italy, Yugoslavia, Thailand, and South Korea. Kroc imbued his people with a belief that opening an institution as American as a McDonald's hamburger stand was a kind of civilizing act. "It's corny," said Steve Barnes, former head of McDonald's International Division, "but I feel like a missionary over here."

In order to get the right version of the gospel across, Kroc opened "Hamburger University" in Elk Grove, Illinois, graduating ten thousand students in 1975 with a "Bachelor of Hamburgerology with a minor in French fries."

Kroc relentlessly tinkered with the original concept. He experimented with drive-through windows (pioneered by Texas's Pig Stands back in the 1920s and highlighted at the Jack in the Box chain opened in San Diego in 1951), and began indoor seating at a Huntsville, Alabama, unit in 1966. He preferred isolated lots without proximate competitors on a block (although very often the emplacement of a McDonald's on a site drew other fast food outlets around it). Parking lots were U-shaped so as to allow for the easiest access and egress. But he never wanted his customers to be so comfortable that they would want to linger, thereby cutting down turnover. Every piece of furniture, every accoutrement, every color was carefully chosen to urge people to order, eat, and leave as quickly as possible. Surfaces were kept hard, thereby maintaining a high decibel level. Intense colors like yellow and orange were used extensively. He prohibited telephones, cigarette ma-

chines, and jukeboxes. As Philip Langdon explains, "Kroc wanted the teen-age trade, yet he hoped to keep the transaction quick and limited; the objective was to prevent adolescents and others from turning his restaurants into social institutions as opposed to mere feeding stations," which was, of course, diametrically different from the traditions of the neighborhood luncheonette or diner where teenagers were encouraged to "hang out" all day sipping on cherry Cokes and malted milk shakes.

Kroc was his own best salesman, of course, never failing to find a speck of paper on the floor, always trying to improve morale among his employees,

rarely ever satisfied with what he saw. The title of his own story about McDonald's is telling: *Grinding It Out.* And the work took its toll. In 1979 Kroc suffered a stroke and soon entered an alcoholism treatment center in Orange, California, because, he insisted, "I am required to take medication which is incompatible with the use of alcohol." (McDonald's revenues also went to pay for the Kroc Foundation's support of Operation Cork, a national education program to help the families of alcoholics.)

McDonald's grew enormously large under Kroc's stewardship, never failing to make a considerable profit even during recessions. By the end of

THE SUCCESS OF MCDONALD'S spurred other fast food companies to come up with their own themes and readily identified motifs, as shown in these units of Long John Silver's in Dallas, Burger King in Miami, Popeye's Chicken & Biscuits (location unknown), and Char-Burger in San Diego.

1984 the company was opening over five hundred new stores each year, and had sold fifty billion hamburgers. The corporation was getting 100,000 inquiries a year about how to get a franchise, the fee for which was $12,500 with a capital investment required of between $286,000 and $340,000. McDonald's became the world's largest owner of real estate. When Kroc died on January 14, 1984, McDonald's had more than 7,500 outlets with worldwide sales of $8.7 billion.

There is no question that McDonald's led the charge for fast food and that all other competitors—even those that had been in business before McDonald's—followed that lead. Hardee's came out of North Carolina; Long John Silver (a seafood operation) began in Kentucky, and Burger King was based in Jacksonville, Florida. There were fast-rising Mexican restaurants like Taco Bell of Irvine, California, and Chi'Chi's (Louisville), roast beef and steak restaurants like Arby's (Atlanta), Roy Rogers (Bethesda, Maryland), and Ponderosa (Dayton, Ohio), and pizzerias, which in the 1980s registered astounding growth, led by Pizza Hut (Wichita, Kansas), Little Caesar's (Farmington Hills, Michigan), Godfather's (Omaha), and Domino's (Ann Arbor, Michigan), whose selling point was the delivery of its pizzas to the customer's door. And there were fried chicken restaurants like Bojangles (Charlotte, North Carolina), Popeye's (Jefferson, Washington), Church's (San Antonio), and the granddaddy of them all, Kentucky Fried Chicken.

The story of Kentucky Fried Chicken is as engaging as that of McDonald's, especially since the originator of the famous recipe, Colonel Harland Sanders, was sixty-five before he began promoting it. There was nothing else he could do. Having run the Harland Sanders Café and motor court in Corbin, Kentucky, since 1940, the Colonel (an honorary state title bestowed by Governor Ruby Laffoon in the 1930s) suddenly faced financial ruin in 1956, owing to the construction of Interstate 75, which would divert customers from his restaurant. If Americans were going to drive the interstate highway system, then he would bring his fried chicken to them. In 1952 Sanders had already taught his recipe to a Utah hamburger stand owner named Pete Harmon, who had made a great success of it. Believing that other restaurateurs might pay to get such a recipe for success, Sanders packed up his car with a pressure cooker and bags of eleven herbs and spices and began calling on roadside eateries where he'd cook up a batch of his chicken for the owner. A good number took him up on the offer, and by 1960 the Colonel had sold two hundred franchises for his chicken, doubling that number within the next year.

Decked out in a white suit and black string tie and sporting a goatee, Sanders was an engaging caricature of the Southern gentleman, and in his affable, grandfatherly way became Kentucky Fried Chicken's completely believable spokesman—especially after dropping in on a franchised store and publicly denouncing the fried chicken he felt was not prepared according to his standards. By 1990 the company (bought by Pepsico Inc. in 1986 for $840 million) had sales of $5 billion and more than 8,000 restaurants in 59 countries.

One of those who took on a KFC franchise was a twenty-four-year-old barbecue-stand owner named R. David Thomas in Fort Wayne, Indiana. An orphan with only a tenth-grade education, Thomas ran the Hobby Ranch House with Barbecue and did fair business. One day in 1956 Colonel

COLONEL HARLAND SANDERS (*above*) of Corbin, Kentucky, did not begin franchising his Kentucky Fried Chicken recipe until he was sixty-five years old. Former KFC franchisee Dave Thomas (*opposite*) named his hamburger empire after his third daughter. The gimmick of Domino's Pizza (*opposite*) was a delivery system guaranteed to bring hot pizza to customers' doors in thirty minutes or less.

Harland Sanders drove up to the restaurant and talked Thomas into taking on a KFC franchise. Before long he was being asked to take over the management of four unprofitable franchises in Columbus, Ohio, and brought them back to fiscal health. He threw himself into the challenge with gusto, working hard to clean up the operations, trading fried chicken for radio and TV advertising time, and soon tripling the business in the Columbus stores. He sold them in 1968 for $1.5 million. He then went on to manage three hundred KFC stores in Florida. He became operations vice-president for Arthur Treacher's Fish and Chips chain.

But Thomas was convinced that the fast food market would gradually demand better burgers and larger portions, so he went off on his own, opening his first Wendy's (named after his third daughter) in downtown Columbus on November 15, 1969. He served a quarter-pound hamburger made from fresh, not frozen, meat, which might be garnished any way the customer wanted, rather than in the restricted forms McDonald's and other hamburger stores sold their product. "I just got sick of seeing hamburgers abused," said Thomas. "How people could precook it, put mustard and catsup on it, wrap it in paper and keep it warm under a heat lamp, I'll never know. But I did know we weren't going to do that at Wendy's." Thomas also made his "Old-Fashioned Hamburgers" square—not intended as a gimmick—but merely to maximize space on the grill.

Thomas offered other items made with high-quality ingredients—chili, a Frosty milk shake that had a soft ice cream consistency, and an array of condiments like pickles, lettuce, onions, and tomato in addition to the standard ketchup. One of the company's most successful advertising campaigns featured a shrewd grandmotherly figure who scorned the paltry amount of meat in other hamburger chains' patties by demanding to know, "Where's the Beef?"

Wendy's restaurants were sit-down operations, complete with Tiffany-style lamps, carpeting, and bentwood chairs. Thomas wanted to attract families to his stores, but in order to dissuade those families from lingering too long, his stores had no booths and his tables had only four chairs.

Together with KFC alumnus Bob Barney, Thomas expanded his Wendy's chain slowly and carefully, offering franchisees an entire region rather than individual franchises to many different people within an area, a strategy that prevented oversaturation and inconsistency within a market area. And they were indefatigable in supporting weaker units by offering coupons and other promotions that brought such stores back to profitability.

When the fast food business slowed in the late 1970s and beef prices rose sharply, Wendy's realigned its concept to include chicken breast sandwiches, stuffed baked potatoes, smaller burgers, breakfasts, and salad bars. The chain also went international, with stores in Germany, England, Spain, Switzerland, Japan, Malaysia, and Singapore. By 1984 Wendy's sales were a very comfortable $2 billion from 3,150 restaurants in 14 countries.

By 1983 fast food restaurants constituted 40 percent of the nation's overall eating and drinking places, with the ten largest chains serving more than half the fast food in America. Fast food restaurants had catapulted the traditionally lethargic restaurant industry into the third largest industry in America by 1978. Fast food restaurants put Americans in the habit of eating out on a very regular basis. By the mid-1980s American families were spending nearly 40 percent of their food dollars at restaurants, with the average American dining out 3.7 times a week, so that *Time* magazine would write, "Nothing is more American today than avoiding a homecooked meal." If that was not an indictment of what fast food had wrought, it is difficult to imagine a more startling alteration of Americans' eating habits.

It was not the quality of the food that mattered on such excursions to such fast food restaurants so much as the experience, the fun of it all. Boxes of fast food were decorated with cartoon characters and could be turned into gameboards. Promotions were built around children's movies coming out of Hollywood, and fast food characters would appear in parades and public functions. And competition was fierce on the market. Fast food had grown steadily in the 1960s, exploded in the 1970s (when sales increased 20 percent annually), then slowed in the 1980s (with sales increases down to 10 percent), owing to a soft economy, higher prices for products, and a saturation of the market. Many Americans had become tired of the same old menu items, so chains began scrambling to bring out new dishes and concepts. Many were flops, like McDonald's "McRib" barbecue (reintroduced in 1990) and Burger King's veal Parmesan. Many of the fast food chains failed in the early 1980s: Arthur Treacher's, Big Bite, Wuv's, and an Italian-Chinese chain called Prusutti & Chin.

The population of the United States was aging, and people in their thirties and forties wanted something more for their money than boxed burgers and bagged French fries. Fast food, which in the 1960s and 1970s had come to be symbolic of American food service with fresh-faced teenagers in funny hats serving up the kind of processed comfort food that people had grown to love, was beginning to trouble communities. Health issues were

raised about the nutritional value of fast foods. But beyond that, fast food restaurants themselves were being perceived as intrusions into many neighborhoods rather than welcome additions.

At one time the opening of a McDonald's in a small American town was cause for rejoicing—it meant jobs, excitement, and seemed as much a natural, inevitable part of community evolution as the establishment of a Sears department store or a Chevy dealership. Having a Wendy's or Burger King in one's midst was almost the crowning touch after churches, schools, and post offices were set up.

But this positive image was being curdled quickly, especially in the East, where fast food restaurants came to be regarded as unsavory, unsightly, and, because of the number of people drawn to them, unsafe. For more than a year and a half Cambridge, Massachusetts, residents protested when McDonald's tore down two pre–Civil War landmark buildings to put up a restaurant. In Washington, D.C., residents formed an Ad Hoc Committee to Prevent Ginocide to protest the replacement of a beloved café with a Gino's Pizzeria. In New York City the news that a McDonald's would be opening would be greeted with neighborhood protests, so much so that, according to an article in *New York* magazine, "Because any such activity is visible nationally, the [McDonald's] corporate strategy has been to go underground about expansion. No job signs appear at construction sites, and the last additions to any new installation are the identifying graphics." The article went on to detail "Ten Ways to Keep McDonald's Out of Your Neighborhood," even advising people to "gather as many people as possible and go into McDonald's during the busiest periods and each order a different burger in a different way . . . thereby playing havoc with the system."

In Europe American fast food restaurants were welcomed by most people with the same delight they did blue jeans and American TV shows, although many others regarded a new McDonald's or Kentucky Fried Chicken restaurant with the same horror they once did the Visigoths and other barbarians. When McDonald's opened its first store in Italy near the Piazza di Spagna in May 1986, it was met by a barrage of criticism and protesters under the "Save Rome" committee banner, while the Communist party proclaimed the intrusion as a "degradation of the historic center." Brandishing placards and T-shirts with pictures of Hollywood star Clint Eastwood (who had recently been elected Mayor of Carmel, California, for his stand against fast food restaurants), the protesters cooked up pots of spaghetti to serve to supporters, and the head of an Italian gastronomic society, Carlo Petrini, immediately formed an organization called the "Slow Food Movement." "Fast food is one of the most powerful and destructive components of our speeded up modern lives," declared Petrini. "We have banded together to stop the undoing of thousands of years of gastronomic civilization, but in a democratic fashion that safeguards the right to pleasure, and, of course, we will act slowly, slowly." In the United States the tongue-in-cheek movement announced it was "committed to promoting the world-wide image of the U.S. as a first class culinary capital and wine-producing nation, not just a country of snacks and soft drinks."

Of course, the Rome McDonald's (the biggest in the world at that time)

TWO EYE-CATCHING ROADSIDE signs with simplistic themes and simple menus

BY THE END OF THE 1970s hamburger stands found they had to diversify their menus to survive in a highly competitive and increasingly saturated market. Thus, Wendy's began offering foods like baked potatoes, salads, pita sandwiches, and baked beans along with its most traditional hamburgers, French fries, and milk shakes.

opened and flourished and spawned many others in cities around Italy. Fast food was never intended to be grand cuisine, but fast food restaurants had come to represent something troubling to those who believed it had corrupted food culture both in the United States and abroad, and many Americans felt embarrassed to export the concepts to other countries that had long suspected the United States to be a nation of bad eaters.

The fast food industry realized that its image was fast becoming tarnished, and that part of that had to do with the garish designs and feed-'em-and-move-'em-out philosophy of mass feeding. It had all worked so well for so long because it seemed to express so perfectly the taste of the era. Indeed, fast food was to food what *I Was a Teenage Werewolf* was to movies and rock 'n' roll was to music—an unstoppable manifestation of a good-natured, rather feckless postwar adolescent pop culture built on the lowest common denominators of taste. Mostly, it was harmless, innocuous, and just good clean fun. But it was, in the 1970s, also out of touch with the new generation of young people who began to regard fast food as a blight on the land.

As a result many chains sought to soften their images by making their units more appealing and more like traditional family restaurants. Even

McDonald's famous golden arches dwindled in size to become little more than a logo that formed a graphic "M." The red-and-white stripes and neon lights were replaced by beige and brown brick and brown mansard roofs. Burger King followed suit. Signage, once flagrantly displayed on the buildings and parking lots to catch the motorist's eye, was reduced and company logos affixed to the buildings themselves. There was a real effort to blend in with the architecture of the neighborhood. A McDonald's in Ann Arbor, Michigan, exhibited scores of photos of old Ann Arbor; Kentucky Fried Chicken brought in hanging plants, wooden tables, and cushioned seats. Refuse bins melded better into the overall interior design, and noise levels were reduced. Some restaurants even enclosed play areas or had playgrounds adjacent to the store. And most of the chains became heavily involved in local philanthropies.

Fast food had radically changed the ways American ate, not only by drawing them away from the home but by creating tastes and flavors that Americans identified with. Southerners who grew up on skillet-fried chicken and homemade mashed potatoes came to prefer the taste and texture of pressure-cooker fried chicken and homogenized potatoes at Colonel Sanders's restaurants. Westerners who once argued over where to find the best, most individualized, hottest chili started to prefer the salty, mild goop at Taco Bell. And those who once sat waiting impatiently at a luncheonette while the aroma of a freshly cooked hamburger tantalized one's nose and tastebuds could no longer abide the wait and so lined up at a McDonald's for a Big Mac and a side of fries.

Regional food, family restaurants, and fine dining continued to evolve during the fast food boom years, but many of these were driven out of business by the onslaught of so many fast food eateries. And many American children grew up never tasting homemade scrambled eggs, freshly cut French fried potatoes, a pizza made from scratch, or an apple pie straight out of the oven. Yet, oddly enough, it was the children who would come to regard fast food as something symptomatic of deeper problems in a disposable society. In the end fast food would survive and thrive, at only a very small cost to its image. But in protesting fast food, the entire food culture of the United States would be altered radically.

A western theme restaurant in Pinnacle Peak, Arizona

Chapter 11

Googie, Mickey, and the Twelve Caesars

New Looks, New Themes in the 1950s

THE EXUBERANT STYLE of California's coffee shops had already been occupying architecture critic Douglas Haskell's thoughts as he drove along Sunset Boulevard in West Hollywood. Then, at the top of the hill, at Crescent Heights, set just below Schwab's Pharmacy, he saw it: an outlandish-looking coffee shop with an angled, cellular steel red roof jutting off into the sky. It had wide expanses of glass from which customers could look down the hills. There were scraggly shrubs hugging its perimeter. And the shop's logo incorporated two eyeballs into the restaurant's name: GOOGIES.

For Haskell, this strange little coffee shop was symbolic of a new kind of iconoclastic California restaurant architecture. So, under the name "Professor Thrugg," in the February 1952 issue of *House & Garden,* he made fun of this outrageous style in words that came to be prophetic. "Googie," he wrote, "brought modern architecture down from the mountain and set ordinary clients, ordinary people free." In mock-academic prose, Haskell addressed the outrageousness of Googie's eye-catching structure, insisting there was a deeper motive to the design than merely to make people brake their cars in surprise at the top of the hill. "You underestimate the seriousness of Googie," he wrote. "Think of it!—Googie is produced by architects, not by ambitious mechanics, and some of these architects starve for it. After all, they are working in Hollywood, and Hollywood has let them know what it expects of them."

179

CALIFORNIA RESTAURATEURS used ports-of-call themes in their establishments, such as Don the Beachcomber in Los Angeles, which featured wildly named cocktails like the "zombie," a dining room named the "Black Hole of Calcutta," and a tin roof splashed with water to create an artificial tropical rain.

Indeed, Googies was designed by a professional architect of some local repute. His name was John Lautner, who had worked under Frank Lloyd Wright at Taliesin and had already made a name for himself for his unconventional house designs when he was asked to undertake the design of Googies in 1949. Lautner was stung by Haskell's remarks, especially since the term "Googie" came to be used as a synonym for what architecture critic Esther McCoy later called "undisciplined design and sloppy workmanship."

Lautner backed sheepishly away from similar projects, but other architects had no qualms about undertaking such an exuberant, if aberrant style. The firm of Louis L. Armet and Eldon C. Davis believed strongly in the vaulting roofs, the wrap-around glass walls, the space-age lighting fixtures, the strong colors of Naugahyde, and the exaggerated signposts out front, motifs that were expressive of a Western mentality accustomed to buildings adapted to the flat expanses of the California landscape in new and daring ways. Armet and Davis created designs for many of the coffee shops that came to signify the California style and to inspire imitators—Norm's, Carnation, Bob's Big Boy, and Denny's (which was originally called Danny's, but changed because it was too much like another chain named Coffee Dan's). In fact, theirs was to become the most pervasive style in coffee shops and family restaurants for decades to come and would cause the diner industry to shift from the streamlined look of the 1930s to a more "contemporary" design closer to the California coffee shop of the 1950s. Yet Armet and Davis's designs were not formulaic, as were those of White Castle, McDonald's, and other fast food restaurants. The California coffee shop was quirky, sometimes bizarre, and partook of many of the favorite design elements of the 1950s—amoeba shapes, boomerangs, diamonds, stars, parabolas, and overhanging lights.

Coffee shops were sit-down restaurants, often open twenty-four hours a day, offering far more comfort than traditional diners or fast food shops. "The California coffee-shop style prevailed in part because it so effectively distinguished coffee shops from other kinds of buildings," wrote Philip Langdon, "and because it was fully the master of the roadside environment, commanding attention whether seen amid a jumble of buildings on a commercial strip or from the approach to an expressway interchange."

The most remarkable thing about Googie architecture was not so much its garish flamboyance as it was its creators' iconoclasm and naïve willingness to try anything. There were rarely any refinements to the Googie de-

DON THE ENTRANCE
BEACHCOMBER

signs because new designs were constantly being concocted to distinguish them from the last one. At its best, Googie exemplified the postwar spirit of dining out in America—casual, comfortable, witty, unpretentious, and accessible. At its worst, it blighted the landscape with awkward shapes and cheap materials. Even Eldon Davis was forced to admit that, despite his efforts to temper the look of the signage used outside the coffee shops, "mostly they were garish." But they were a whole lot of fun too. Going to such a restaurant was a kick, an escape from the humdrum into a futuristic microcosm where you could order pancakes at any hour of the day or have a hamburger cooked fresh before your eyes.

For better or worse, Googie was the most exciting new form of vernacular architecture in America, elements of which were picked up in other public buildings where attracting attention was the whole point of the exercise. Traditionally the high-end hotel and restaurant business had been extremely conservative. The architecture of the stately, formal dining rooms of the 1930s and 1940s hotels was not much different from that of hotel dining rooms in the 1890s, with a preponderance of French rococo or Italianate baroque decor. The flowered carpet, the gilded mirror, the dark mahogany bar, the crystal chandeliers, and the red brocade wallpaper—these were the marks of a "fine restaurant," and there was little deviation from that fussy, often intimidating decor until the 1950s.

It was in Miami Beach that this mold was altered—one might say, mutated—into an overblown, exaggerated style that Googie architects could easily identify with. The most salient examples of this new glitz were in the work of Morris Lapidus, author of *The Architecture of Joy* and a man for whom excess was no vice. Lapidus's Fountainebleau and Eden Roc hotels had more to do with Cecil B. DeMille than they did classical Greece, Rome, or Louis XIII—all styles he intermixed within one building, even within one room. "I designed what I did for *them*," said Lapidus in an unsettling display of popular demagoguery. "The immensity of a meaningless lobby; the overabundance of beautiful antiques; the feeling of great opulence. When they walk in they *do* feel, 'This is what we've dreamed of, this is what we saw in the movies, this is what we imagined it might be.'"

In his book *Populuxe* (1986), Thomas Hine cunningly contrasts architect Mies van der Rohe's zenlike dictum "Less is more" with Lapidus's straightforward statement, "Let's just say you like ice cream. Why have one scoop of ice cream? Have three scoops." Yet Lapidus had a condescending view of the Mi-

CALIFORNIA COFFEE SHOP architecture, like that of Ships in Los Angeles, utilized the horizontal landscape of the desert to create sprawling designs based on popular 1950s space age shapes.

ami Beach visitor. "These weren't essentially cultured people," he insisted. "Some of them may have been, but they'd forgotten their culture."

Following Lapidus's lead, Miami Beach architects built gigantic seaside resort hotels with design elements assembled to dazzle the onlooker through sheer (if often cheap) extravagance. Ignoring the indigenous Art Deco architecture that had characterized Miami Beach's boom era of the 1930s, they aimed instead for a completely new look full of curving terraces, stairways that led nowhere, pools that meandered through grottoes of poured concrete, Greek and Roman murals, and candy-striped awnings—all coexisting, however inaptly, for the delectation of visitors who could not help but be overwhelmed by it all.

The visual assault began with the size and height of the buildings, then continued through serpentine lobbies and into the restaurants and rooms themselves. The kineticism of materials and textures—bright-hued tiles, fluorescent lights, brass and copper fixtures, plaster statuary, and plastic everywhere—shimmered in the Miami Beach sunlight, and the tropical heat gave it all a steamy glamour.

GRECO-ROMAN DECOR and overly stylized service distinguished the lavish hotels of Miami Beach, where vacationers bask in the sun while being served a Caesar salad by a formally dressed waiter.

In this regard the restaurants in these hotels more than lived up to visitors' expectations. Chandeliers dwarfed those sitting below them. Pure white, unchipped Greek and Roman statuary stood gazing out over buffet tables. Gilded mirrors gave everything a dusky glimmer, and distressed finishes gave the premises a veneer of "antique class," all used as a backdrop to lavish food preparations in the "continental" style—a little French, a little Italian, some steaks and chops, and, since Miami Beach had a huge Jewish population, some Eastern European delicacies like lox, gefilte fish, and bagels.

Sunday brunch was a Lucullan feast, as much for the eye as for the palate. Chafing dishes were full of egg rolls, Swedish meatballs, Italian lasagne, and scrambled eggs and bacon. Crêpes were flamed, slabs of roast beef carved on a groaning board, desserts were mounted in tiers. For a set price everyone was invited to fill their plates to overflowing and to come back for seconds and thirds.

No matter what this steam-table, heat-lamp food tasted like—and it was often a lot better than visitors could find at their local family restaurants—it was there in profusion, and the experience of being in such a dining room with so much to choose from was the adult equivalent of a child being set loose in a candy shop.

There was no attempt at sophistication in such resort restaurants, and their appeal to a postwar generation of American travelers was as much sensory as gustatory. As a result their success was copied in the extravagant hotel dining rooms of Las Vegas, Reno, Lake Tahoe, and Atlantic City, which ultimately made the restaurants of Miami Beach look downright conservative.

The gargantuan size of these eateries was geared to the amazing postwar prosperity that allowed Americans to travel farther and more frequently than ever before. These were people who sought to indulge their fantasies about food, service, and atmosphere in ways never before open to them. The average American, who would have been intimidated at restaurants like Le Pavillon in New York, The Pump Room in Chicago, Perino's in Los Angeles, and Locke-Ober in Boston, felt coddled and welcome in dining rooms ten times more opulent than they could have imagined and offering many of the same "gourmet" food items like beef Wellington, oysters Rockefeller, and cherries Jubilee that were found on the menus of more exclusive supper clubs.

The common man had never learned nor respected moderation when it came to eating out—whether it was in the oyster cellars of the Bowery, the saloons of the Great West, or the speakeasies of Chicago. Gluttony had long been a measure of one's success in society, as Diamond Jim Brady had amply demonstrated at Delmonico's, and to gorge oneself on great quantities of food and drink proved one's mettle, stamina, and well-being.

It was no different in the 1950s, and by then more people could afford to eat out more often than ever before. And while fine food was certainly much appreciated by a small number of discriminating diners who could afford to eat at the Colony or Le Pavillon, it was atmosphere and concept that mattered to the average guy and his family looking for an exciting night out.

The real thrill of going out was in being somewhere special—not at a diner, Howard Johnson's, or Schrafft's, where you knew exactly what to expect—so that style took precedence over the food itself, and the theme restaurant, à la Trader Vic's, and the fantasy restaurant, à la the Fountaine-bleau, were in the ascendancy.

In fact, there was a great void waiting to be filled. In much the same way the railroads and steamboats determined the direction restaurants would take in the nineteenth century and the automobile had guided the forms restaurants took in the first half of the twentieth, it was the airplane (later the jet) that helped determine the future of the American restaurant in the 1950s and 1960s.

Air travel was still a novelty for most Americans in the early 1950s, but its promise—and the dream of space travel—clearly fascinated people and provided much of the style of the period. More important, air travel was becoming a common method of transport for business people, many of whom traveled to Europe, where, with a strong American dollar in their wallets, they were exposed to a much more sophisticated—if highly tradi-tional and classic—form of dining experience.

The airports themselves grew from simple Quonset hut buildings into magnificent examples of commercial architecture, with grand spaces de-signed to promote a sense of wonderment at the marvel of air travel. Simply going to an airport was an adventure for most Americans, who'd dress up for the excursion and partake of the excitement of seeing friends and associ-ates off on a trip.

It was not surprising, therefore, that one of the most important restau-rants of the modern era was installed at an expanded airport in Newark, New Jersey, in 1952. It was called the Newarker Restaurant, and it was built by a fledgling company called Riker's Restaurant Associates, headed by a coffee importer named Abraham F. Wechsler, who in 1945 had taken over a chain of thirty-five mismanaged coffee shops and turned them around to profitability. Although the company had no experience in running a full-service restaurant, Wechsler and his son-in-law, Jerome Brody, had managed a snack bar at the old Newark Airport, so they were given the contract to develop a luxury res-taurant to be installed at the new Newark Airport. Wechsler had qualms at first, having no reason to believe an airport restaurant could possibly attract enough customers interested in eating a fine meal, especially since the dining room was to be set two floors up—with no escalator. But they took the job on anyway and hired an energetic young hotelier out of Florida named Joseph H. Baum to manage the new restaurant. Baum in turn hired a classically trained chef named Albert Stockli to oversee the kitchen.

The Newarker Restaurant opened its doors in 1953, and Wechsler's fears seemed well founded: Within a year The Newarker had lost twenty-five thousand dollars. "People thought we were nuts to start a restaurant of this calibre in the swamps of Secaucus," Baum later told a reporter for *The New Yorker*, "[because] the public's image of airport restaurants was every bit as bad as its image of railroad-terminal restaurants. But Jerry Brody recognized the restaurant's values and supported it. We never cut corners. The more money we lost in those early days, the more trouble Albert Stockli and I took to make the food good and cooking outstanding." Baum also brought in the finest china and silverware, served a lobster and a half per portion (he called it the "three-clawed lobster"), and adapted the Pump Room's specialty of flaming food on skewers and in chafing dishes. Indeed, Baum would try almost anything new and different to draw the customer to the swamps of Secaucus. Within two years The Newarker was not only drawing crowds but had earned the reputation as one of the most innovative restaurants in the United States, and the company, now called Restaurant Associates—and referred to as "RA"—was ready to shake the industry right down to its tradition-bound nineteenth-century roots.

Baum was born in 1920 in Saratoga Springs, New York, where his father ran a summer hotel. After attending the Cornell School of Hotel Administration, the younger Baum joined the Navy, served on a minesweeper in World War II, went on to learn hotel accounting, and got a job as manager of New York's flamboyant Monte Carlo Hotel, which was complete with a waterfall and a clientele drawn from the theater district. Baum had a flare for the dramatic and, under the tutelage of his boss, William Zeckendorf, Jr., developed an extraordinary eye for detail and never took anything for granted—a talent he'd cultivated at a series of Shine hotels in Florida before taking over the operation of The Newarker.

Baum had long been disappointed in the restaurant business, finding it somewhat seamy, bound by outmoded traditions, and run by people with little imagination and much bad taste. "I found it dull, boring, sort of faceless in terms of trying to imitate the international classicism of the time," he told an interviewer in 1986. "What I've done along the way is to try to make the industry what I wanted it to be for me." Baum wanted to build restaurants that would be exciting for both the customer to dine in and himself to work in, restaurants full of life, energy, and passion. Thus, bolstered by the success of The Newarker, Baum assembled around him the brightest young talent he could find—Stuart Levin, George Lang, Alan Lewis, Jim Armstrong, Brian Daley, John Clancy, Tom Margittai, Paul Kovi, and others who would, together and individually, all make their own mark upon the restaurant industry in the decades to follow—and hired two of America's greatest cooking teachers, James Beard and Julia Child, as consultants on RA projects and menus. Baum was one of the first to publicize and advertise restaurants in newspapers and magazines as places of wonderment and fantasy and hired public relations man Roger Martin to get out the news.

Within the next few years, RA opened dozens of restaurants, each one uniquely conceived and constructed with a degree of sophistication, wit, and polish utterly unknown in the industry at that time. No detail was left unquestioned, from the size, shape, and function of a piece of silverware to the provenance of each individual ingredient on the plate. There might be a dozen different glasses for service of a dozen different beverages. Tables were measured and adjusted for the most comfortable height. Waiters' uniforms were designed from scratch to reflect the theme of the restaurant.

RA refined the idea of the theme restaurant but never created a formula. This was the opposite approach from the fast food concept of repeating an ef-

RESTAURANT ASSOCIATES created a series of eateries built around different themes, such as at Zum Zum in New York's Pan Am Building, where a variety of authentic German sausages was featured.

ficient formula, with minor variations, again and again, so as to become as familiar as a church steeple and as consistently welcoming. RA restaurants had the effect of titillating some and intimidating others. Every project was radically different from the next. None looked like another.

The glamour attached to RA projects also derived from the striking modernity of the public buildings in which they were set. La Fonda del Sol (a deluxe Latin-American restaurant) was built on the ground floor of the Time & Life Building on the Avenue of the Americas. Zum Zum (a fast food German eatery), the Trattoria (a snazzy Italian restaurant), and Charlie Brown's Ale & Chop House were implanted in the controversial Pan Am Building near Grand Central Terminal. And The Four Seasons and the Brasserie were integral parts of Mies van der Rohe's awesome Seagram Building on Park Avenue.

Suddenly, an industry most Americans had long regarded with skepticism and condescension had become a corporate world of high finance, artistic enterprise, and real vision. Suddenly, like Molière's bourgeois gentleman, restaurateurs discovered they were speaking prose.

By 1965 RA ran more than 130 restaurants as disparate as the Hawaiian Room at the Lexington Hotel, Tavern on the Green in Central Park, the food service facilities at the Orange Bowl in Miami, and the Festival of Gas Restaurant at the New York World's Fair of 1964, where one of the company's restaurants—Festival 64/65—was the first to showcase regional American cuisine.

One of the most extravagant of RA's concepts was the Forum of the Twelve Caesars, which was built around the acquisition of twelve portraits of Roman emperors by seventeenth-century Italian artist Camillo Procaccini. Baum and Brody decided that New York in the 1950s bore strong similarities to Imperial Rome—"a time of lusty elegance," Baum called it, "in which the good things of life are presented to the leaders of the world." And so RA set about replicating the Appian Way in the vestibule, setting a smiling Bacchus in bronze on specially designed plates (at fifty dollars a piece), and dressing the waiters in togalike outfits. Wine bottles were plunked into ice buckets shaped like Roman helmets. Baum and his associates visited Roman sites in Italy, read Suetonius and Apicius to the staff, and ran the menu by classics professor Dr. Harry Levy of Hunter College to make sure the Latin names were correctly parsed.

The menu itself was a tongue-in-cheek screed full of dishes no Caesar had ever eaten, along with a few they probably had. There was "Fiddler Crab à la Nero . . . Flaming, of course," "The Noblest Caesar [Salad] of Them All," "Chicken Varius in a Shell of Centurion Almonds," "Sirloin in Red Wine, Marrow and Onions—a Gallic recipe Julius collected while there on business," "Tart Messalina," "Nubian Chocolate Roll," and "Peaches of the Blushing Poppaea."

Fanciful menu language had long been an American restaurant gimmick, and RA's menu writers played it to the hilt, fracturing French along the

THE HEIGHT OF POSH DINING in the 1950s was Restaurant Associates' Forum of the Twelve Caesars, which featured faux-Roman dishes like "Tart Messalina" and "Fiddler Crab à la Nero" amid an atmosphere based on Imperial Roman banquets.

ONE OF THE MOST BEAUTIFULLY designed restaurants of its era, La Fonda del Sol, set at the base of the Time & Life Building, had a Latin-American theme and could seat 420 people at a time.

way, resorting to pidgin Polynesian when necessary, and punning every chance they got. A Riker's Coffee House menu listed "Sodalicious Ice Cream Sodas." The Newarker offered a "Parisian frivolity" dessert called "Tra-La-La." The Mermaid Tavern used mock colonial spelling and lettering to describe "Tater Sallett" and "Stake." And the Hawaiian Room's "pu-puu" were described as "Veree Plenty—Veree Pupulee."

At the same time, RA took its food very seriously, and tried to serve dishes that would both entice and educate the public in the varieties of the world's cuisines. Thus, the lasagne and freshly made ice cream at the Trattoria was closer to what one might find in Rome than in most Italian-American restaurants in New York, and the homemade sausages at Zum Zum were far more savory than the heavy-handed food served at German restaurants in Yorkville. And the menu at La Fonda del Sol listed innovative dishes like shrimp with coriander and bacon on a skewer and corn-crusted scallop, shrimp, and crab casserole.

La Fonda del Sol was RA's most ambitious attempt—at the incredible cost of three million dollars—to court the sophisticated diner in New York. Here the theme was elegant Latin American, as interpreted by designer Philip Girard. The room was decked out with hundreds of Latin-American folk dolls and human figures made from bread. A magnificent open oven dominated the dining room, which could seat 420 people.

Yet of all the restaurants RA built in the 1950s, none was more impressive than The Four Seasons, opened in the Seagram Building on July 20,

1959. Here Baum and his associates poured everything they had learned thus far—and much they could only envision—into one of the most extraordinary restaurants ever built. The cost was $4.5 million, financed by the Seagram wine and spirits company that gave the building its name. The space for the restaurant, originally intended as a Cadillac showroom, challenged every rule of traditional restaurant planning. For one thing it was set on three levels, and the ceilings on the second floor soared to twenty feet.

The project was given to Ludwig Mies van der Rohe, who turned it over to his associate Philip Johnson. Baum wanted the restaurant to have an elegant serenity of a kind he found when reading Japanese haiku poetry, and Johnson gave it to him. The first floor was used merely as a lobby, with coatroom and rest rooms. From there a broad stairway led to the Bar Room (later called the Grill Room) that was unlike any watering hole ever seen. The majesty of the high ceilings combined with curtains of shimmering metal beads that rippled with the slightest movement of air. A sculpture of gleaming metal rods by Robert Lippold hung over the bar. The lighting was subdued and seductive. And, echoing the theme of the four seasons, potted trees were changed each summer, fall, winter, and spring, as were the colors of the waitstaff's jackets. There was a richness in every texture of the wooden walls, the plaid carpet, and the use of metal throughout.

Coming up the stairs of The Four Seasons, the guest feels as if he were entering the throne room of Oz, yet there was no extravagance in the Grill Room's decor, its quiet broken only by the drinkers at the bar. The room was built to attract a serious expense account crowd who would adopt The Four Seasons as a kind of corporate lunch room, which is exactly what it eventually became.

The entrance to the main dining room was through a passageway hung with a Picasso stage curtain (two Mirós hung in the lobby); this opened to what was called the Pool Room, because a gurgling, lighted pool dominated the floor space (where any more sensible restaurateur might have placed six more tables). Tableware, glassware, and silver were designed by the team of Garth and Ada Louise Huxtable, and the chairs (some costing nearly $500 each) were designed by Eero Saarinen, Charles Eames, Ludwig Mies van der Rohe, and Philip Johnson.

The Pool Room was lighter at day and more seductive at night, but the key to everything at The Four Seasons was the studied but palpable calm that prevailed, both in the service and in the way the clientele conducted themselves, with worldliness and reserve.

Food might well have been beside the point at The Four Seasons, and Baum himself once remarked, "People don't go to restaurants like the Forum and The Four Seasons . . . primarily to eat—they go for the excitement and entertainment." Yet every effort was made to produce food prepared from the finest ingredients available and with consummate skill on the part of the kitchen staff.

Baum saw his role as twofold—to be an entertainer and to be an educator. A stern taskmaster with a volatile temper, he insisted on getting exactly what he wanted, even if he wasn't sure what it was until he tasted it. He

DESIGNED BY PHILIP JOHNSON and set in Mies van der Rohe's magnificent Seagram Building, The Four Seasons served *haute* American *cuisine* amid a splendor of art by Picasso and Miró, chairs designed by Eero Saarinen and Charles Eames, and silverware by Garth and Ada Louise Huxtable. Its Grill Room (*right*) was set for "negative reservations," that is, tables were available only when regulars said they were not coming that day.

believed wine was the natural complement to good food and so he stocked the best wines in the world, including those from then-unknown California vineyards. He set up lines of distribution to purveyors, and demanded they send RA only the best. And he insisted that menus evolve and change with the seasons, as well as with a public taste he was trying hard to sway as much from steak and baked potatoes as from contrived, tiresome clichés of French-American restaurants of the day.

Menus were changed dozens of times until they came up to RA's ideal—ideals that were constantly being invented and revised as they learned more about what customers would and would not eat. At a time when most deluxe restaurants in New York were serving Le Pavillon-inspired *haute cuisine,* The Four Seasons pioneered what eventually came to be called the "New American Cuisine," with dishes like smoked salmon soufflé with onion sauce, minted lobster parfait, and a signature dessert known as chocolate velvet cake.

RA's contributions to the American dining scene were obvious to anyone who entered one of its restaurants in the 1950s and 1960s. They were theatrical, unique, entertaining, even intimidating. There was never anything cheap about them, whether it was a fast food operation like Zum Zum or a deluxe dining room like The Four Seasons. RA gave the restaurant business in America a new image and corporate clout that helped attract the kind of bright, young college-educated entrepreneurs who might once have gone into publishing, marketing, advertising, and design. RA opened the doors for architects, graphic artists, interior designers, fashion designers, acoustical experts, and efficiency experts to enter a glamorous business that was both fun to work in and receptive to innovation and creativity.

Yet most of RA's finest restaurants were not commercial successes. The eclectic menus and high prices were tough to swallow at a time when most Americans were not used to dining on such a scale. Such restaurants as The Four Seasons, La Fonda, and Forum were a bit ahead of their time, and the public could not be coaxed to spend quite so much money for something with which they didn't truly feel comfortable.

Thus, despite the fact that Restaurant Associates became one of the most famous and important corporations of its era, despite the fact that several of RA's outlets were grossing millions each year, and despite the rise of their stocks to forty-eight dollars a share in the mid-1960s, the company, of which Baum assumed the presidency in 1963, was making little in the way of profits and paid next to nothing in dividends.

Expansion had been too fast (in 1968 alone, RA bought the Barricini Candy Company's 131 shops, took over the operation of the Treadway Inns chain, and got into airline food service); European operations had fared poorly; money had been spent too lavishly; and many of RA's brightest personnel had left, including Baum, who resigned in 1967.

In 1969 RA grossed $110 million, but lost $720,560, then $1.3 million in the first quarter of 1970. Eventually its stock slipped to four dollars a share. After massive retrenchment, closings of units, and divestitures (The Four Seasons was sold to Tom Margittai and Paul Kovi in 1973), RA emerged in the 1970s leaner but on more solid financial footing, retaining such money-making properties as Mamma Leone's, Brasserie, and Charlie Brown's pubs.

In addition to building great restaurants, RA also created the profession of the restaurant consultant, and many of RA's alumni went on to become master restaurateurs on their own. One of the most brilliant was George Lang, who in his native Hungary was headed for a career as a violinist (during the war he once played for eight hours straight at gunpoint for a group of Russian soldiers). He escaped Communist Hungary in 1946, and came to America, where, like de Kooning at the lunch counter, Lang found the workings of the Horn & Hardart Automat a perfect expression of American verve and spirit. After a brief stint as a violinist in the Dallas Symphony Orchestra, he decided instead on a career in food service, working every position in the industry from busboy to waiter to cook to catering manager, eventually taking a job at the Waldorf-Astoria, where, under chef Charles Philippe, he learned the disciplines of working in a high-volume kitchen and got a taste for the kind of theatrics that made dining out more than just eating out. Lang was later hired by Restaurant Associates, first to head up their Tower Suite restaurant, next to manage all the RA restaurants at the New York World's Fair of 1964, then to direct The Four Seasons. In 1970 he left the company to start his own consulting firm, the George Lang Corporation, which was the first of its kind to offer restaurateurs guidance of every conceivable kind—from financial planning to interior design to menu conceptualization.

Lang brought to restaurants a degree of European polish and sophistication few in his industry possessed. He authored several authoritative books on gastronomy, including the classic *Cuisine of Hungary* (1971), wrote travel columns that taught generations of Americans how and where to eat abroad, and bought and refurbished New York's historic Café des Artistes. He counted among his friends as many musicians and artists as he did restaurateurs, collected art and rare books, and brought a witty, philosophical mind to the pleasures, vices, and virtues of restaurants in modern society, speaking to his colleagues and clients as a gastronomic guru given to one-liners and platitudes in the same breath. In his "Sure-Fire Recipe for an American Bistro," Lang included the following ingredients for success in the restaurant business:

- Several sackfuls of money, preferably not yours and without strings attached.
- 1 well-seasoned chef . . . preferably one whose ego has to be fed only once a day.
- 1 fully ripened interior designer (do not remove backbone).
- The combined leadership qualities of de Gaulle and Genghis Khan.
- The optimism of a person who is getting married for the seventh time.
- 1 public relations person, whipped until a froth has formed.

"I represent the small fraternity that believes in considering the total picture before deciding on the goal and the road toward this goal," said Lang. "Perhaps our professional bible should say: 'In the beginning was the feasibility study.'"

Lang exported his American business acumen and enthusiasm to the world, developing restaurants in Montreal, Budapest, Hamburg, Manila, Thessalonika, and Monte Carlo, where he went deliberately against the French grain by featuring hamburgers, barbecue, and chili in the dining room. Lang set up innovative dining facilities in department stores, boutiques, shopping centers, corporate headquarters, and aboard the *Queen Elizabeth 2*. He pioneered the pasta bar for a chain restaurant called Jennie's Cookery in Mission Viejo, California, refined a concept for storing food in a flexible pouch for up to a year without refrigeration, and insisted on incorporating a region's culture into any ethnic restaurants he helped design.

The creation of novel restaurant concepts was, by the mid-sixties, a booming business in the United States. Americans had always loved theme restaurants whether it was a hamburger stand in the shape of a dragon, a Hollywood nightclub done up with waterfalls and tropical rain forest, or a deluxe Manhattan dining room set with Roman antiquities. Now the designs and concepts became more sophisticated and far more costly, though often the themes were strained and mawkish. "Old English pubs" proliferated in places with names like Ye Olde Bull & Bush in Atlanta, The Golden Bee in Denver, and His Lordship's in St. Louis. At Atlanta's Abbey restaurant, waiters came to the table dressed as monks (a sartorial gimmick also featured at New York's Monk's Inn). In Pinnacle Peak, Arizona, a casual, yippee-i-oh Western theme was carried through to the point of having waiters cut the necktie off any man fool enough to wear one. A dentist named Joe Santo opened a Moorish restaurant in New York in 1964 called the Salum Sanctorum, where the menus looked like illuminated medieval manuscripts, smoking and hard liquor was forbidden in the main dining room, and sacramental candles burned in the stuccoed dining room. In Los Angeles at the Magic Castle Dinner Club, which counted Cary Grant, Paul Newman, and Arthur Godfrey as members, bookcases were creaking doorways, stools mysteriously revolved with the customer atop them, and food was served in bubbling cauldrons or magicians' top hats. In Boston Anthony Athanas built a gigantic seafood restaurant on a decrepid pier in 1963, and had a lobster fisherman regularly tromp through the dining room with his catch to the delight of the customers. He even hired a one-legged doorman whom he had fitted with a wooden pegleg.

NO THEME SEEMED TOO OUTLAND-ISH for restaurateurs to copy, as long as it was done for fun and profit, as in Chicago's Ivanhoe Restaurant.

ONE OF THE STRANGEST restaurant concepts of the 1960s was the Autopub in New York (situated in the General Motors Building, of course), where customers had food served to them in cars.

One of the most outrageous was New York's Autopub, located, appropriately enough, in the General Motors Building on Fifth Avenue. Here customers sat in bucket seats and were served by beautiful waitresses in racing uniforms. Lighting came from racing helmet lamps, an entire wall was done in chrome, and there was even a drive-in movie. You might choose a table in the Classic Car Lounge or sit in the Grandstand, and for romantics there was Lovers Lane, where you'd snuggle in cars made to look like those at a tunnel-of-love attraction.

Then there was a whole genre of restaurants set atop a tall building or other structure, like Seattle's Top of the Needle, which was opened May 22, 1961, at Seattle's Century 21 Exposition. Set at the 500-foot level of a 600-foot totem called the Space Needle, the restaurant, designed by John Graham & Co., sat 260 people and revolved once an hour.

What any of this had to do with good food was not of much concern to the average customer. "Look, we are a very rich country," Donald Greenaway of the National Restaurant Association told *Newsweek* magazine in 1966. "And not everybody is interested in theater, opera or concerts." Restaurants had become pure entertainment and big business, which several industry magazines like *Restaurants & Institutions, Restaurant Business, Restaurant Hospitality, Nations Restaurant News,* and others charted each month, as restaurant chains emerged solidly among the Fortune 500.

This new freedom to create new forms in ever more sophisticated ways was not lost on those whose livelihood had long been built on fantasy and futuristic vision. Nowhere was this more evident than in the food service operations of the Walt Disney organization, which had made its reputation as the world's foremost "Dream Factory" with its animated cartoons and movies. Perhaps the most remarkable thing about Disney was his own child like view of the world, a view that never allowed for skepticism or negativism when in the pursuit of something that had never been done before. Whether it was the perfecting of an animation process or the building of a "family" atmosphere in his organization, Disney never asked why a thing could not be done, but only how in fact it could be accomplished—an attitude that gave birth to the most wondrous playground any child could possibly have imagined.

This was Disneyland, opened in Anaheim, California, in 1955. The idea had been on Disney's mind for almost twenty years and grew out of his disenchantment with the kind of unstructured, tawdry amusement parks then prevalent in the United States. In 1952 he set up an arm of his company called WED (his initials) to conceptualize and build a clean, modern, efficiently run amusement park that would appeal to both young and old. The result was an amalgam of theme parks within a central location—Main Street patterned after the kind of Midwestern towns he had grown up in (Disney was born in Chicago, and lived in Marceline and Kansas City, Missouri), Adventureland, Frontierland, Fantasyland, and Tomorrowland—all cunningly associated in one way or another with Disney movies and TV shows.

Disneyland opened on July 17, 1955. By the end of the fiscal year four million visitors had made the trek out to Anaheim, where they were amazed at the size, the scope, and the wholesomeness of a park built to resemble a movie lot. There were rides through African jungle rivers, rocket ships to the moon, a submarine journey (which coincided with Disney's 1954 movie based on Jules Verne's *Twenty Thousand Leagues Under the Sea*), Sleeping Beauty's castle (a *Sleeping Beauty* animated feature was due in 1959), a pirate ship flight to Peter Pan's Never-Never Land (Disney's *Peter Pan* was released in 1953), and trolley cars on Main Street. And in every corner of the park were food facilities perfectly suited to the contrived themes, with waiters dressed in period costumes, wastepaper baskets painted to look like part of the landscape, and menu language adapted to the particular fantasy being spun, even though the food was not much above a fast food level in those early years.

To sit and eat hamburgers on a porch on a idealized Tom Sawyer's Island as a Mississippi riverboat plied its way through impeccably muddied waters was a reverie any American family would cherish. Americans brought up on Western movies could dine in a Wild West saloon, complete with chorus girls and cowboys shooting up the bar. On Main Street you could eat fried chicken and biscuits on a Victorian veranda or get a vanilla cone at what looked like the model for the perfect corner ice cream parlor. And in Tomorrowland Googie architecture was adapted smoothly and rationally into the futuristic Spaceport setting.

The theme park was an ideal place to develop novel ideas in food service, and Disney made sure that everything was prepared and served with the highest regard for cleanliness, wholesomeness, and entertainment value. Disney read well the appetite of Americans for sentimentality cloaked in the element of surprise. As the man who created Mickey Mouse was fond of saying as Disneyland was being conceived, "You've got to have a wienie at the end of every street."

A swinging singles' bar of the 1970s—the Brown Derby, Columbus, Ohio

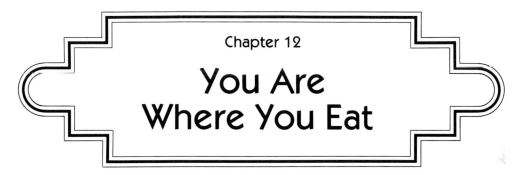

Chapter 12

You Are
Where You Eat

Where Everyone—But Not Anyone—Was Welcome

"CIVILIZATION HAS TAUGHT US to eat with a fork," Will Rogers once observed, "but even now if nobody is around we use our fingers." Such a statement may well be true of most people in the world, but it has a particular relevance to the way Americans dined out in the 1950s and 1960s. The success of fast food would seem to prove the point. But even at the refined level of white tablecloth restaurants like Le Pavillon and The Four Seasons in New York, Scandia and Perino's in Los Angeles, The Pump Room and the Cape Cod Room in Chicago, the London Chop House in Detroit, Brennan's and Antoine's in New Orleans, Ernie's and the Blue Fox in San Francisco, The Chesapeake in Baltimore, The Zodiac Room and Arthur's in Dallas, Maisonette and Pigall's in Cincinnati, and others around the United States, it was a slow process of education to turn even well-traveled Americans away from the conservative menus of the past.

"People don't give a rap what they eat," remarked the long-time chef at the Waldorf, René Black. "They just know filet of sole, sirloin steak, broiled lobster, and don't forget the hot biscuits." In fact, after the war, the Waldorf kitchens got nine orders of steak for one order of anything else.

Restaurants from the beginning had, of course, functioned as much more than feed houses, however fine the feed, and Americans had always regarded certain restaurants like Delmonico's, Louis Sherry's, and Peacock Alley at the Waldorf-Astoria as the exclusive reserves of the rich and powerful. Workingmen had their own favorite restaurants where they could

197

THE "POWER LUNCH," enjoyed by male executives over martinis, steaks, and lobsters, was an everyday event at New York's Palm steakhouse, which now has several branches around the United States, attempting to imitate the no-frills atmosphere of the original.

carouse with their families and friends, writers and artists had their bars, and various segments of American society claimed certain restaurants for their own. But the speakeasies of Prohibition and the populism that followed World War II broke down many of the artificial barriers—or velvet ropes—and made it easier for a much wider swathe of America's middle class to get into the better restaurants. Also, there was more money to be spent in and earned by restaurants.

More people could afford to eat and drink out on a frequent basis, and the restaurant-going experience itself had in the big cities become an evening's entertainment. Fine food was rarely a strong enough magnet to draw crowds, and theme restaurants tended to flare brightly, then fade as soon as the novelty wore off on the public.

The restaurants that hung on, prospered, and became objects of intense scrutiny by the media and the public were those that catered to specific segments of society and to specific industries like show business, publishing, advertising, sports, and fashion. A society ball at a city's ritziest hotel no longer elicited the kind of public excitement that now erupted over the spotting of a prizefighter like Rocky Marciano or a TV celebrity like Jack Paar at a restaurant, and drinking often took precedence over dining in many of the most famous restaurants of the era.

One of New York's most popular restaurants after the war was Toots Shor's, run by a tough, wisecracking graduate of the speakeasies who prided himself on being able to drink any of his customers under the table. During one week's time Shor put his reputation on the line three times, challenged in turn by an actor, a publicity man, and a radio comedian to see who could consume the most liquor without losing consciousness. The last bout began at two in the afternoon and lasted till four; when the challenger collapsed trying to make his way to the men's room, Shor stopped his staff from re-

THE SINGLES' BAR CAUGHT ON quickly in the 1960s, owing to an influx of young, sexually liberated baby boomers who found places like San Francisco's Henry Africa's (*left*) and New York's T.G.I. Friday's (*below*) affable meeting places for their ilk.

moving the man from the doorway. "Leave the bum there," roared Toots. "I want everybody to see him, so it'll be a lesson to any other creep who gets ideas about messin' with the champ." And for twenty minutes customers had to step over the snoring body.

Newspaper columnists wrote more about "watering holes" (the "21" Club was still one of the most renowned in the 1950s) than they did fine restaurants, whereas in Hollywood a celebrity hangout like The Brown Derby or Chasen's would be flippantly dubbed a "beanery" rather than be dignified with the word *restaurant.* In Washington, D.C., which had never developed much of a fine restaurant scene, watering holes like Duke Zeibert's catered to politicos, lawyers, and lobbyists. The Monocle, opened by Connie Valanos up on Capitol Hill in 1960, attracted the young entourage and cabinet members of President John F. Kennedy, and Valanos learned to keep food warm when legislators were called away from lunch for a vote on an impending bill. The only President who did not eat at least once at The Monocle was Lyndon Baines Johnson, who, after having once been turned away for lack of a table when he was Vice President, refused ever to enter the restaurant again.

A restaurant that drew a President to its dining room would achieve immediate and enduring celebrity, so when President John F. Kennedy favored the Jockey Club with his presence in the 1960s, it became, overnight, the most fashionable spot in town, buoyed further in the 1980s when Ronald and Nancy Reagan chose to dine there on special occasions. The Washington press corps hung out at the Old Ebbitt Grill or, when interviewing a particularly high muckamuck, at deluxe French restaurants like Maison Blanche (French for the White House) or Le Lion d'Or. Whenever First Lady Nancy Reagan gave an interview to *Time* magazine, it was always at Table 25 at the elegant Le Pavillon. Presidents Lyndon Johnson, Richard

Nixon, Gerald Ford, and Jimmy Carter showed little interest in dining out and therefore lent no luster to any new restaurants during their regimes. Indeed, President Carter sent a shock wave through the American business community when he attempted—unsuccessfully—to take away tax deductions on business meals he called "three Martini lunches." But when George Bush showed to eat up at an Italian restaurant named i Ricchi soon after his inauguration in 1988, the restaurant's fame was made overnight, and Bush, very much the Sinophile, made the fortunes of a restaurant called Peking Gourmet Inn in Falls Church, Virginia, where he goes seemingly at the drop of a hat, whenever he and his wife feel like "going for Chinese."

In Los Angeles the old warhorse restaurants like Perino's, Chasen's, and The Brown Derby endured through the 1950s and 1960s, and the Polo Lounge at the Beverly Hills Hotel has long been the most important breakfast nook in the city because it draws Hollywood executives and movie stars there for morning business meetings.

The more exclusive the restaurant's policy toward customers, the more regulars love it. Thus, Detroit's London Chop House continued to attract the most important men of the automobile industry, the Brahmins of Boston took their meals at the downstairs Men's Grill (which banned women until 1970) at Locke-Ober Café, and the society crowd of San Francisco congregated nightly in Trader Vic's Captain's Cabin room.

In New York, various industries adopted certain restaurants as their special enclaves. La Grenouille, La Côte Basque, and Orsini's drew the most fashionable of the Seventh Avenue designers and retailers in the 1950s, 1960s, and 1970s. The actors, agents, and producers of Broadway shows frequented places like Patsy's, Barbetta, Joe Allen, the Stage Deli, and the Russian Tea Room, while the advertising community on Madison Avenue lunched at Giambelli. One Chinese restaurant, Pearl's, was actually bankrolled by a number of executives and editors from Time-Life, Inc., who wanted a good place to go near their new offices on Avenue of the Americas. And it became something of a ritual for a young business executive to be taken to one of the old New York steakhouses like The Palm or Christ Cella. New York society made it a tradition to dine on Sunday nights at The Coach House or Trader Vic's in the Plaza Hotel, which also housed the exclusive Oak Bar, where women would be not seated after 3:00 P.M. until well into the 1970s.

The "21" Club continued to draw a wide range of affluent, older clients, but The Four Seasons, under new owners Margittai and Kovi, was giving "21" strong competition for the younger glamour industry executives from publishing, advertising, and retailing. Margittai and Kovi honed in on precisely that crowd. They lightened the menu, simplified service (no more tableside flaming), and patterned the Grill Room after the great European models like London's Savoy and Paris's Ritz. By the end of the decade The Four Seasons Grill was christened the home of the "power lunch," after an article by Lee Eisenberg in the October 1979 issue of *Esquire* entitled "America's Most Powerful Lunch" published a diagram of the room indicating where New York's most powerful executives sat—Lois Wyse of Wyse Advertising was at Table 35, TV producer Mark Goodson took Table 17,

editor Michael Korda of Simon and Schuster dined at Table 33, real estate developer Lew Rudin would be at Table 11, fashion designer Calvin Klein lunched at Table 41, and, most days of the week, the restaurant's designer, Philip Johnson, could be seen at Table 22. The frequency of this clinetele's appearances and their claim to specific tables eventually led to what was called the "negative reservation," which meant a regular would call to say he or she was *not* coming to dine that day and would therefore free up the table for someone else.

The power lunch had an early-morning corollary in the "power breakfast," begun in 1976 by Preston Robert Tisch, president of the Loew's Corporation that owns New York's Regency Hotel, which afforded business people the opportunity to wedge an extra meeting into the workday at breakfast in its 540 Park Avenue dining room.

One of the most celebrated cult restaurants in New York was Elaine's, a dingy-looking Italian-style restaurant reclaimed from what had been an Austro-Hungarian bar. Owner Elaine Kaufman managed a Greenwich Village restaurant called Portofino, where she'd made friends with several writers and artists who came calling when she opened a place under her own name at Eighty-eighth Street and Second Avenue in April 1963. Before long Elaine's had a reputation as a writers' hangout, where Kaufman would save tables for regulars, offer liberal credit to those between books or writing assignments, and serve as surrogate Jewish mother to the literary egos that

THE EXTRAVAGANT AND ECCENTRIC decor—full of Tiffany glass, hanging ferns, a brass railing—of New York's Maxwell's Plum had an enormous influence on restaurant design throughout the 1960s and 1970s.

dropped in night after night. On any given evening one might run into Norman Mailer, Woody Allen, William Styron, David Halberstam, Gay Talese, and George Plimpton—few of whom ever had anything good to say about the run-of-the-mill Italian-American food. If you were not of that ilk, you were made to feel like an outsider by her and by her staff. "I don't like people who just pass through and eat a meal and take a look," Kaufman once said. "I save my tables for my family, the ones I know and care about. I don't have any family of my own—who needs all those problems? I prefer my restaurant because no matter if I have a rotten day, I know that come night I'll be in my place and it'll revive me and I'll have a good time."

Elaine's functioned as a home away from home for writers, an oasis not of serenity but of security, and a place where like-minded people expected not good food but camaraderie. In a lengthy homage to Elaine's in *New York* magazine, celebrated authors tried to describe the essence of what made the place so special. Roy Blount, Jr., poeticized about its special character: "Where else but Elaine's do they welcome/Writers, again and again?/Remember the night that Malcolm/X and Solzhenitsyn came in?" Wrote Irwin Shaw, "At the busiest hour there is always one more chair ready for the poor devil who has just finished the first act of his play or been locked out of his apartment by his wife."

Unlike the self-conscious literary cafés of Europe like Paris's La Coupole, debate and philosophizing were not key to Elaine's success. For more than anything else, it was a place to relax and gossip. "No one talked much about the books themselves, nor, even though those years were politically charged, about politics," David Halberstam explained. "If there was a hot subject in the late sixties, it was not Vietnam; it was the [New York] Knicks."

The exclusivity of such restaurants may not seem much in the great traditions of democracy, but in fact anyone could make a reservation, order a meal, and ogle those whose presence gave the place a special aura. Were you to be accepted in such a circle, you would become part of the aura itself, and you were thereupon regarded by outsiders with a certain awe the restaurant had conferred upon you.

A far less exclusive, but quite ritualized form of restaurant exploded onto the urban scene in the 1960s. Between 1940 and 1970 more than twenty-eight million people moved from the countryside to the cities, so that by 1970 the rural population had dropped from 40 percent of the national population in 1940 to only 26.5 percent. Add to this a postwar baby boom of young people moving into the job market and a liberalization of social dating mores, and it is easy to see why bars and restaurants would thrive in the large urban centers.

On Manhattan's Upper East Side there had been an influx of young people with good jobs and plenty of spending money moving into high-rise apartment complexes, which drew a large number of attractive young models and airline stewardesses (there was one apartment building called the "Stew Zoo") who were well traveled and sexually active. Alan Stillman, a flavors industry salesman, noted that these people had few nice places to meet and eat, so he decided to augment his income by opening an informal bar-restaurant on Manhattan's Upper East Side, which he called by the initials T.G.I. Friday's, short for "Thank God It's Friday." There were, of course, plenty of bars in New York and other cities where young people got together to meet and eat, but Stillman decided to upgrade the quality of the standard American bar menu of burgers, spareribs, salads, and sandwiches so as to attract a crowd who would come, drink, meet, and sit down to a decent meal, and fill the place Monday through Sunday.

AN EFFUSIVE ROMANTICISM was the theme of New York's Sign of the Dove—known as one of the "big splurge" restaurants of the 1970s.

T.G.I. Friday's opened on March 15, 1965, and was an immediate success. Within months it was featured in *Life* magazine as an example of how social patterns were changing in America. The "singles' bar" was born.

When asked to explain the phenomenal success of T.G.I. Friday's, Stillman said, "I can tell it to you in one word: the Pill. The opening of T.G.I. Friday's coincided precisely with the introduction to American singles of the birth control pill."

Suddenly the strictures that had always given bars their "den-of-iniquity" image loosened. "Nice girls" were now free to go to a bar like T.G.I. Friday's, meet young men, and, if they so chose, strike up a relationship on the spot.

T.G.I. Friday's functioned as a less frantic, more acceptable alternative to the traditional bar scene, and fully 50 percent of the restaurant's profits came from food service rather than from liquor sales. Within months singles' bars (sometimes called "fern bars" because of the ubiquitous hanging ferns used as decorative devices in such establishments) dotted the Upper East Side, and the "swinging singles' scene" spread like wildfire to other cities. Stillman himself opened branches of T.G.I. Friday's around Manhattan called Tuesday's, Wednesday's (which was also a discotheque for a thousand people), and Thursday's, and then built thirteen T.G.I. Friday's in various cities, before selling off the chain in 1975.

The singles' bar phenomenon not only manifested a new style of restaurant but also drew into the business people who, like Stillman, had never thought of opening a restaurant. This brought to the industry fresh blood and new ideas.

One of the most flamboyant of these new restaurateurs was Warner LeRoy, son of film director-producer Mervyn LeRoy. The younger LeRoy spent much of his youth surrounded by Hollywood fantasy and grew up to produce his own shows on Broadway, ventures that added measurably to his already considerable wealth. Well-traveled and familiar with the great restaurants and grand cafés of Europe, LeRoy thought it would be fun to open his own café, where he might even exhibit some of his own artwork. He took over a small luncheonette (located next to a movie theater he already owned), redecorated the place in a quirky, idiosyncratic style with etched mirrors, Tiffany glass, and stuffed animals hanging from the ceiling, added a sidewalk café, and came up with a meaningless name that somehow evoked the jaunty style of the mid-sixties—Maxwell's Plum.

Maxwell's opened in April 1966 and was overwhelmed with young people from the neighborhood on its first night. Like T.G.I. Friday's, Maxwell's became an "in" spot seemingly known to every out-of-town vistor within months. "LeRoy had positioned Maxwell's perfectly," wrote Charles Bernstein in his book *Great Restaurant Innovators*. "Airline stewardesses, secretaries, and nurses flocked to the place, and it became a highly respected singles spot. It arrived just as the women's liberation movement and casual lifestyles were finding their niches. The openness, casualness, and uniqueness of this sidewalk café combined for maximum customer appeal."

LeRoy played it all to the hilt. With his showman's eye for the theatrical, he would dress in outrageous outfits that might include a tuxedo jacket that seemed cut from drapery fabric or a Moroccan costume done up with flashlights and silver bells. Within three years he'd expanded Maxwell's from 80 to 240 seats, installing a lighted ceiling composed of ten thousand sheets of stained Tiffany glass (which created an industry look for singles-style restaurants that continues to this day), a magnificent, horseshoe-shaped oak bar, and an amalgam of antiques and just plain kitsch that passed for real glamour with most of his customers and made everybody else just feel good being in such a lavish, overly decorated space.

LeRoy also put a great deal of thought into his menu, which ran the gamut from hamburgers to classic French cuisine, all prepared from top-quality ingredients, and he paid his French chef nearly $100,000 a year.

The singles' scene rolled across the country and combined with the discotheque craze that hit first in the mid-1960s, then again in the 1970s. The manufacturer of the popular French men's cologne (Canoe) even published a "where-the-action-is guidebook" entitled *How to Make It from Coast to Coast*. Writer John Foreman explained in his introduction, "There's a new type of bar springing up in the land, known loosely as the 'singles' bar—a term that seems to invite a put-down in some quarters. But tonight, no matter who says what, fine-looking women will be sitting on barstools all across the country. Barstools in places of every possible description, from engineer-boot-hip to 1930s-revival-surly-chic. They're out there a million strong with and for every taste conceivable." And most of them had provocative names like Lucifer (Boston), She-Nannigan's (Chicago), The Final Approach (Cleveland), Whiskey à Go Go (Los Angeles), The Climax (Miami), Adam's Apple (New York), and Your Mustache (Detroit).

Many of the tenets of the sexual revolution of the early 1960s were promulgated by what was the most popular men's magazine in American history—*Playboy*—which promoted a philosophy of hedonism that made drinking and dining out very much part of the seduction process. The singles' bars, therefore, fit perfectly into this new alluring lifestyle, and *Playboy* magazine's founder, Hugh Hefner (who himself never drank anything stronger than Pepsi-Cola and rarely went out to a restaurant), expanded his empire into private Playboy Clubs, where members were served by young women dressed up in abbreviated "bunny" costumes. These clubs were masterminded by Arnie Morton, a Chicago restaurateur who joined Playboy in 1959 and took the club concept around the world to Europe and Asia, where it was enormously successful for more than a decade. While it cannot be said that good food ever stole the limelight from the sexual titillation of the Playboy Clubs, for many young men of the sixties and seventies, the clubs represented their first experience of just how glamourous dining out could be. And the idea of belonging to a restricted club (even though anybody could join for a membership fee) gave even more cachet to the experience.

Truly exclusionary clubs, where members had to be invited to join and strict requirements based on wealth, position, social background, heredity, school, or industry flourished in the 1950s and 1960s. After the war there were far more people with sufficient money to set up their own preserves, be they urban gentlemen's clubs, sports' clubs, university clubs, or family country clubs. The management of these clubs realized that one of the ways to bring in capital was to charge annual "dining fees," which meant that members had either to eat at the club's restaurant or pay the fee anyway. Since money spent on drinks at the bar was rarely allowed as part of satisfying the enforced dining fee, club dining rooms had captive audiences and the food was, in general, much inferior to that found in an outside white tablecloth restaurant.

Club menus were a mix of standard American fare like roast beef, green peas, and baked potatoes with a few continental clichés thrown in, like sole amandine and chicken curry. Most of it was overcooked, spooned out of chafing dishes (or carved under a heatlamp), and served in frozen pastry shells in surroundings that resembled a prep school dining hall.

More than anything else in the postwar period, the country club restaurant prevented serious restaurants from developing in many parts of the United States, because the people who could best afford to eat out at a good restaurant preferred to dine with their ilk (and pay off their dining fees) at their clubs. Add to this a number of states and counties—especially in the South and Midwest—that continued, long after the repeal of the Eighteenth Amendment, to prohibit the sale of liquor by the glass at restaurants, and clubs became even more attractive. Many restaurants got around these atavistic "blue laws" by selling temporary "memberships" to on-premises "clubs" for a fee of a few dollars. A customer would merely purchase a membership for the night and drink to his heart's content—although in some states like Mormon-controlled Utah, customers still had to mix their own drinks after making separate purchases of liquor and mixers.

On the other end of the social ladder were restaurants whose customers were from narrow ethnic groups who discouraged "outsiders" from eating at their favorite places. Sometimes these were private "social" or "sporting" clubs in Little Italy or perhaps a second-floor Chinese restaurant with no sign to indicate its existence. *New York* magazine food writer Gael Greene once even wrote an article entitled, "The Mafia Guide to Dining Out," noting that "Little Augie Pisabo was shot to death with Gian Marino's recipe for clam sauce in his pocket." Jewish restaurateurs who kept strict glatt kosher rules could be purposely hostile to any Gentile who would ask for an item to be prepared differently.

But the most exclusive restaurants of all were those that, with legal sanction, kept out large segments of the American population solely on the basis of their race or sex. Although most prevalent in the South, restaurants in every region of the United States excluded whomever they wanted on the supposition that a public restaurant was also a privately owned business. Thus, it was a rare thing to find blacks, Mexicans, or Orientals dining in most upscale restaurants until well into the 1950s. Even in cafés, cafeterias, and lunchrooms blacks and other people "of color" would be served only in separate sections of the establishment. This form of segregation held particular irony in the South, where most of the food preparation in the kitchen was being done by blacks.

Even in those regions where local laws did not specifically encourage or allow such segregation, many restaurants made it clear that blacks and other minorities were not welcome. In a 1955 study entitled *The Tables Are Turning,* the Committee on Civil Rights in East Manhattan, Inc., explained how it sent black couples into restaurants serving meals at four dollars or

less and found that 42 percent were treated rudely, had to wait for a table out of turn, were seated in an obscure room, given either slow service, or rushed out as soon as possible—all practices that defied the New York Civil Rights Law of 1938. After the Committee sent members back to those same restaurants to interview the owners, complain to them of their policies, and threaten legal action, the percentage of restaurants acting so disagreeably dropped to 16 percent.

The same kind of moral suasion had little effect on restaurant owners in the South, where local law helped enforce segregation. And so in the early 1960s restaurants came to be among the most important battlegrounds in the Civil Rights Movement in America, when blacks began "sit-ins" at lunch counters that refused them service or attempted to segregate them in any way. While there had been similar actions earlier in Washington, Oklahoma City, and Louisville, a sit-in on February 1, 1960, at a Woolworth

MORE FANTASY THAN FINE FOOD was served up at the Playboy Clubs, which tied into the sexual revolution and the philosophy of *Playboy* magazine by having waitresses dress in tight-fitting "bunny" outfits designed to appeal to their predominantly male membership.

lunch counter in Greensboro, North Carolina, set off a wave of such incidents in more than fifty Southern towns that year.

And, with the coming of the Women's Liberation Movement, restaurants that excluded women became targets that fell easily to social and
economic pressure. On August 26, 1970, Boston's male Brahmin strong-
hold—the downstairs dining room at Locke-Ober Café—was successfully
broached by a party of women led by a professor from the Massachusetts
Institute of Technology, who demanded to sit where previously women had
only been allowed if accompanying a man—and then only on two days a
year, New Year's Eve and the evening of the Harvard-Yale football game.
Locke-Ober was liberated forever afterward.

Where you ate in America had gone from signifying privilege and affluence to manifesting a more sinister form of social convention. The social
conscience stirred at America's lunch counters by the Civil Rights Movement was soon to evolve into even more primal concerns about the healthfulness of America's eating habits, so that what you ate and where you ate
it told a lot about what you were.

PUBLIC IN NAME ONLY, many restaurants in every region of the
United States shamelessly catered
to an exclusive clientele while rigorously excluding others on the
basis of race, color, or profession.

Health food restaurant in Dearborn, Michigan, circa 1970

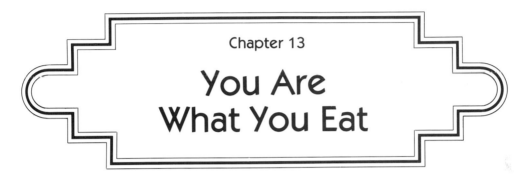

Chapter 13

You Are
What You Eat

The Counterculture Cooks Up a Storm

NINETEEN SIXTY-NINE was one weird year in American history. The social fabric of the United States was being stretched into new forms and torn to tatters by dissidence. The Vietnam War raged on, with deepening doubts about its effect on the American psyche, especially after the massacre of Vietnamese civilians at a hamlet called My Lai. Senator Ted Kennedy pleaded guilty to leaving the scene of an accident that involved the death of a female companion in Chappaquiddick Island, Massachusetts. Actress Sharon Tate was savagely slain by cult murderer Charles Manson and his followers. Norman Mailer won the Pulitzer Prize with his book *The Armies of the Night* about a protest march on the Pentagon. American astronauts landed on the moon. And the *Saturday Evening Post* published its final issue.

In Woodstock, New York, 400,000 people assembled at Max Yasgur's farm that August to listen to rock and folk music and to join together in an idealistic spirit of brotherhood, peace, and not a little sex and drugs. There, in a field of mud, where three deaths and three births occurred that weekend, a disparate array of musicians played everything from folk ballads to acid rock. At first *The New York Times* asked on its editorial page, "What kind of culture is it that can produce so colossal a mess?" The next day, the paper proclaimed the festival "a phenomenon of innocence."

One of the performers that weekend was Arlo Guthrie, son of the legendary American folk singer Woody Guthrie. As other musicians ripped their way through dissonant versions of "The Star-Spangled Banner," shouted out protest songs, or feverishly played Indian ragas, Arlo picked and talked his way through a rambling, lilting semifictional narrative about his adventures at a Massachusetts commune and a woman named Alice Brock, who served as cook and surrogate earth mother to just about everybody. "You can get anything you want," went the chorus, "at Alice's Restaurant."

With equal shares of disarming wit, social satire, and praise for Alice's cooking, the song, which Guthrie had debuted two years earlier, went on to become a kind of hippie anthem to whose refrain people attached whatever fantasy they wished. "Alice's Restaurant" seemed to sum up the gentler facet of the American counterculture movement at a time when fanatics on both sides were opening wounds that threatened to bleed the country of its traditional values.

Guthrie's song even became the basis for a motion picture directed by Arthur Penn in 1969, which further enriched the legend of Alice's Restaurant, making it into the same kind of tourist's shrine as Thoreau's Walden Pond. The problem was, by the time the song made it famous, Alice's Restaurant had long since closed.

There had been a restaurant called The Back Room, a luncheonette opened in 1965 in Stockbridge, Massachusetts, by Alice Brock, a college dropout who had become politically active in the area and the kind of good, old-fashioned American cook who could make anything taste delicious. In this little luncheonette Brock served fresh, healthful food—no hot dogs or French fries—dutifully baked her own bread and, as she said, ran the place as "an act of love."

Brock closed The Back Room in 1965, before Guthrie's song immortalized it as Alice's Restaurant. In 1971, having written *The Alice's Restaurant Cookbook* (1969), Brock took over a roadside stand she called Take Out Alice, then enlarged it and renamed it Alice's Restaurant, where she served far more refined food than before. Eventually she moved to Lenox to larger quarters she called Alice's at Avaloch, and even penned a book entitled *My Life as a Restaurant* (1974). Brock closed that restaurant in 1979, and moved to Provincetown, where she now lives.

The Alice's Restaurant of the song symbolized a kind of wholesome, nostalgic throwback to a culinary past that some felt had been corrupted by the processed food industry, fast food purveyors, and big city restaurants serving eccentric food at unconscionable prices to people who ate too much, drank too much, and didn't think enough about where their food was coming from. American babies were being fed poor substitutes for mother's milk, American teenagers were getting fat on burgers and fries, and American businessmen were swigging Martinis at swank restaurants that refused to serve anyone with long straggly hair.

Like everything else that grew out of the protest movements of the sixties, food became politicized. In *The Making of a Counterculture,* which also appeared in 1969, Theodore Roszak railed against "technocratic totalitarianism in which we shall find ourselves ingeniously adapted to an existence wholly estranged from anything that has ever made the life of man an interesting adventure."

Food, one of the basic elements for sustaining life on planet Earth, therefore, took on all sorts of polemical associations among the counterculture. The American food industry was vilified for everything from robbing food of its natural flavors to creating new "plastic" products like soft drinks and snacks concocted from chemicals. The nutritional value of a sugared breakfast cereal, a package of bacon pumped full of nitrites and red dye, orange juice strained of all pulp, eggs dehydrated into powder, tomatoes picked while green—all were called into question by those who wanted a return to "natural" foods and "organically grown" foods free from pesticides and chemical treatments.

Americans' cherished love of red meat was assailed as responsible for our blood lust for war, while vegetarianism was seen as a purer, less violent assault on nature. The slaughter of animals was regarded by some as tantamount to murder, and anything associated with the word "pig" (an epithet flung at the police) was looked upon with utter disgust. As Warren J. Belasco notes in his book *Appetite for Change: How the Counterculture Took on the Food Industry, 1966–1988* (1989), "Pig was related to fat—itself a long-standing metaphor for bourgeois affluence, softness, and corruption. In advising readers not to 'pig out,' food writers were more concerned for readers' minds than waistlines."

The same connotations were hurled at any foods that were artificially white, including refined, bleached flour, white bread, white rice, and dessert toppings. Whiteness, especially among black dissidents, was associated with White Supremacy, while the consumption of more "naturally" colored foods like brown rice, brown sugar, and brown eggs demonstrated one's ethnic awareness. The food traditionally cooked by Afro-Americans—basically Southern farm foods like chicken, chitterlings, collard greens, okra, yams, and black-eyed peas—came to be called "soul food." "One thing is certain," wrote Al Calloway in an article in *Esquire* in April 1968, "soul would be nowhere without the great savior, soul food. Black people brought to the Americas a tradition of how to make good food. Being close to the earth was their nature. . . ."

Calloway went on to describe the kind of collaborative cooking process that went on at a Harlem eatery called the Victory restaurant. "A plate of knuckles, black eyes and rice, a thick slice of corn bread, a glass of lemonade and a small home-made sweet-potato pie, and you're straight. . . . Soul food is why it is still chic to have a soul sister in the kitchen."

Whether or not "chic" was the politically correct word to use among counterculturists, "ethnic" cookery (a term popularized in the sixties), and especially that from Third World countries, became extremely fashionable during the sixties. An infatuation with Southeast Asian, particularly Vietnamese food, developed among those who regarded American participation in the Vietnam War as destructive of an entire culture. Indian food was immensely popular, especially after major rock 'n' roll groups like the Beatles embraced Indian philosophy and culture, which they saw as more spiritual and transcendant than Western civilization. And vegetarianism, which wreaked havoc only on flora but not fauna, was very much a part of the way one achieved an Oriental state of consciousness.

Rich in aromatic seasonings, Indian food was so different from bland Western food that it became something of an adventure to go to a Bengali or Bangladesh restaurant, sit on cushions under ceilings hung with colorful fabrics, listen to sitar music, and eat exotic food so fiery it would bring tears to the eyes of the first-time consumer.

For those receptive to the powers of suggestion, such foods were thought to have mind- and body-altering properties, a side effect that also led believers to investigate the cookery of Mexican and American Indians of the Southwest, where wild "magic" mushrooms were used to enhance drug experiments. Indeed, such cookery was called "head food."

In all this there was a high degree of unadulterated, generational rebellion against the way Americans had been "conditioned" to eat in the postwar period, and restaurants were an easy target of scorn by those who felt strongly that the elitism of "gourmet" restaurants was at odds with the aims of the egalitarian Age of Aquarius. The very foods that seemed to define American culinary abundance—a two-inch-thick steak, a baked potato crowned with sour cream, chocolate layer cake, and a few good belts of whiskey or beer to wash it all down—became symbols of one's parents' gluttony and decadence. Simply going to a restaurant serving that kind of food was regarded as counter-revolutionary in some quarters.

The association of the food movement with the more general anti-establishment ideas was easy enough to make, and some made the most of it. In the summer of 1976 in Arcata, California, a group of seven bakeries met to form what was to become The Cooperative Whole Grain Education Association, whose cookbook used a wry double entendre in its title—*Uprisings, The Whole Grain Bakers Book*. A more extreme tack was taken by the Communion Restaurant in San Francisco, where all meals were priced at only sixty cents (dropped from eighty cents after the group felt guilty about turning a profit). "But the customer had to be willing to *learn* while enjoying such a cheap meal," notes Belasco. "Although customers were free to take as much as they wanted, they were politely urged by not-so-discreet signs to 'take only as much as you need. There is a difference between want and need. Want is all ideas and need is real.' For further self-examination, customers made their own change at the open cash register. And finally, to keep the pupils intent on their lessons, the restaurant enforced a 'No talking' rule. By doing away with useless talk as well as 'distracting' music and wall paintings, Communion hoped 'to let people have a chance to learn how their bodies feel about food—how to pay full attention to their food and their eating.'"

More typical of the counterculture restaurants of the sixties and early seventies was the Moosewood Restaurant, established in a former school building as a collective in Ithaca, New York, in 1973. Here everyone pitched in to manage, clean, cook, devise menus, and serve (at very low wages). The emphasis was, of course, on vegetarian and ethnic foods, and the healthfulness of the diet was prominent in the self-educational process the commune built upon. The members would hold brunches to benefit day-care centers, ecology groups, and wildlife preservation. Moosewood was one of

several such counterculture kitchens that evolved over the years into a formidable restaurant in its own right. One of the great vegetarian restaurants in the United States today—Greens in San Francisco—was established in 1979 by a group of nonproselytizing American Zen Buddhists led by Deborah Madison back in the 1970s.

Some of the best-selling books of the era were counterculture publications that included ample material on food preparation. America had had a long history of health food movements dating back to the nineteenth century, and the Temperance Movement itself had a strong streak of moralism about it that reverberated in tracts published in the 1960s and 1970s. Books like *The Last Whole Earth Catalog* and *Our Bodies Ourselves* were as didactic as Deuteronomy in their precepts on how to eat well *and* morally. The

THE EQUATING OF ETHNIC FOOD and health food with sexual allure was one of the hallmarks of the counterculture's appeal to a wider audience, as evidenced by Pierre's mobile falafel stand in New York, circa 1970.

editors of *The Last Whole Earth Catalog* recommended that commune leaders buy good cooking equipment, because "the best way to attract and keep
good people is with outstanding food" and urged followers to do their own
butchering so that "you get to thank the animal personally." At the same
time they added a new scientific twist—ecology. Proponents of natural
foods, organic farming, and consumerism pointed the finger at an American
food industry that was chewing up our amber waves of grain at an alarming
rate, spraying DDT on our fruits and vegetables, and injecting chemicals
into our meats—not to mention ignoring the atomic fall-out in our milk
supply. In a land of unparalleled plenty, we were, said the critics, poisoning
our own food chain.

Many of those who attacked American food culture did so with an off-
putting stridency from a self-serving platform of political ideology. But the
sounding of an alert about problems with the way Americans raised, har-
vested, slaughtered, and prepared their food was to have enormous impact
in the supermarket, in the home kitchen, and in the restaurant business,
which was coming under severe attack for ignoring the basic tenets of good,
wholesome nutrition and for promoting forms of food that were attenuated,
far removed from their source, transubstantiated into something almost unrecognizable as food, or were just plain gimmicky.

However well intentioned food cultists were in the sixties and early seventies, polemics did not move pork chops in the restaurant industry, which,
despite a downturn in business in 1969, was surging ahead during the same
period. The end of the Vietnam War in 1973 defused the more radical political dissenters, as more young people, fresh out of college, turned their ener-
gies to more long-term domestic issues, which included concern for the
environment, problems in the food chain, better nutrition for everyone, and
a fervid interest in the way our food was cultivated and prepared.

The crusading impulses of the sixties were turned inward to health issues, diet, and consumerism. By the mid-seventies, vague, often meaningless
terms like "natural," "organic," and "light" moved out of the health food
stores and commune restaurants into the mainstream markets and onto restaurant menus as ways to seduce a new generation of eaters fearful of con-
taminating their own bodies with adulterated foods. The very idea of
adulteration was easy to expose in the food industry and, to a lesser extent,
in restaurants, where ethnic foods had been adapted to please a so-called
"American palate" that seemed to prefer blander, sweeter forms of Italian,
Chinese, Mexican, and other foods to the real thing.

With impressive academic training to back them up, the graduates of the
sixties' counterculture began to investigate food culture with the same fervor
they had applied to civil rights, the anti-war movement, and industrial pollu-
tion. Inquisitive American youths who had backpacked their way through
France, Turkey, and India in search of some primal truths found themselves
entranced with the food cultures of those countries and came back to write
about them in scrupulous detail. In the preface to her authoritative *Couscous
and Other Good Food from Morocco* (1973), a book that seemed more influenced by Lawrence Durrell than Betty Crocker, Paula Wolfert wrote, "The
moment the Yugoslav freighter touched at Casablanca in 1959 I boarded a bus

and rushed to Marrakesh, in search of the adventurous and exotic life. I felt immediately that I belonged in this country, and have never gotten over that feeling—I am still enchanted by all things Moroccan."

Travel abroad had become for so many college-educated Americans part of the ritual of growing up, and familiarity with the culinary culture of a foreign land became a mark of one's sophistication. These Americans gobbled up Ernest Hemingway's reminiscences of Paris in the twenties, *A Moveable Feast,* published posthumously in 1964, as much for its descriptions of café and bistro meals as for its literary gossip, and Alice B. Toklas became a cult figure among drug aficionados with the publication of her *Alice B. Toklas Cookbook* (1954), which included recipes for hashish-laced brownies.

The act of cooking itself, once considered drudgerous and unfulfilling, was taken up with a real passion, especially by women in the early seventies, before the Women's Liberation Movement shamed their sisters out of the kitchen and into the workforce. Writers like M.F.K. Fisher, Elizabeth David, Jane Grigson, and other women who wrote seriously about food culture were idolized, and a California-born Bostonian named Julia Child revealed

NO MATTER HOW MAKESHIFT the presentation, health food restaurants sold a menu of moralism and funk, like "smoothies" made from pureed vegetables and exotic fruits.

the true joys of cooking when she debuted on the local educational television channel, WGBH-TV, as "The French Chef." There had already been cooking shows on television (James Beard had one in the 1950s), but Child, six feet tall and possessed of a voice that swooped over several octaves in the course of a recipe, won over not just those who wished to know a bit more about cooking but those who had never before even considered mastering the intricacies of French cuisine.

In some ways she seemed like the most unlikely candidate for television stardom, for she was anything but glamorous and made the kinds of mistakes—like dropping food on the floor—that would drive more professional performers to tears. It was just such nonchalant candor that took the starch out of fancy cookery for millions of Americans who came to regard Child as a kind of eccentric New England aunt who could cook rings around anyone in the family.

Child grew up in Pasadena, California, and as a girl went to many of the Hollywood restaurants popular before the war. "I really don't remember much about the food in those restaurants," she recalled. "I do remember that they were terribly glamorous and you could see movie stars. I remember things like the breadsticks at Perino's and the revolving doors at The Biltmore. And of course strawberries Romanoff at Romanoff's and Caesar salad at Caesar's Place in Tijuana. I'd go with my white gloves on and have an awfully good time, but food was not of much interest to me back then."

Child's interest in food burgeoned during World War II when she and her husband, Paul, who was in the OSS, were stationed in the Far East. "We lived in Ceylon, India, and China, and there were marvelous restaurants with all kinds of unusual foods that were full of flavor. You'd sit at big round tables with the whole family, and if you didn't like the food, you just threw it over your shoulder onto the floor. It was great fun!"

After the war the Childs lived in France, where Julia took cooking courses and became an excellent home cook, eventually teaming up with Simone Beck and Louisette Bertholle to write *Mastering the Art of French Cooking* (1961), which was intended for "the servantless American cook who can be unconcerned on occasion with budgets, waistlines, time schedules, children's meals, the parent-chauffeur-den-mother syndrome, or anything else which might interfere with the enjoyment of producing something wonderful to eat."

Child moved back to the United States, settled in Cambridge, Massachusetts, and began hosting "The French Chef" on a shoestring budget for the local public television station, WGBH-TV. When the show went on nationally, a whole generation of Americans woke up to the pleasures of cooking, where before it had too often been regarded as drudgery.

Child tapped into Americans' developing interest in international taste at a time when more Americans were traveling abroad and dining at the best restaurants in Europe. Back home, they wanted to reproduce these flavors and recipes, and it was Child who took them by the hand into a non-threatening encounter with once-feared dishes like quiche Lorraine and chocolate soufflés.

* * *

Perhaps you couldn't get such fancy French cuisine at Alice's Restaurant, but what Alice's represented was a return to an idealized family-style cookery of a sort that had at best gone out of style in American gastronomy and at worst stood in danger of being forgotten.

One of those who picked up on the significance of the song title was another Alice—Alice Waters—a French cultural history major at the University of California at Berkeley who had grown up in Chatham, New Jersey, eating what she called "very plain, New Jersey cooking." At the age of nineteen she and a college roommate took a year off from school and toured France in order to learn the language. But along the way she found herself falling deeply in love with the flavor of French cooking and the quality of French ingredients.

On her return to Berkeley, by then a hotbed of political activism, Waters began working on a left-wing newspaper called the *San Francisco Express Times,* for whose staff and friends she'd do a little cooking. Eventually writing a column entitled "Alice's Restaurant," which vied for space with jeremiads against the Vietnam War and J. Edgar Hoover. "And I didn't know *anything* to be doing that," she later told an interviewer for *The Journal of Gastronomy.* "I didn't think I could make mayonnaise unless I stuck a potato on the end of a fork and stirred it like that. All those little folk ways. But it was a great way to learn. There's nothing like cooking for people who encourage you. . . . The more you cooked good things, the more they liked you."

After graduation Waters trained to be a teacher at a Montessori school in London while indulging her newfound love of cooking, drawing inspiration from the works of British food writer Elizabeth David and American expatriate Richard Olney, both of whom had written in-depth studies of French bourgeois cooking. She returned to Berkeley to teach at a local Montessori school, but soon friends were encouraging her to open her own little café in the university neighborhood. In 1971, with ten thousand dollars and not a whit of professional knowledge about how to run a restaurant, Waters naïvely opened a little place she called Chez Panisse, after a character in the films of French director Marcel Pagnol. "It was just that time," she said. "It was *assumed* that if you were doing something you wanted to do and people liked it that the money would come." Within months, Chez Panisse was forty thousands dollars in debt.

But everybody helped out, eventually the little place prospered, and Waters bought half the business. At first she didn't do much of the cooking, nor did she want to, but little by little she trained herself to make the kind of food she remembered in France—culled from the best local sources, based on seasonal ingredients, and utilizing nothing that had been processed. She thereupon began to cultivate sources for fresh herbs, vegetables, and meats, sometimes trading meals at Chez Panisse for a farmer's produce. People would bring mushrooms or tomatoes or a vinegar made from local wine grapes to her back door, and she delighted in trying them all.

She also promoted the new varietal wines from the Napa and Sonoma valleys and made up her menus every day according to what was freshest and best from the market. And, convinced that she was making dishes so good that everyone would like them, she offered only one set menu each

A FORMER FRENCH LITERATURE student and political activist named Alice Waters successfully married the counterculture's iconoclasm to strict ideals of French culinary classicism at her Berkeley, California, restaurant, Chez Panisse.

evening and seemed sad when people didn't savor a dish like roast kidneys or risotto in squid ink.

Later on she opened a smaller, casual, more inexpensive café upstairs from Chez Panisse, where she featured the hearty foods of the Mediterranean and Provence, including pizzas—which until then had never been regarded in America as anything more than fast food.

Chez Panisse began to get national attention, and Waters's reputation was such that it brought to her kitchen a long line of people from various disciplines who wanted to share in the experience of what she was trying to do at Chez Panisse. Mark Miller, who had come from Massachusetts to Berkeley to study Chinese art history and Japanese anthropology, started a newsletter called *The Market Basket,* assembled a formidable scholar's library of culinaria, and eventually came to cook at Chez Panisse. Jonathan Waxman had studied political science and planned to become a jazz trombonist before taking a job in a restaurant in Hawaii ("so I could lie on the beach all day," he later said), then trained in France before finding an American kitchen sympathetic to his talents—Chez Panisse.

This attraction of well-educated, middle-class young people like Waters herself to the restaurant profession was something quite new in American gastronomy. Before Chez Panisse, the job of chef was regarded by most Americans as a minor profession, requiring certain skills but little intellectualism. What Waters and her followers showed was that the application of intelligence, inquisitiveness, and a fervid interest in food culture could remake American gastronomy in a way that the more radical counterculture food groups could hardly understand. Indeed, Chez Panisse's cuisine—which would be the basis of what would later be called "California cuisine"—was derived from the French bourgeoisie. And however revolutionary that might have been back in 1789 or in the Paris Commune of 1871, to the revolutionaries of the 1970s it had entirely the wrong, revisionist connotations.

Waters also ran counter to the long-cherished belief in a male-dominated industry that held females had no business in a restaurant kitchen, and she helped moderate the views of some women's liberationists who had criticized kitchen work and cooking as a demeaning, outmoded traditional role for women. Waters's high standards and commanding knowledge opened the door for women chefs like Joyce Goldstein of Square One in San Francisco, Jackie Etcheber of Jackie's in Chicago, Lydia Shire of Biba in Boston, Anne Rosenzweig of Arcadia in New York, Mary Sue Milliken and Susan Feniger of City Restaurant in Los Angeles, Johanne Killeen of Al Forno in Providence, Susan Spicer of Bayona in New Orleans, Leslie Reis of Café Provençal in Evanston, Elizabeth Terry of Elizabeth on 37th in Savannah, and many others who entered the profession in the seventies and eighties. Indeed, the number of female students enrolled in culinary studies at Rhode Island's Johnson & Wales University jumped from 10 percent of the class in 1973 to 40 percent by the end of the eighties.

Chez Panisse's fame grew rapidly, and Waters soon found herself being written about as a guru, an earth mother, a guiding light of a new style of American food that differed formally and by intent from the kind of elaborate, gimmicky fare served at most restaurants in the United States. Long-time professional chefs marveled at the taste of her food, the intensity of flavors, and the audacity of her conceptions. "I know I have a certain aesthetic, because that's my taste," she explained in 1984. "It's what people have done in Italy and France for years. . . . But on the whole I don't think there is anything mysterious about it. The one thing that seems maybe different about Chez Panisse is that we're never content to stay as we are. I always want to change it a little bit. I don't want to stop where we are and let it settle because we're right at the beginning, just a little bit into kindergarten."

New York's The Palace—the most expensive restaurant of the 1970s

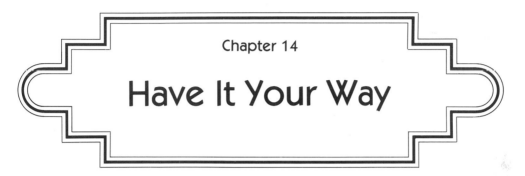

Chapter 14

Have It Your Way

Eating Out in the "Me" Decade

MUCH AS THE RESTAURANT INDUSTRY might have liked to ignore the counterculture food movement, there was no stopping its momentum, coming as it did on a wave of young, well-educated, well-traveled Americans who entered the labor market in the mid-1970s. These were customers who craved new flavors and new styles of restaurants and took their food *very* seriously, whether it was learning to discuss the different vintages of First Growth Bordeaux with a sommelier at a deluxe French restaurant or sitting on a stool at an Ethiopian restaurant, where using one's fingers was the only correct way to eat a millet-flour pancake called *injera* stuffed with chili-spiked meats.

After decades of eating at bland Chinese-American restaurants, Americans began showing a keen interest in the hot, spicy foods of the provinces of Szechuan and Hunan, especially after President Richard Nixon's visit to China in 1972. Restaurants featuring the food of those regions sprang up in American cities and, before long, in suburban shopping malls. Indian restaurants garnered increased popularity, and the regional cookeries of that subcontinent were amply represented at places that offered everything from sumptuous Moghul rice dishes called *biryanis* to Goan curries.

Any sensible owner of a restaurant above the level of fast food had to adapt to these new demands for authenticity and culinary excitement. A Fred Harvey restaurant in Los Angeles even put Japanese-style teriyaki chicken on its menu, and Burger King adopted the slogan "Have It Your Way" for what writer Tom Wolfe came to call the "Me" decade in 1976.

Ironically, the counterculture's infatuation with ethnic "peasant" foods paralleled a burgeoning connoisseurship for European *haute cuisine.* For most of America's gastronomic history, finickiness about the way one ate had represented the height of elitist, European pretension. Except as specimens of decadence, like James's Daisy Miller or Fitzgerald's Jay Gatsby, characters who make a fuss over fine food, wine, and restaurants are almost nonexistent in American literature and popular culture. But as Americans traveled abroad more and became more comfortable with deluxe dining and gourmandism, this image began to change appreciably.

One of the pop culture figures who helped alter Americans' perception of connoisseurship was the fictional British agent James "007" Bond, whose creator, Ian Fleming, larded his spy novels with sumptuous meals served at some of the world's great restaurants, or, as might happen in the world of international intrigue, at the palatial home of one of the world's great mad villains. There was much decadence in the Bond character, and he was a man of finicky tastes—he preferred champagne to red wine, had his coffee beans blended by De Bry on Oxford Street, specified Scottish smoked salmon with his scrambled eggs, believed that sushi cured a hangover, and became famous for demanding that his unorthodox vodka Martinis be "shaken, not stirred." But no one would ever accuse the man with a "license to kill" of being effete. Indeed, women found 007's connoisseurship seductive. Bond remarked on his interest in food and wine in *Casino Royale* (1953), saying, "I take a ridiculous pleasure in what I eat and drink. It comes partly from being a bachelor, but mostly from a habit of taking a lot of trouble over details."

Bond was the fictional symbol of the modern Renaissance Man—intelligent, well educated, sexually irresistible, an unbeatable sportsman, powerful, egotistical, dangerous, honorable when it suited his purposes, and possessed of an unlimited expense account. His understated connoisseurship became even more pronounced in the tremendously popular movie versions of Fleming's books, beginning with *Dr. No* in 1962. In fact, the sales of Dom Pérignon soared after Bond showed his preference for that champagne in the early movies, so much so that other champagne houses paid hefty fees to the movie producers to have 007 drink *their* bubbly in subsequent films.

The worldliness exhibited by Bond was enthusiastically advocated by American men's magazines like *Esquire* (which did several features on Bond movies) and *Playboy* (which published several of Fleming's stories), so that by the 1970s many American men had begun a process of self-education about food, wine, and restaurants, along with cars, stereo equipment, and clothing. Committing vintages to memory, learning the difference between sevruga and beluga caviar, specifying one's favorite brand of whiskey at a bar, and tipping maître d's to guarantee a good table and superior service—these became hallmarks of the American man-about-town in the 1970s, so that familiarity with the grand luxe restaurants of Paris and New York became a matter of self-image in a generation that needed the kinds of new stimulants traditional restaurants simply did not provide.

This new appetite for exciting food served in exciting surroundings was happily nurtured by a new breed of journalist who covered the food and restaurant "scene" with the same enthusiasm newspapers and slick magazines had long brought to entertainment and fashion. Before the 1950s the concept of candid, informed restaurant reviews really didn't exist, except as an adjunct to gossip columns or in travel guides like those by Duncan Hines. Although the New York *Herald Tribune*'s food editor Clementine Paddleford wielded considerable clout for her euphemistic restaurant write-ups, the man who raised restaurant reviewing from being little more than a trade-off for advertisers to a respectable critical standard was Craig Claiborne, a Mississippian who'd studied at a Swiss hotel school, worked in various restaurants, written a few articles for *Gourmet* magazine, done some public relations, and spoke French. At a time when most food editors were women and most Wednesday food sections were devoted to recipes, Claiborne's appointment as food editor at *The New York Times* on September 9, 1957, was an unusual and unorthodox move.

Before long, the *Times* was encouraging Claiborne to try his hand at occasional restaurant reviewing, even though he protested he hadn't eaten at enough of the great ones to be a real authority. But the public enjoyed his write-ups and as of May 24, 1963, they became weekly hundred-word columns.

Claiborne did not think much of the restaurant scene in those days—in his autobiography, *A Feast Made for Laughter* (1982), he called New York a "hick town" when it came to fine dining—but he applied rigorous criteria and helped elevate the standards of both the restaurants he covered and food writing itself. Backed by the full faith of his newspaper and a lavish expense account, Claiborne was as scrupulous as he was incorruptible, so that his praise for a restaurant could guarantee its success overnight, while his pan, to his dismay, could close it down within days. He also heralded those chefs whom he believed were headed in the right direction—that is, away from the clichés of continental cuisine—and his enthusiasm for a style of cookery, such as Szechuan Chinese or Cajun, could literally start a fad for such food.

After five years, however, Claiborne had became bored with restaurant reviewing, and, after a period away from the *Times,* continued on at the paper solely as food editor. While he would be the first to tell people that the job of restaurant critic was not all "cake and ale, champagne, truffles and caviar," he did at one point write an article that seemed to sum up the decadent food culture of the mid-1970s. Having bid on and won an American Express-sponsored meal-for-two anywhere in the world for a charity benefit, Claiborne and his *Times* colleague, chef Pierre Franey, flew off to Paris to dine at the renowned Chez Denis. After a grand gorge that would have impressed Diamond Jim Brady, Claiborne and Franey paid a bill of four thousand dollars—which Claiborne wrote about in a front-page article in the *Times,* eliciting a thousand letters split equally between those who praised him for his stamina and gourmandism and those who considered it a vulgar, cold-blooded, and heartless act while people elsewhere in the world went without food. Even the Vatican called the dinner a "scandalous" act.

NEW YORK TIMES FOOD CRITIC Craig Claiborne, seen here celebrating the good life of the "Me" decade with restaurant consultant George Lang, helped elevate both the gastronomic standards of Americans and the professionalism of restaurant criticism.

By the mid-1970s restaurant critics had become fixtures at most city newspapers, although many were summarily drafted, without any proper credentials, into the job from other sections of the paper. Too often the aging gardening editor or the sportswriter who liked to eat out got the assignment, whether or not he knew much about food. Sometimes reviewers were deliberately chosen *because* they had a working man's antagonism to fancy restaurants with fancy food. Even at the *Times* Claiborne's successor was the recently retired art critic, John Canaday, followed by investigative journalist John L. Hess, who by his own admission could not have handled the job without the assistance of his wife, food writer and historian Karen Hess. Not until 1975 did the *Times* hire a specialist, Mimi Sheraton, as full-time restaurant critic and food reporter, who brought a knowledge and dedication to the job that was daunting.

For some time, however, the food press had been drawing a diverse group of young writers who, with the same kind of zeal manifested by the counterculturists, tried to bring an irreverent, often unorthodox, sometimes eccentric approach to their subject. These were writers who may or may not have had wide experience eating out in great restaurants but who brought to their task an unjaded openmindedness, an unflagging energy, and a fresh palate to the dining table. Most came to food writing as a sideline or hobby, like graphic designer Milton Glaser and art director Jerome Snyder, who, under the hip name "The Underground Gourmet," began noshing their way through cheap restaurants of every ethnic stripe for the New York *World-Journal-Tribune*. Some, like Steve Raichlen of *Boston* magazine and Jim Quinn of *Philadelphia* magazine, had themselves come out of the counterculture. Thus, Quinn once began a 1983 essay on restaurants with the completely irrelevant remark, "Fifteen years ago, when Lyndon Johnson was still fooling many of the people much of the time about the war in Vietnam and I first started reviewing restaurants . . ."

One of the most influential restaurant reviewers of the era was Gael Greene, who began writing for *New York* magazine in 1968. Under the title "The Insatiable Critic," Greene brought a literary sensibility and a sensualist's palate to the job, echoing the sybaritic prose style of Colette or Proust. Of the pasta at an Italian restaurant, she would write, "Gnocchi-celebrants may crack under the blissful pain." Of an egg dish at a hotel dining room: "Alas, les oeufs à la coque, mouillettes Beluga, is a solo soft-boiled egg with pitiful dry dots of caviar on ribbons of toast, a $16 despair." On a famous chef's occasional mistake: "Oh, Soltner misses. One could weep. It's a little like Nureyev tripping on a shoelace."

Greene reported on which celebrities dined at which tables at which restaurants and would begin reviews with romantic questions like "Must fidelity inevitably dull passion?" She'd wail in mock heroic tones over her loss of gastronomic innocence, "Does the feverishly indulged mouth lose its sense of reality . . . become inevitably jaded? Can the pilgrim who has tasted the perfect panaché de poissons aux petits légumes stay in touch with the raison d'être of a fast-food hamburger?" and once called her job "slow death by mayonnaise."

As a matter of fact, Greene admitted to loving fast food, and may have been the person who coined the term "junk food." "I love Fritos and tacos and Chunkies and Fresca *with* cyclamates [an artificial sweetener] and peanut butter," she exulted, "especially with something called Smoky Crisps which the Great God Skippy giveth and tooketh away."

This tongue-in-cheek style, balanced between the Apician and the Rabelaisian, coupled with her on-the-job-training attitude, suited perfectly the aspirations of those like herself who were just discovering the joys and pleasures of food both for its own sake and for the excitement restaurants could afford. It was quite a compelling style at that, and more than a few restaurant critics in other cities copied it, although more often than not the results were an embarrassing jumble of swoons and orgasmic groans used to describe some wholly pedestrian fare.

Guidebooks began rating restaurants by stars or other symbols à la France's *Guide Michelin.* Most notable was the *Mobil Travel Guide,* first published in 1960 in collaboration with the Mobil Oil Corporation, which, in addition to detailed information on sights and attractions, awarded (without comment) one to five stars to restaurants in all fifty states. The modus operandi of the ratings system (one star meaning "good," five stars "one of the best in the country") was never made clear, except that the *Guide's* editors admitted that their "inspectors" were often senior citizens, retired schoolteachers, and other nonprofessionals. Restaurateurs who made it into the *Guide* with a high rating milked the publicity for all it was worth, while others complained that inspectors seemed to show more interest in the cleanliness of the rest rooms than in bothering to eat a meal in the dining room.

The *Mobil Travel Guide* ratings also baffled professional food critics who found it difficult to imagine that a city like Montgomery, Alabama, could sustain three three-star restaurants or that Las Vegas could have twenty, especially since the editors insisted they applied the same standards in those cities as they would in New York or Los Angeles. Nevertheless, the *Mobil* awards were announced each year with the solemnity of the Nobel Prizes, and, along with the Automobile Association of America's fine dining awards (which used diamonds instead of stars), they helped set certain standards for service, hospitality, and deluxe dining in America.

A whole slew of new food magazines encouraged young writers to avoid the upturned-pinky prose of their predecessors and to create excitement about their subject. *Gourmet* magazine, which dated back to 1941, had long upheld the most conservative traditions of American food culture, but newer magazines like *Bon Appétit, Food & Wine,* and *Cook's* championed young chefs and innovative restaurants in ways that created a real enticement to want to see what all the fuss was about.

For restaurants had, by the middle of the 1970s, become entertainment on their own—not because of dancing girls or live music, but because the places themselves formed a dramatic backdrop for a new generation of people—including millions of women no longer content to stay home and cook every night—who could afford to go out to eat often and at more expensive places than ever before. These people had passed through the singles' bar scene and were ready to put their connoisseurship on the line.

Though no longer a young man, Joe Baum saw this as clearly as anyone

in the restaurant industry, and, despite his being deposed at RA in 1968, he had already envisioned a restaurant for a new age that would make his previous efforts pale by comparison. In 1970 New York's Port Authority contracted him to create a broad range of food facilities for what was to be the tallest building in the world—the World Trade Center—in New York's downtown financial district, a region not then known for its fine restaurants. There were fears the Center would never attract enough tenants to make the enterprise commercially viable, but Baum, who remembered hearing much the same thing about the viability of The Newarker, believed the grandiosity of the Center would make it a tourist attraction. Who wouldn't want to eat at a restaurant called Windows on the World set on the 107th floor of New York's tallest skyscraper?

Baum threw himself into the creation of Windows with a childlike wonder he expressed to a reporter who came to cover the opening of the complex. "What can I do?" Baum exclaimed. "What's possible?"

A minimum of twenty-two food service units was planned at a cost of at least twenty-six million dollars. There were to be corporate dining rooms, delicatessens, a steakhouse, and a sprawling fast food facility called The Big Kitchen on the ground floor, with striking graphics done by "The Underground Gourmet" himself, Milton Glaser. From individual counters customers could buy anything from a salad or sandwich to oysters and hamburgers to ice cream and muffins. Hamburger meat was specially ground for maximum flavor; all steaks were U.S. Prime; chicken soup was made from scratch; lamb was roasted on a rotisserie, and breads were baked twice a

THE MOST SPECTACULARLY situated restaurant in the world—Windows on the World opened in 1976 atop the 107th floor of New York's World Trade Center.

THE GRAND BUFFET at Windows on the World was testament to the belief that too much was not necessarily too much in the hedonistic 1970s.

day to ensure freshness. The Big Kitchen was the prototype of what would later become known in the industry as the "food hall," with many food purveyors selling various American and ethnic foods from stalls built around an open core.

But the Center's crowning glory was Windows on the World, reached via a freight-sized elevator that seemed to soar to the top (even though the elevator's fifty-second ascension did not exceed seventeen miles per hour). The ear-popping trip was but a titillating prelude to what was to come. On exiting onto the 107th floor, you were greeted by a young, attractive hostess in a well-tailored uniform and taken through a mirrored gallery to the main dining room wrapped with the gigantic windows that gave the room its name. The grandeur of the New York landscape below gave way to a shimmering, endless sheet of ocean that receded to what seemed to be the end of the earth.

Windows on the World had glamour and finesse in every detail. Designed by Warren Platner, the room gleamed with brass and marble. Every table had a spectacular view (sometimes blanketed over by fog on a bad night) and none was more than twenty-three steps from the kitchen, which maximized the efficient flow of service traffic.

The dinner menu was created from the best ingredients available and, while not cheap, offered good value and was aimed at pleasing just about every taste. There would be pâtés and terrines, steaks and chops, but there

RESTAURANT DEVELOPER JOE BAUM (*eating*) together with chef Jacques Pépin (*right*) would taste-test dozens of recipes in order to come up with one that would be delectable for both gourmets and casual diners at Windows on the World.

would also be Japanese sesame noodles, bass in aspic, lamb stew, and a sumptuous array of desserts, all complemented by one of the finest wine lists in the United States that included some of the finest wines *from* the United States. During weekdays Windows functioned as a private business people's club. After three o'clock the Grill Room opened to the public as the Hors D'Oeuvrerie, where one could choose from a dazzling array of appetizers and finger foods from around the world—everything from Russian *zakuska* to Chinese *dim sum* and American spareribs—all expertly prepared and rigorously authentic.

Windows was, of course, an overwhelming success. Within weeks of opening in the spring of 1976, the restaurant needed twenty-five operators just to take reservations, and tables were booked six months in advance. It was a one-of-a-kind restaurant, and so completely realized in its details that it immediately became the model for similar big projects in other cities, such as the 95th Restaurant atop the 95th floor of the John Hancock Center in Chicago. More than anything else, Windows showed the industry what was possible in a market hungry for a thrill or an adventure in dining out. Baum showed that theme restaurants could no longer depend for their effectiveness on a puerile, visceral response from a public who had grown far more sophisticated about food and service.

This meant that, now, the restaurant industry had to put its money where the public's mouth was and to spend more on better ingredients and better chefs. Having for so long served a public that seemed to care more

about atmosphere, the cocktail lounge, the celebrity tally, the exclusivity, and the fun to be had at a restaurant, the industry now had to contend with a public that was in many ways far in advance of the old-line chefs who were still turning out gallons of béarnaise sauce to be poured over inferior cuts of meat amid a setting that reeked of Paris in the Belle Epoque rather than the United States in 1975.

None of this was lost on the food and beverage planners for a new Walt Disney project to be called EPCOT (an acronym for Experimental Prototype Community of Tomorrow), which was to be the second stage of an enormous amusement park area outside of Orlando, Florida, at Lake Buena Vista. The first stage, called the Magic Kingdom, opened in 1971, had been a much enlarged version of the Anaheim Disneyland, and food outlets did not evolve much beyond the burgers-and-fries restaurants of the original. But EPCOT was to be something far more innovative. Disney himself, who had died in 1966, had envisioned an adult theme park devoted to new technologies and the ecological and environmental problems facing the world in the next century, including the development of new sources and kinds of food.

The man put in charge of EPCOT's food service was an RA alumnus named Jim Armstrong, whose mission was to create exciting new food service facilities that reflected the theme of the park. There would be more emphasis on seafood, fresh fruits and vegetables, and salads. There would also be a number of World Showcase restaurants keyed to national pavilions and run by outside restaurateurs. There was to be a serious commitment to wines (Disneyland and the Magic Kingdom sold no alcohol at all) and white tablecloth service. Fruits and vegetables raised through hydro- and aeroponics at the Land Pavilion, which was devoted to the history and future of agriculture, were used in the pavilion's restaurants.

When EPCOT opened on October 1, 1981, visitors could choose from a wide range of theme restaurants that included everything from fast food to deluxe cuisine. Disney had attracted first-rate outside restaurateurs who would, as had been the case at the 1939 World's Fair, introduce Americans to ethnic foods prepared with real integrity. Armstrong said he aimed at "authenticity to the point of acceptability," which meant that the food had to be true to its native land but not so exotic as to put off the average American. The Italian Pavilion restaurant replicated Venice's Piazza San Marco and housed an offshoot of Rome's famous Alfredo's restaurant, which had created fettuccine all' Alfredo. At the Japanese pavilion, visitors dined on tempura, yakitori, and other specialties prepared by Tokyo's renowned Mitsukoski restaurant, and the food at the San Angel Inn (the original is in Mexico City) was not the usual Tex-Mex fare but authentic Mexican dishes not easily found elsewhere in the United States. The Chinese restaurant, Nine Dragons, was built to be one of the most elegant and best serviced in the United States. The French restaurant, called Chefs de France, would be run by three of France's most illustrious chefs—Paul Bocuse, Roger Vergé, and Gaston LeNotre—and set in an idealized copy of a Parisian bistro. Eventually there would be a German *Biergarten,* a Moroccan restaurant, a Norwegian restaurant, and an English pub.

THREE OF FRANCE'S most illustrious chefs of the *nouvelle cuisine* era of the late 1970s and early 1980s (*left to right*), Paul Bocuse, Gaston Le-Notre and Roger Vergé, were contracted by the Walt Disney Company to develop and run a French restaurant at EPCOT Center in Lake Buena Vista, Florida, which opened in 1981.

In 1987 EPCOT debuted an extraordinary seafood restaurant called the Coral Reef whose main design feature was a six-million-gallon aquarium that was part of the Living Seas exhibit. Diners would sit down to choose from a wide range of seafood as giant groupers, octopuses, and blue sharks swam by their table.

Nothing like this existed anywhere else in the United States, nor, for that matter, anywhere else in the world. Few independent restaurateurs had the resources for such thematic developments, and most independents were content to follow the standard menus and thematics of the past rather than risk going out of style after a few years.

The overwhelming majority of the fine restaurants in America at the beginning of the seventies were content to keep on serving all the clichés of "continental cuisine" or to appeal to a traveling businessman looking for a two-inch-thick steak with mushroom caps and a good strong Martini. Very few restaurants paid much attention to wine service, although the improvement of varietal wines from California did spark the interest of the public and better bottlings began showing up on restaurant wine lists after 1975.

Cities like Boston, Chicago, Detroit, Cleveland, Washington, Miami, and Los Angeles had but a handful of truly superior restaurants, while New Orleans plugged along with its own highly developed restaurant scene, which paid little attention to what was going on anywhere else. Cities like Houston and Dallas did not even allow liquor or wine by the glass until the early 1970s, which kept the country club dining rooms full but did nothing to promote fine dining in Texas. From a 1990 vantage point *Washington Post* restaurant critic Phyllis Richman recalled the dismal caliber of the capital's dining scene in the 1970s: "Fifteen years ago, even the most revered restaurants (which were of course, French) routinely served canned petits pois and canned baby carrots. . . . Breads were not made in-house nor were pastries. Fish was more likely to be frozen than fresh. Sauces were stodgy, menus were predictable, and the higher the tab, the haughtier the waiter."

Even in New York, which had always been the inspiration to the rest of the country when it came to deluxe restaurants and new ideas, there was still a stultifying number of restaurants that merely copied each other's menus, so that one could dine out at such *haute cuisine* establishments as Le Cheval Blanc, La Côte Basque, Le Marmiton, Le Madrigal, Le Périgord, and La Grenouille and believe the food all came out of the same commissary kitchen named in honor of Henri Soulé.

The same might also be said for the majority of restaurants in France, where the codification of classic French cooking by Georges Auguste Escoffier had wrapped a straitjacket around chefs since the turn of the century. This, however, began to change in France in the 1960s when young chefs like Paul Bocuse, Roger Vergé, Jean and Pierre Troisgros, and others, inspired by Fernand Point of La Pyramide en Vienne, broke free from the strictures of hotel dining rooms and began to cook as they wished, bringing new ideas, new cooking techniques, and new ingredients into the classical repertoire. The best of these never strayed far from that repertoire, but they recognized that French cuisine had become boring and predictable, as well as heavy-handed and out of touch with modern nutrition.

EPCOT'S INTERNATIONAL pavilions featured restaurants from Mexico, Germany, England, Italy, Japan, China, Morocco, and Norway. One of the most successful was Les Chefs de France, which served more than a thousand people a day.

The result was a somewhat lighter, though still very rich, cuisine that sparkled with creativity and showed off the chef's personal imagination in preparing and presenting dishes that were both delicious to eat and breathtaking to behold. This new style of cooking was formally christened *"la nouvelle cuisine"* by French food writers Henri Gault and Christian Millau in the October 1973 issue of their *Gault-Millau* magazine, wherein they pronounced what they called the ten commandments of this modern cookery to be:

1. Avoid unnecessary complications.
2. Shorten cooking times.
3. Shop regularly at the market.
4. Shorten the menu.
5. Don't hang or marinate game.
6. Avoid too-rich sauces.
7. Return to regional cooking.
8. Investigate the latest techniques.
9. Consider diet and health.
10. Invent constantly.

As with the original Ten Commandments, Gault-Millau's were made to be broken, or at least ignored by those who took up the crusade for *nouvelle cuisine.* Others took the commandments to the extreme, so that in an effort to "invent constantly" young chefs concocted the most eccentric dishes they could, blending together ingredients that had never before coalesced (usually with good reason), combining fruit sauces with seafood, serving lobster with vanilla sauce, and puréeing vegetables into baby food. Most of these chefs eschewed the use of flour in sauces, but built them with gobs of butter. The most expensive ingredients like truffles and *foie gras* were used with abandon. Fish and game was barely cooked and often came to the table bloody. And always, presentation on an oversized plate was given a high priority in such kitchens, so that sauces would form mosaics, vegetables would sprout forth like antennae from a *terrine* of goose liver, and desserts would be mounted in gaudy Technicolor displays that literally looked too intimidating to eat.

Nouvelle cuisine became all the rage in France, and it was duly reported on in the American press, at first as a curiosity and then as a bandwagon onto which chefs hopped with dispatch. For the first time in American gastronomic history, food for its own sake had become pure fashion, so that acquaintance with the progenitors of *nouvelle cuisine* bolstered one's sophistication level several notches in culinary and social circles.

It also indicated you were a person of some wealth, for the prices at *nouvelle cuisine* establishments were usually exorbitant and portions quite small. The acceptance of French *nouvelle cuisine* in the United States had a certain irony to it, for the service of small portions of very precious food flew directly in the face of American food service tradition, which was to give a hefty portion of food at a fair price. Devotees of the *nouvelle* style insisted, rather obnoxiously, that it was neither chic nor healthy to eat so much food and that the "esthetics" of a dish would be ruined by having too much food cluttering up the plate design.

By the mid-seventies *nouvelle cuisine* had started to make amazing inroads into the American restaurant scene, first in New York and Los Angeles, then throughout the major cities. Curiously enough, the beachheads were established by young American chefs and entrepreneurs who had fallen in love with the *nouvelle* style (and saw its promotional value) rather than by French expatriates. One of the first was a former lawyer Robert Pritsker and his wife, Karen, who opened a *nouvelle* restaurant called Dodin-Bouffant (named after a fictional gastronome) in Boston before moving it to New York in 1979. The first woman chef at the Waldorf-Astoria, Leslie Revsin, left there to open a storefront restaurant in Greenwich Village called Restaurant Leslie that served her own very personal cooking. In a sliver of a dining room named Le Plaisir partners Steven Spector and Peter Josten concocted menus with innovative items like hot shellfish sausage, green pasta with black truffles, red snapper in a red wine sauce with beef marrow, and blood-rare breast of duck with fig mousse.

Foreign hotel chains like the Meridien (owned by Air France) and the Four Seasons (a Canadian company) installed deluxe *nouvelle* dining rooms in its United States properties, and by 1980 the *nouvelle* craze was in full flourish. Every major American city had its *nouvelle* restaurants, which were glowingly reported on by local food writers who more often than not began their reviews with a line like, "At last we have a great modern restaurant in our fair city!" In Boston there was L'Espalier, Apley's, and Julien (named after that city's first French restaurateur in 1794); in Philadelphia, Le Bec Fin and Frog; in Washington, Jean-Louis and Le Pavillon; in Cleveland, The French Connection; in Minneapolis, the New French Café and 510 Haute Cuisine; in Dallas, the French Room, Calluaud, and Café Royal; in Houston, Restaurant de France and La Réserve; in St. Louis, Chez Louis; in Denver, Dudley's; in San Francisco, Fournou's Ovens and Le Castel; in Seattle, Rossellini's Other Place, and in Honolulu, Bagwell's 2424.

Chicago was a particularly fertile field for the *nouvelle* style, with restaurants like Ambria, Le Perroquet, and particularly Le Français, which was actually forty minutes away in Wheeling, Illinois, ranked by many food critics among the finest restaurants in the United States. Under chef-owner Jean Banchet, Le Français became a training ground for several young chefs who themselves would establish *nouvelle* restaurants in other cities, such as Vincent Guerithault of Vincent's in Scottsdale, Arizona.

But it was in Los Angeles that the style of *nouvelle cuisine* really took hold and evolved into something that took on its own Southern California characteristics. This might have been expected in a city built on entertainment value. By the mid-seventies, restaurants had become their own form of entertainment. Add to this a population explosion and tremendous affluence, and you had a city whose natives and visitors had by 1983 outspent New York by half a billion dollars on eating out (although much of that money was spent at drive-ins and taco stands).

The prime mover of the *nouvelle* style in Los Angeles was chef Jean Bertranou, who opened the elegant L'Ermitage in February 1975. On November 28, 1977, Bertranou held an event for which two of France's greatest *nouvelle* gurus, Paul Bocuse and Roger Vergé (who dueled with comedian Danny Kaye using baguettes of French bread) cooked a spectacular, four-hour *nouvelle* dinner. For the assembled Los Angeles chefs and food lovers the evening was an epiphany, opening their eyes and freeing their imaginations to the possibilities. As *Los Angeles* magazine restaurant critic Bruce David Colen wrote of that evening, "The hosts in white toques discovered that Jean Bertranou . . . was able to supply them with California produce the equal, if not exactly the same, of any in France. Perhaps coming as an even greater surprise to Bocuse and Vergé was the realization that their guests knew a great deal about food and wine, were conversant with the cuisines of many nations and could tell a fine vintage by color and nose without having to sip. That night, the continuing myth of the unsophisticated Californian with the pastel polyester palate was finally laid to rest."

Not only were Los Angelenos ready and willing to support *nouvelle* restaurants, but an influx of foreigners in the early eighties to the Los Angeles region gave further impetus to the fine dining movement there. The *nouvelle* style fit glamorously into the city's show business foreground, and restaurants like Bernard's in the Biltmore Hotel and L'Orangerie, which sat catty-corner to L'Ermitage on La Cienega Boulevard, set new standards for elegance, design, and savoir-faire in a city trying hard to shed its image as Tinseltown.

One of the new-style restaurants that came to synthesize French *nouvelle*-ism with a more casual California swagger was Ma Maison, opened in October 1973. At first this quirky-looking dining room with its patio furniture, lawn-party tent ceiling, garish green carpet, and pompous service seemed merely a bad joke (the restaurant's phone number was snobbily unlisted), but it did draw a Hollywood crowd, and celebrities like Orson Welles would hold forth in a corner, while owner Patrick Terrail walked through the room with a carnation in his lapel and clogs on his feet. It was only after Terrail installed Austrian-born chef Wolfgang Puck in the kitchen that the food got better, more *nouvelle,* and more noticed by the food press. Soon Ma Maison had everything going for it—a high-caliber celebrity clientele, a savvy, eccentric chef who made for good copy, and a style that, despite its goofy glitziness, clicked in the context of Southern California's lifestyle.

The fashion for *nouvelle cuisine* unquestionably contributed greatly to the improvement of fine dining in the United States. The emphasis on fresh, local ingredients, the more careful attention given to cooking time, the preference for grilling and steaming over frying and sautéing, and the loosening of the frayed apron strings of "continental cuisine" all engaged the passions and talents of the brightest people in American food culture. Indeed, when *Playboy* magazine surveyed 120 food writers, chefs, and gastronomes around the country as to what were the top twenty-five restaurants in America in 1980, nine were *nouvelle* establishments, with most of them open less than five years.

There was not a little soul-searching during that period among food lovers who thought perhaps things had gone too far too fast and cost too much. There seemed a deliberate attempt by some *nouvelle* practitioners to shock the palate rather than please it, and more flash than substance to a lot of it. Chefs were becoming celebrities themselves, and people would spend whatever was necessary to prove their restaurant savvy. And there was the troubling, even sickening feeling that it was all too Lucullan and perhaps somewhat amoral to spend so much on the care and feeding of one's appetite. In a review of what was then the most expensive restaurant in the United States in the 1970s, New York's The Palace, Gael Greene voiced concern over what had begun to bother many. "Decadence never goes out of style," she wrote. "It simply convolutes into greater surrealism. Rome burns . . . fiddlers play. Empires teeter . . . there's no room at the orgy. . . . As children we sunned at the beach while millions went hungry. Grown up, we debate the relative grandeurs of a '53 Margaux and a '55 Palmer behind a montage of the swollen bodies of Biafra and Bangladesh. Still, I really feel uneasy spending $197 for two at The Palace."

And American restaurants had strayed very far from Alice's.

Downhome American food made a comeback in the 1980s

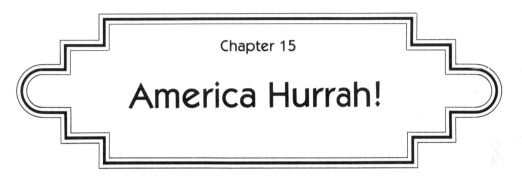

Chapter 15

America Hurrah!

The Rise of Regional and New American Cuisine

IN THE APRIL 1972 ISSUE of *Playboy* magazine, peripatetic author Calvin Trillin wrote, "The best restaurants in the world are, of course, in Kansas City. Not all of them; only the top four or five."

The unqualified, thumb-in-your-eye forthrightness of this statement, had, in its own way, as much impact on American food culture as "Call me Ishmael" had on American literature. Written in response to an article in the same issue by gastronomic writer Roy Andries de Groot entitled "Have I Found the Greatest Restaurant in the World?" about a *nouvelle cuisine* establishment in France's Rhône Valley, Trillin entitled *his* article, "No!" A native-born Kansas City boy, Trillin loved the kind of basic, all-American grub he ate at places like Arthur Bryant's Barbecue, Snead's B-B-Q, Winstead's Drive-in, Stroud's fried chicken restaurant, and Jess & Jim's steakhouse, and hated the kind of food served in continental restaurants (usually set atop bank buildings) with names like "La Maison de la Casa House." "Its food will sound European," Trillin wrote, "but taste as if the continent they had in mind was Australia."

In this and subsequent articles, Trillin sang the praises of the kind of "downhome" dishes most American food writers had long ignored or regarded as little more than rib-sticking fast food that had *nothing* to do with fine dining. For Trillin, a dingy, sit'em-and-serve'em, black-owned barbecue joint like Arthur Bryant's represented everything places like Windows on the World were not, and vice versa. The slowly roasted meat, the peppery, smoky sauce, and the French fries cooked in lard at Bryant's had all been

THE SECOND SYMPOSIUM on American Cuisine, held in New Orleans in April 1983, brought together food authorities from all over the world to discuss the past, present, and future of American gastronomy. Present that weekend at a dinner celebrating the 100th anniversary of Commander's (*opposite*) were Jerry Berns of New York's "21" Club, Commander's Palace owner Ella Brennan (*left of Berns*), food writer James Villas (*far left*), and French food critic Christian Millau (*holding glass*).

GUARDING HER ANONYMITY as a restaurant critic under large hats, *New York* magazine's Gael Greene brought a flamboyant sensuality to food writing balanced by a social conscience that helped bring good food to the ill and infirm through the Meals on Wheels program.

refined over decades into food so delicious, so dependable, and so satisfying that the bland, fussed-over clichés served at most white-tablecloth restaurants made Trillin dyspeptic or simply sad at the thought that places like Bryant's would soon recede into American gastronomic history.

Trillin would go on to write pieces about a crawfish festival in Beaubridges, Louisiana, a barbecue cook-off in Memphis, about the phenomenon of Cincinnati chili as concocted by Greek immigrants, and of how he feared going into "garlic shock" if he allowed himself to eat too much sausage at Buster Holmes's restaurant in New Orleans.

The reason Trillin's articles (collected in three volumes, jokingly referred to as "The Tummy Trilogy" and entitled *American Fried* [1974], *Alice Let's Eat* [1978], and *Third Helpings* [1983]) struck such a nerve in American food culture was that he brought to his subject a refreshingly dry wit along with formidable credentials as the author of a long series of "U.S. Journal" pieces for *The New Yorker* magazine, whose prestige lent a good deal of cachet and credibility to his ruminations on the savoriness of the burned edges of the Bryant's beef brisket. Not only did Arthur Bryant's become famous overnight, but Trillin awoke to find himself a leading proselytizer (what he called his "cheerful glutton persona") for American grub.

Nothing could have surprised Trillin more, for he had never written much about food before, and his only real interest in the subject was in what it said about the culture that produced it. "It was very weird," he later remarked. "Even though I kept protesting that I really didn't know anything about cooking or restaurants, people would use my books as guides to the best American restaurants. That wasn't my intention at all." Eventually Trillin gave up writing articles about food entirely, because, as he puts it, "I just couldn't participate in discussions with people about the relative merits of one potato chip over another."

Before Trillin, there were, of course, food writers who had long championed honest, old-fashioned American cookery—foremost, James Beard, Waverley Root, and Evan Jones—but the food media of the seventies was in the grip of what John and Karen Hess called the "Gourmet Plague." "We would like to see a revival of genuine American cooking," they wrote in *The Taste of America.* "Traces still persist, but fewer and fewer cooks make Maine Lobster Stew, or the chowders, the gumbos, the crab cakes, the baked beans, the oyster loaves, and other great dishes of our past."

The average American might well have been eating those very dishes at home or in local eateries, but among food writers coverage of restaurants serving such food was rare, with the dishes themselves usually relegated to the recipe page of the local newspaper's Wednesday food section along with the tuna casseroles and Jell-O salads. Higher-minded food writers tended to neglect American food and restaurants in favor of *haute cuisine* European models, so that the same 1980 *Playboy* poll of food critics that placed nine *nouvelle cuisine* establishments among the top twenty-five greatest restaurants in the United States listed only six that might be termed "American," and most of those, like New York's "21" Club and Detroit's London Chop House, were more in the "continental" mold than strictly American.

Spurred by the Trillin article, a number of America's foremost food

writers began turning their attention to American regional cooking. The erudite food writer James Villas wrote articles for *Esquire* and *Town & Country* extolling the virtues of real country ham, the glories of hash, the neglect of American cheeses, and the only correct way to make Southern fried chicken. In a style that was both sophisticated and at the same time crusading, Villas would declare, "I don't hesitate for a second to state that I'm as mad about all-American hamburgers as anybody else and am proud that this is still by far the most beloved of our yummy staples." His championing of American restaurants like New York's Coach House, Boston's Locke-Ober, and San Francisco's Jack's conferred on such places a classic status and evocative charm that helped revive an interest in such traditional American dining rooms that might otherwise have been forgotten.

Also in the late seventies former *New York Times* restaurant critic Raymond Sokolov began a series of authoritative articles in *Natural History* magazine chronicling the richness and diversity of what he called "disappearing American regional foods," while in the *Times*'s food pages Craig Claiborne began to profile distinctive American cooks like Cajun Paul Prudhomme, black cook Edna Lewis of Virginia, dessert expert Maida Heatter of Miami, restaurateurs Rose and Richard Cernak of Obrycki's Crab House in Baltimore, and Mexican food authority Diana Kennedy, showing how their work exemplified the finest traditions of gastronomy on a par with anything coming out of Europe.

Two of the most engaging writers to celebrate old-fashioned American restaurants were Jane and Michael Stern in their books *Roadfood* (1977)

CHICAGO-STYLE PIZZA cooked in an iron skillet was created by Ike Sewall and Ric Riccardo in the 1940s at their Pizzeria Uno restaurant in Chicago, and it proliferated throughout the United States, becoming more a standard American item than an Italian dish.

and *Goodfood* (1983), updated and combined into one volume in 1986. In the hallowed "On the Road" tradition of Walt Whitman, Woody Guthrie, and Ken Kesey, the Sterns, who had met while Yale graduate students in 1968, crisscrossed the United States looking for America. Jane Stern had already written a book called *Trucker: A Portrait of the Last American Cowboy* (1975), and the two of them had chronicled some of this country's weirdest and eccentric roadside attractions in *Amazing America* (1977) before setting out to find the purest examples of American food culture at soda shops in Tennessee, tearooms in Georgia, pancake houses in New Hampshire, delis in New York, drive-ins in New Jersey, barbecue pits in North Carolina, boardinghouses in Mississippi, fish camps in Arkansas, oyster bars in New Orleans, bakeries in Minnesota, cafeterias in Oklahoma, coffee shops in California, and steakhouses in South Dakota—all lovingly described with a keen interest in getting at the source and finding out the reasons individual foods took root in certain parts of the country. The Sterns would search out the origins of Buffalo chicken wings (The Anchor Bar in Buffalo, New York), the muffuletta (Central Grocery in New Orleans), the fried dill pickle (The Hollywood in Robinsonville, Mississippi), the best crabhouse in Baltimore (Obrycki's), the best Dungeness crab in Dungeness, Washington (Three Crabs), and the best Indian fry bread in Arizona (the Gila River Arts and Craft Center Restaurant in Sacaton).

The Sterns were savvy enough to realize that they could not treat the atmosphere and service at a Cajun restaurant featuring boiled crawfish with the same fastidious attitude a critic might bring to reviewing a deluxe French restaurant in Manhattan, but their understanding of the simplicity and goodness of the food along the American highway came through without affectation and with a tremendous respect for the people who cooked it. Their admiration for the cooking of blacks, Hispanics, and backwoods people was genuine and their dedication to eating everything they came across was daunting, even when it meant downing a brain sandwich at The

JANE AND MICHAEL STERN chronicled American pop culture in a series of books that included two guides, *Roadfood* (1977) and *Goodfood* (1983), which pinpointed traditional American restaurants serving everything from Buffalo chicken wings to spiced Maryland crabs.

Haven in St. Louis or Rocky Mountain oysters at the Wolf Lodge Inn in Coeur d'Alene, Idaho. Their strict criteria for inclusion in the books were, "Is this restaurant the best of its genre?" and "Does it express the culinary soul of its region?"

The reappreciation of American food was not without its political associations, and it is interesting to note the way those individuals who occupied the White House during the sixties, seventies, and eighties influenced the way certain foods were perceived. During John F. Kennedy's tenure, he was credited with bringing a worldly international style of entertaining to the White House, but despite his New England heritage, did nothing to promote American food or wines. Texan Lyndon Johnson, on the other hand, was ridiculed for entertaining foreign guests at down-on-the-ranch barbecues, which to the counterculture food press represented insidious American machismo in its most carnivorous form. Richard Nixon's Imperial Presidency did little for American food (he much preferred French wines to American), but his trips to China had a decided effect on helping to popularize Chinese restaurants in this country. Gerald Ford's Michigan background failed to stir any interest in the food of that region, but when Georgia peanut farmer Jimmy Carter rose to the office in 1977, there was a good deal of interest in the foods of the South, just as there was in the California style of entertaining when Ronald and Nancy Reagan entered the White House. And George Bush endeared himself to the common man when he expressed his fondness for fried pork rinds and his dislike of broccoli.

Oddly enough, the infatuation with *nouvelle cuisine* was itself causing a reexamination of American food and an appreciation for fresh, local provender, which, according to *nouvelle* tenets, was the first requisite for good cooking. Indeed, even the inventors of the term *nouvelle cuisine,* Henri Gault and Christian Millau, exhorted Americans to develop their own style of cooking. "Cuisine is a reflection of a culture," they said, "and it would be absolutely abnormal for Americans to allow foreigners the exclusivity of nourishing them."

There was much more variety in the marketplace and American wines were not just getting better in the 1970s; they were being successfully promoted in a series of blind tastings designed to show their competitiveness with the best wines from France.

It was only a matter of time before young American chefs would try to wed what they'd learned of French technique and ethnic ingredients to their own culinary traditions in an effort to create something both new, while at the same time rooted in American tradition. Repeating the pretty patterns and recipes of the French masters was just another kind of conformity, one that simply did not allow enough room for self-expression. It was time for a "new" American cuisine to be formulated and publicized.

Despite her devotion to French Provençal and Mediterranean cooking, Alice Waters continued to be a maternal source of inspiration to young chefs who saw in her work at Chez Panisse the single-mindedness to run a restaurant exactly as she pleased. Chez Panisse became a mecca for those who would cook with only the very best the land had to offer and to utilize the bounty of California's farms and vineyards as the basis for personal experimentation.

One of those drawn to Chez Panisse with somewhat less lofty ambitions (he was down to his last five dollars) was a Harvard graduate student named Jeremiah Tower, who had emigrated to California in 1972 because he figured it was the only place where he could use his training as an underwater architect. Finding no work in his field, Tower bluffed his way into a job as cook at Chez Panisse by adding a little salt and cream to a soup Waters asked him to improve. Before long he'd became, almost by default, head chef at the restaurant. Six years later he opened his own place, the Balboa Café, where he featured a simple menu based on meats, fish, and vegetables grilled over a native American wood called mesquite that gave off an intense, smoky heat and flavor. Tower next took over the Santa Fe Bar & Grill, where he specialized in using Southwest ingredients in novel dishes like black bean cakes with sour cream and grilled salmon with lime butter, and he delighted in refining old-fashioned items like vanilla ice cream with caramel sauce and pecans. By the time Tower sold off those restaurants in 1984 to open what he called "an American Brasserie" named Stars, he had developed a reputation as one of the innovators of what was being heralded as "California Cuisine," a subject he discussed in May 1984 at a week-long exposition in Hong Kong.

Yet Tower later scoffed at the label because he found it too confining and too full of overnight clichés. For the hallmarks of California Cuisine had developed quickly—a reliance on mesquite-grilled foods, a sublimation of salads to main-course status, a tendency to undercook vegetables, meat, and fish, an explosion of colors on the plate (including items like baby vegetables, purple potatoes, and exotica like kiwi fruit), goat-cheese-covered pizzas, and a chauvinism about California wines from the Napa and Sonoma valleys. And chefs throughout the United States picked up on them more as gimmicks than as the starting points for a new gastronomy.

"California Cuisine really wasn't about goat cheese and Sonoma lamb and fresh herbs and baby this and baby that," said Michael McCarty, who at the age of twenty-five in 1979 opened a *nouvelle* French restaurant called Michael's in Santa Monica that mainifested a glamorous but casual Southern California lifestyle. "It was more of a philosophy. Just as the young chefs in France caused the *nouvelle* revolution, so we in California said, hey, everything was fine and we're not demeaning the kind of food then being cooked, but we've got another generation of diners out there, of fashion and art, and food and wine that are all part of *our* revolution. And as Californians we're very susceptible to new ideas and very eager, almost like pioneers, to try anything and just be fascinated by the new ingredients we were able to bring in."

McCarty's realization of these new developments was seamlessly synthesized at Michael's with its cool peach-colored walls, its striking artwork by painters like David Hockney and Jim Dine, its open-air garden patio, and its beautifully arranged *nouvelle cuisine.* McCarty had grown up in suburban New York, trained in business at the University of Colorado, lived in France, studied art, and learned to cook at the Cordon Bleu and Académie du Vin, all influences he brought to bear at Michael's. He dressed his waiters in khaki chino slacks, pink Oxford shirts, and knit ties, a uniform much copied by other restaurateurs, and he encouraged a friendly, sometimes win-

some, but always knowledgeable approach to service that came to epitomize the California style. And, even though his food was *nouvelle*-inspired (and the menu entirely in French), McCarty proclaimed proudly that "it's American food because *I'm* American." With his gift for self-promotion and a skill for picking young American chefs attuned to his philosophy, McCarty, more than anyone else of that era, gave the California Cuisine movement its panache and its dazzle.

But it was another Los Angeles chef—an Austrian named Wolfgang Puck—who made it resonate loudly across the country. Puck's own background had involved the usual slow, disciplined, European training process in both classic and *nouvelle* restaurants like L'Oustau de Baumanière in Les Baux de Provence and Maxim's in Paris. He came to the United States at the age of nineteen, worked at a French restaurant in Indianapolis called La Tour, and was then hired in 1975 by Patrick Terrail to take over the kitchen of Ma Maison in Los Angeles. "It was losing eighteen thousand dollars a month when I got there," Puck remembered, "but three months later it grossed one hundred fifty thousand dollars." The turnaround came when Puck introduced a lighter *nouvelle cuisine* to a clientele constantly on a diet,

THE STYLE of so-called "California Cuisine" derived many of its hallmarks from Michael's in Santa Monica, where owner Michael McCarty popularized casual, chic outdoor dining together with American adaptions of French *nouvelle cuisine*. He was also one of the first to hang first-rate artwork by modern American painters and sculptors in his dining rooms.

although he never sacrificed flavor and never stinted in his use of butter sauces or cream in his desserts. He also provided very good copy for the California press, who found in him the kind of exuberant personality most chefs of the day lacked. By 1980 Ma Maison was the most exciting restaurant in Los Angeles, with equal measures of Hollywood celebrities and food markedly different from anyone else's.

Puck had another idea—he wanted to open a really good pizza restaurant of his own—so, after a falling out with Terrail in 1980 and with the financial backing of a local dentist named Don Salk, Puck and his wife, Barbara Lazaroff, took over an old Russian-Armenian restaurant on Sunset Boulevard, gave it a whitened, casual barnlike interior with a grill kitchen open to the dining room, and called it Spago (Italian for "string"). The original pizzeria idea was quickly expanded into a full-service restaurant with an enticing menu of savory dishes like black pepper noodles with smoked duck and radicchio lettuce, red snapper with a spicy pecan butter, and an array of desserts that ran from classic French chocolate *marjolaine* cake to an old-fashioned (but much refined) blueberry buttermilk tart. He did offer pizzas, but they were a far cry from the traditional tomato-and-mozzarella pie found around town. Puck topped his pizza with smoked salmon and golden caviar (he called it "Jewish pizza"). His food had snap and color to it, and so did Puck, who wore a baseball cap in the dining room instead of the traditional chef's white toque, and his wife Barbara worked hard to attract and keep happy the show business community who made Spago into the most publicized restaurant in America at the beginning of the 1980s.

Puck would try anything to keep things exciting. "I never considered myself a trend-setter," said Puck. "I just get bored easily." And he dismissed those critics who complained his food had strayed too far from traditional restaurant fare by saying, "I'd rather make a great pizza than make some dish with canned truffles."

Puck's next move was even more daring—a restaurant called Chinois on Main that created a hybrid form of French and Chinese cuisine that applied all his European cooking techniques to exotic Oriental ingredients. Lazaroff designed a deliberately dissonant dining room full of life-size cloisonné cranes, Chinese artifacts, and modern California artwork, so that the room's eccentric decor mirrored the iconoclastic style of Puck's cooking.

Puck's unique flair for public taste flourished in a city that thrived on showmanship. But the style of California Cuisine—and the decor of California restaurants—were just as irresistible to the rest of the country, so that the stark, breezy look, casual service, and gorgeous-looking food burst upon the national restaurant landscape with a seductive power to enthrall customers and to excite chefs in a decade when Americans were becoming increasingly serious about dining out as entertainment.

Many chefs and restaurateurs saw the promotional value of slapping a regional label onto such a style, so that restaurateurs in various parts of the United States would proclaim that their use of fresh local ingredients cooked by classic techniques could be conveniently fitted out with a name like "New Southwest," "New Texan," "New New England," "New South,"

NO AMERICAN CHEF since Henri Soulé did more to influence the style and taste of restaurants than Austrian-born Wolfgang Puck, chef-owner of Los Angeles's Spago, which featured an open kitchen, a devil-may-care attitude toward dishes like pizza, lots of grilled foods, and a nightly crowd of Hollywood celebrities.

"New Midwest," "New Northwest," or, as an umbrella term, "New American Cuisine," all of which shared, to one extent or another, the style points set by California chefs like Waters, Tower, McCarty, Puck, and others.

For many, "New American Cuisine" (or the more proletarian "New American Cooking") was nothing more than a fashion or a way to spike up a menu and a dining room decor. One might as soon find a goat cheese pizza with fiddlehead ferns on a menu in Boston as one would a goat cheese pizza with andouille sausage in New Orleans or a goat cheese pizza with chile peppers in Tucson. In the hands of a recent convert to the New American style, many dishes were concocted according to concepts rather than good taste and were designed to attract attention rather than to please the palate. Too often, the results were disastrous, sometimes hilarious, and occasionally disturbing. There was a good deal of Yankee hubris involved in the exploitation of the New American Cooking movement, although some did it with a naïve belief that anything was all right as long as it was something new. As Ellen Brown wrote in *Cooking with the New American Chefs* (1985), "The new American chefs have no sense of inferiority."

For the best of them, however, the idea of a serious, orderly development of an genuine regional gastronomy came as a true challenge worth more than a season's fancy. One of the earliest and most dedicated of these young chefs on the East Coast was Lawrence Forgione. Born in Long Island, New York, Forgione was a physical education major at a West Virginia college before he developed an interest in cooking that landed him in the Culinary Institute of America, from which he graduated in 1974. After a low-paying stint at London's famed Connaught Hotel, Forgione returned to New York in 1977 to learn the French *nouvelle* style under master chef Michel Guérard at a nightclub-restaurant called Regine's, then became head chef at a beautifully situated restaurant under New York's majestic Brooklyn Bridge called the River Café. Here Forgione was given free reign to develop his own eclectic style that impressed both critics and customers with its extravagance and unorthodox look. But the success of the River Café also allowed Forgione to establish sources for first-rate provender, even to coaxing an upstate farmer named Paul Kaiser to raise free-range chickens for the kitchens of the Café and other restaurants.

By the time Forgione opened his own restaurant, An American Place, in 1983, he had fallen under the influence of the recognized "dean" of American cooking, James Beard, who urged the young chef to cook and to refine the foods of America's great culinary tradition, whether it was a chowder from New England, a grilled rib-eye, or an apple pandowdy. Forgione came to believe fervently that no great cuisine could ever be based on imported ingredients, and he became manic about using only American products. "I want to give American food of the future an integrity by looking to the past," Forgione told Ellen Brown, "but I'm cooking in the present. My food must reflect that present, and I don't do slavish recreations of historic dishes, even those dishes with distinct roots in the past."

To bolster his philosophic stance, Forgione, like the grand restaurateurs of the Gilded Age, listed the provenance of his ingredients right on the menu, so that a typical night's offerings might include Key West shrimp with mustard sauce, Olympia oysters over pasta, herb crêpes filled with Calistoga goat cheese, Albermarle Sound pine bark fish soup, veal steak with Montana jerky sauce, New York State duck *foie gras,* Louisiana soft-shell crabs with sweet potatoes, and a salad made from endive raised on a farm in the Bronx.

Forgione was one of the first to take this line of culinary logic, but colleagues in the New American movement adopted it and proudly announced their preference for local products. The movement gained speed quickly. In the same year An American Place opened, Jasper White opened a restaurant in Boston under his own name, where he specialized in and refined the foods of New England, using cranberries, beach plums, Vermont Cheddar cheese, cob-smoked hams, apple cider, maple syrup, and the entire bounty of the North Atlantic to make modern versions of chowder, New England boiled dinner, Indian pudding, and pumpkin pie. At his restaurant The Trellis in Historic Williamsburg, Virginia, Rhode Island-born chef Mar-

SEVERAL OF THE YOUNG LEADERS of the "New American Cooking" movement are shown here celebrating a Meals on Wheels charity dinner. *From left to right* are Alfred Portale, unidentified, Lawrence Forgione, and Jonathan Waxman.

cel Desaulniers adapted the style of California cooking to seasonal menus based on local delicacies like Smithfield ham, Urbana ducks, Surry sausage, Chesapeake seafood, and wines from Virginia and Maryland. Michigan-born Brad Ogden reveled in creating new dishes with old-fashioned Midwestern ingredients at The American Restaurant in Kansas City, and later, at the Lark Creek Inn in Larkspur, California, while Richard Perry, at his namesake restaurant in St. Louis, took his inspiration from the kinds of foods traditionally served on Midwestern farms and at boardinghouses and then modernized them in dishes like roast pheasant with country sausage and apricot and gooseberry sauce, or grilled rabbit sausage with Ozark honey mustard. In Santa Fe, New Mexico, Chez Panisse graduate Mark Miller opened a restaurant called the Coyote Café that prided itself on its support of local farmers paid to raise an entire range of chile peppers, blue corn, and livestock to the restaurant's specifications. Nothing so delighted Miller as coming upon exotica like *huitlacoche,* a corn fungus that tastes like morel mushrooms.

A whole group of young Texas chefs appeared in the eighties who sought to sublimate the image of their state's cuisine, which had long been a mix of Southern farm cooking, cowboy ranch cooking, and bowdlerized Mexican cooking, into a cuisine as complex as anything to be found in Escoffier. They sought out the best seafood from the Gulf, game from the prairies, fruits and vegetables from the farms, and wines from a growing number of vineyards in regions around the Hill Country of Lubbock, Tow, and New Braunfels.

At the Mansion on Turtle Creek in Dallas, chef Dean Fearing would take an old idea like tortilla soup and turn it into a signature dish or an old-fashioned childhood dessert like sweet potato pie and make it a dish fit for the most demanding gourmet. So, too, Dallas chef Stephan Pyles (who started out to be a musician) of the Routh Street Café, Anne Greer (a former art major) of the Nana Grill in Houston, and Robert Del Grande (with a Ph.D. in biology) of Café Annie also in Houston would radically alter Texas's image as a state whose restaurants had only recently been hopelessly dated.

No chef was more important to the New American Cooking movement than the redoubtable Paul Prudhomme, who singlehandedly stirred up a national appetite for a kind of cooking barely known outside of the Louisiana bayous and not even much appreciated in Creole-loving New Orleans. Prudhomme came out of Opelousas, the youngest of thirteen farm-born Cajuns who loved nothing better than to eat, as was obvious from his girth, and he emanated the very soul of his people in his laugh and in his obvious relish for the good things in life. As a media personality, he even had the right résumé: Prudhomme started out at the age of seventeen running a hamburger stand called Big Daddy-O's Patio in Opelousas, then in the mid-seventies became a cook, then head chef, at the renowned Commander's Palace, run by Ella and Dick Brennan in New Orleans's Garden District. There, with the full support of owners Ella and Dick Brennan, Prudhomme proceeded to establish himself as one of the best chefs in a great eating-out city by refining and updating Creole cooking. In 1979 he and his wife, Kay Hinrichs, opened a second-story po' boy sandwich shop called K-Paul's on Chartres Street in the French Quarter, but before long the tiny storefront was serving complete meals in surroundings cunningly designed to look makeshift and downhome but that also reflected Prudhomme's stubborn belief that the lunchroom atmosphere, the sharing of tables with strangers, and the sassy waitresses who stuck paper stars on the cheeks of those who cleaned their plates were crucial to an appreciation of his people's food culture.

Prudhomme did not just set the standards for Cajun food; he created a whole cookery all on his own, for the richness of his food and the liberal use of hot peppers were but derived from bayou cookery and manifested Prudhomme's own individual and distinctive taste for complex, multilevel flavors coaxed out of the best possible ingredients. "I used to wonder why

the simple boiled red potatoes my mother used to make tasted so different from those I got in restaurants," Prudhomme recalled. "Then I realized that it was because my mamma's were plucked right out of our farmland that morning and cooked that afternoon."

K-Paul's Louisiana Kitchen was a local novelty at first, but after being "discovered" by the national press, the restaurant's reputation soared and long lines of customers (most of them out-of-towners) stretched down Chartres Street every night of the week. Prudhomme's food was stunningly seasoned; even his "Cajun Martini" had a chile pepper in it, and his "blackened redfish" (a local catch heavily spiced and seared in plenty of butter in a black iron skillet) became the most copied dish in America since Antoine's invented oysters Rockefeller in 1899—so much so that the federal government had to ban commercial fishing of the species so that it would not be completely fished out within a few years.

Prudhomme's fame spread like a Gulf oil fire. His cookbook sold in excess of seven hundred thousand copies when it was published in 1986, and his TV cooking video became a best seller. Nationally, Prudhomme-style Cajun restaurants popped up from Maine to Oregon, and the "rage for Cajun" became a culinary phenomenon like nothing ever seen before in American gastronomic history.

But then, American food was all the rage in the mid-eighties, from diners to *haute* dining rooms. Older American restaurants like New York's Coach House and Peter Luger's, Kansas City's Savoy Grill, Miami's Joe's Stone Crab, New Orleans's Arnaud's, Galatoire's, Brennan's, and Antoine's, San Francisco's Jack's and Sam's, and Los Angeles's Musso & Frank's came to be regarded as keepers of the flame of America's gastronomy, while barbecue pits, crabshacks, and fish camps took on folkloric proportions as writers began to research America's food culture with gusto and a kind of scholarly interest unimaginable a decade before.

Restaurant chefs published scores of cookbooks, and collections of regional recipes poured out of the publishing houses. There was even a campy book called *White Trash Cooking* (1986), by Ernest M. Mickler, that set down the kinds of food (like potato chip sandwiches) supposedly enjoyed by poor Southern whites.

American cooking had become all the fashion. In restaurants, the waiters wore their khaki trousers and Oxford shirts and the cooks all sported baseball caps. The kitchens were open for all to see and belched forth the aroma of mesquite. New Age music wafted from unseen speakers. And people came to talk of free-range chickens, poblano chilies, and Willamette Valley Pinot Noirs.

Chefs became celebrities and hit the talkshow trail, leaving their kitchens frequently in pursuit of national recognition. There were symposiums held in every state to debate the question of just what *was* American cooking, and Julia Child, long known as PBS-TV's "French Chef," began featuring American food on her shows and founded an organization called the American Institute of Wine and Food to promote scholarly investigation of American food culture.

By the mid-eighties the New American Cooking movement seemed securely on track, rushing forward with momentum, conviction, money, and a crusading impulsiveness that made it seem bound for glory. And then, suddenly, it all slowed down and came to a grinding halt.

IN THE 1980s, PBS-TV's "French Chef," Julia Child (*left*), began to champion American cooking, while chef Paul Prudhomme (*above*) elevated downhome Cajun cooking to a national fad at his restaurant K-Paul's Louisiana Kitchen in New Orleans.

251

The Sci-Fi Dine-In Theater Restaurant at the Disney-MGM Studios, Lake Buena Vista, Florida, 1991

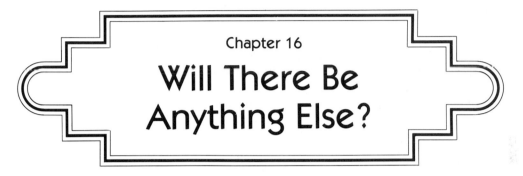

Chapter 16

Will There Be Anything Else?

The Future of the Restaurant in America

ANEW WORD ENTERED the English language in 1982 to describe a person for whom food becomes as much a hobby, pastime, and topic of discussion as art, politics, or sports—"Foodie." The term was first used in an article entitled "Cuisine Poseur" in the English magazine *Harper & Queen* in August 1982, two years later amplified into a satiric book called *The Official Foodie Handbook,* whose cover line read, "Be Modern—Worship Food."

"A Foodie is a person who is very very interested in food," wrote authors Ann Barr and Paul Levy. "Foodies are the ones talking about food in any gathering—salivating over restaurants, recipes, radicchio. They don't think they are being trivial—Foodies consider food to be an art, on a level with painting or drama."

The authors went on to pinion New York as the "hot-plate of Foodism," just as the London *Times* in December 1983 called New York the "eating capital of the world, a city devoted to its stomach," and by any measure that would seemed to have been true. With its concentration of more than sixteen thousand restaurants, its competitive food media, and a business community that subsisted on lavish business lunches, New York's capacity to absorb the best and worst in food culture, both domestic and foreign, had indeed made it the eating capital of the world. It had outstripped Paris not because the quality of New York's cuisine was higher (although it was gaining fast), but because it was generating the food world's news just as its panoply of restaurants created an excitement all of their own.

The city had acquired not only a solid core of classical, as well as *nouvelle* French and Italian restaurants and enjoyed an explosion of other ethnic restaurants. It had also been a crucible for the New American Cooking movement with restaurants like An American Place, Huberts, Arizona 206, Jams, Gotham Bar & Grill, and Arcadia. And it was also a standard-bearer of traditional American cookery with historic restaurants like Gage & Tollner, Peter Luger, The Palm, The Coach House, The Gloucester House, "21" Club, Fraunces Tavern, The Homestead, The Grand Central Oyster Bar & Restaurant, and many others. It had a large, thriving Chinatown, a picturesque Little Italy, and new ethnic communities were forming and reforming throughout the five boroughs—all of them feeding off what seemed an unlimited supply of customers night after night.

As a Foodie City par excellence, Los Angeles was easily a close second to New York and teemed with restaurants that looked like Hollywood sets and germinated out of a show business beatitude that novelty for its own sake was sufficient reason for existing. A glorious French château-style restaurant named L'Orangerie would be flanked by stretches of dreary retail stores on La Cienega Boulevard. A restaurant at the Santa Monica Airport was named after the workhorse airliner, the DC-3, and resembled a sound stage fitted out for a movie about the Twenty-third century, yet the menu was full of French bourgeois and American downhome classics.

Chicago was more of a copycat town when it came to restaurants, led by one of the most imaginative restaurant companies ever to appear on the American scene. It was called Lettuce Entertain You Enterprises, Inc., a double entendre linking a vegetable to the title of a song sung by stripteasers in the musical *Gypsy*. The real mover behind Lettuce was a college dropout and macrobiotic food enthusiast named Rich Melman, who on June 10, 1971, with real estate agent and haberdasher Jerry A. Orzoff, opened a singles' bar/restaurant in Chicago named R. J. Grunts, whose main gimmick was a "salad bar" offering forty different items from which customers (many of whom were hippies or members of the counterculture) concocted their own salads. (R. J. Grunts was named after "Rich," "Jerry," and a sound one of Orzoff's girlfriends made when she ate.) With the same sense of personal style that had characterized all the great American restaurateurs, Melman (Orzoff died in 1981) deliberately went against the prevailing, rather conservative status quo in Chicago and conceived a series of theme restaurants that were fun to be in, attracted enormous crowds of young people, and were unlike anything else in the city.

Melman would take concepts he saw in cities like New York, Los Angeles, and San Francisco, and adapt them to his targeted market. Every project was based on a thorough examination of the market and involved an extraordinary attention to detail, whether Lettuce was designing a deluxe *nouvelle cuisine* dining room like Ambria (1980) or a send-up of 1950s diners like Ed Debevic's (1984). He would build an authentic, if garishly decorated, Spanish *tapas* restaurant and give it a hipster's name—Café Ba-Ba-Reeba! (1985)—or install a Japanese sushi bar at a Mexican restaurant called Hat Dance (1988), whose principal decorations consisted of umbrellas hanging upside down from the ceiling. When Lettuce opened an enormous trattoria called Scoozi! (1986), the walls were aged to simulate those in a Tuscan

CHICAGO'S Lettuce Entertain You Enterprises, led by Rich Melman, in the 1980s lovingly re-created the nostalgic appeal of 1950s diners at several Ed Debevic's restaurants (named after a fictitious Polish-American proprietor), complete with stainless-steel accents, Formica tables, and menus, full of meat loaf, mashed potatoes, and Jell-O desserts.

restaurant hundreds of years old, while the woodwork at Shaw's Crab House (1985) was thickly varnished to make the place look as if it had always been there.

Melman's philosophy almost seemed to be, "How much fun can we possibly have with this concept and still get away with it?"—an attitude manifest in Bub City Crab Shack & B-B-Q, which was set up in 1990 in an old industrial building, fitted out with cheap plywood walls, animal heads, chicken wire, and bar stools, and made to look like a Southern road house.

Melman seemed equally adept at conceptualizing the most elegant dining rooms as he did barbecue joints: Having taken over the management of the revered Pump Room in the Ambassador East Hotel in 1976, Melman opened Chicago's acclaimed restaurant The Everest Room in 1986. But his forte was in plumbing young Americans' abiding affection for casual, reasonably priced restaurants where there was a party atmosphere every night of the week.

Melman read well Americans' nostalgia for the era of good feelings and prosperity that seemed to characterize the decade of the 1950s, and he drew on the iconography of the neighborhood luncheonette or roadside diner. In creating the concept for the Ed Debevic's diners, Melman invented a fictitious Polish-sounding owner and re-created not the streamlined diner look of the 1930s but a 1950s California coffee shop design that to Americans born after 1960 had an old-fashioned, slightly campy atmosphere, right down to having employees act out stereotypical roles like the fast-talking waitress or nerdy-looking waiter. The menu listed everything from meat loaf and mashed potatoes to a whole array of Jell-O salads—foods once relegated to the dumpster of gastronomic history and deliberately at odds with modern concerns about lighter, healthier foods. Ironically, the meat loaf/milk shake/cole slaw foods came to be called "comfort foods," a buzzword that depended on nostalgia for its hard sell.

Ed Debevic's was a good joke, and it worked. Melman opened units around Chicago, in Beverly Hills, in Phoenix, New York, and even Osaka, Japan. After all, how seriously could you take food and restaurants anyway? In this, Melman was at once making fun of the Foodies' mentality while at the same time devoting as much intelligence, diligence, and attention to detail as Joe Baum might to Windows on the World.

In fact, the nostalgia for diners reached its peak in the 1980s, with brand-new ones built from scratch to incorporate various design elements so as to represent an American dream of diners—sleek, spick-and-span clean, ribbed with neon and glittering surfaces. The apotheosis of this kind of nostalgic reverie was Boogies Diner, opened in 1987 in Aspen, Colorado, by Merry-Go-Round Enterprises, Inc., with another opened in 1990 in Washington's Georgetown, which combined a retail clothing store with a spectacular-looking restaurant whose motto was "Eat Heavy, Dress Cool." Taking the cue from the enormously successful Hard Rock Cafe chain of upscale American eateries (whose leitmotiv was a classic 1950s car sticking out over the doorway), Boogies was originally conceived by an offbeat renegade clothing retailer named Leonard "Boogie" Wineglass, whose antic behavior inspired a character in the 1985 movie *Diner* set in Baltimore.

The Georgetown Boogies, set on two levels, evoked the style of the 1950s diner with its soda fountain counter, vinyl-covered booths, and speckled laminated surfaces in fifties colors like avocado, grape, and bright red, all of it dominated by a unique forty-foot, stainless-steel clock tower whose pendulum sported a 1947 Harley-Davidson motorcycle. The early rock 'n' roll theme was carried through in the menus, which broke down foods into categories like "Oldies But Goodies" and "Boogies Greatest Hits," and featured dishes like "Elvis' Favorite—The Hound Dog" (a chili-sauced hot dog with cheese, onions, and sauerkraut) and "The Garden Party" salad (named after a popular song of the 1970s by the late rock star Rick Nelson).

Not all of the new diners served the kind of old-fashioned roadhouse fare that gave the original models the sobriquet of "greasy spoons," offering instead the kinds of dishes that went under the banner of the New American Cooking. Places like San Francisco's Fog City Diner, Atlanta's Buckhead Diner, and New York's Empire Diner featured more sophisticated food that almost seemed the antithesis of the fare offered at the early immigrant-owned diners, and even a simple item like a BLT sandwich might be made with freshly made brioche bread, just-whipped mayonnaise, local hickory-smoked bacon, and tomatoes and lettuce from an organic farm. The ice creams and desserts would be made on the premises and the chocolate sauce prepared from imported Swiss chocolate.

It was all part of the new fantasies that stirred Foodies' passions for novelty (even wrapped in the guise of the past) and a quest for the quintessential recipe—what Calvin Trillin called the "One Perfect Raspberry" school of cooking. Fueled by an overheated economy built on two-career couples' incomes, restaurants became larger, more theatrical and, on the whole, much more concerned with the kind of quality for which Americans would happily pay.

No longer were restaurants a once-in-a-blue-moon extravagance or saved for a celebratory occasion. No more were posh dining rooms at places like the "21" Club and La Côte Basque in New York, Chasen's in Los Angeles, and Tony's in Houston the restricted enclaves of high society. More people than ever had more money than ever (and in the big cities larger expense accounts) and were more interested than ever in the experience of dining out. So much so that the cover story for *New York* magazine for November 26, 1984, was entitled "Sex, Exercise and Apartment Hunting Can't Match Restaurant Madness," in which author Patricia Morrisroe wrote, "More and more people feel entitled to what was once the preserve of the wealthy, and in accommodating these people, restaurateurs have democratized dining."

They also had to figure out how to keep those customers coming back, or how to get them to come in to a new restaurant in the first place.

The result was more and more extravagance, more eighty-seat restaurants costing millions of dollars, larger, grander cafés with deafening decibel levels, more reliance on public relations than good taste, and an urgency to come up with still another gimmick, which might appear in the form of a bright young chef who was trying to meld elements of American, French, Italian, Spanish, Thai, and Chinese cuisine all on one menu—what came to be called "Fusion Cuisine."

Restaurateurs who had never set foot in the Caribbean would get a chef to design a menu of upgraded dishes like Stamp and Go or conch fritters, while others indulged themselves in what was termed "Pacific Rim Cooking," incorporating all the flavors from cultures as disparate as Micronesia, Burma, Japan, and Southern California into their sauté pans.

In 1989 San Francisco's Jeremiah Tower opened a restaurant called "690" (the number of his address on Van Ness Avenue), where he served everything from Indian pappadum wafers to a duck Calalu stew and lobster with Thai basil sauce. In Los Angeles at City Restaurant (opened in 1985) Mary Sue Milliken and Susan Feniger would list Italian pasta, Austrian Linzer torte, Thai melon salad, and Portuguese mussel-and-cockle stew all on the same menu. In Washington, D.C., a restaurant called Cities featured the cookery of a different international city each month, and at New York's Quilted Giraffe, owners Barry and Susan Wine served everything from classic French duck *confit* to tuna-topped *wasabi* pizza to full *kaiseki* Japanese tasting menus. Lydia Shire, one of the early proponents of "New New England Cooking" opened a place in Boston in 1989 called Biba, where she featured dishes like calf's brains with brown butter, tuna sashimi, roast suckling pig, Italian mascarpone soufflé, and Indian tandoori breads. Echoing Wolfgang Puck's remark, Shire said, "Boredom sets in at a certain point cooking the same old dishes. I still keep classics like finnan haddie chowder and mashed potatoes on my menu, but there's so much competition out there, that you need to look for unusual, challenging foods to satisfy the public."

Concomitant with all this experimentation was a growing sentiment among Foodies that fused Americans' ancient Puritan abstemiousness with the counterculture's holistic view of food and the environment. The more enjoyment experienced by an eater, the more guilt he was made to feel, so that those who could easily afford to indulge their appetites for any food or restaurant found that such behavior took its toll on the waistline, the internal organs, and the psyche. It was ironic then that The Four Seasons, which when it opened in 1959 had dedicated itself to all the unalloyed pleasures of the epicure's table, in 1983 created special menus that were lower in calories, cholesterol, sodium, and fat for those regular customers who were "forced" to dine there on business several days a week. Chef Seppi Renggli in consultation with Dr. Myron Winick, the director of the Institute for Human Nutrition at Columbia University's College of Physicians and Surgeons, came up with a trademark name for this new menu—Spa Cuisine—and the idea took flight immediately.

The concerns for nutrition, long life, and youthful appearance took hold of American gastronomy in the eighties, so that foods were often characterized as "good" or "bad," and the use of the word "healthy" on a menu came to have a certain elitist snob appeal for some customers while thoroughly depressing others. Butter and cream, once the mainstays of classic cooking, were discarded in favor of saffron oil and yogurt. Seafood was steamed rather than fried, sauces were left off entirely, and rich desserts eschewed in favor of exorbitantly priced, often out-of-season berries. Mineral water was to be preferred to spirits or wine.

The dilemma of affluence had come down to a choice between hedonism

RESTAURANTS IN THE 1980s began catering to diet-restricted customers with low-calorie, low-salt, low-fat dishes on their menus, as in the "Alternative Cuisine" items offered by **The Four Seasons'** Hotel chain, whose **Fountain** restaurant menu in Philadelphia lists such "nutritionally balanced" dishes. Savvy restaurateurs also began offering special items for their international clientele, as shown by the Japanese breakfast offered at the Four Seasons' Aujourd'hui restaurant in Boston (see page 260).

WEDNESDAY, JUNE 12, 1991

Cold Gazpacho Soup with Basil and Cucumber 4.00

Caesar Salad with Croutons 5.00

Black Ink Capellini with Sautéed Squid, Shrimp and Baby Scallops, White Wine Jus 5.50

* Grilled Tuna Fillet with Corn Salsa and Coriander Jus 6.00

* Carpaccio of Beef with Mesclun Salad, Goat Cheese and Walnut Vinaigrette 5.50

Baby Vegetable and Thai Noodle Salad with Oriental Honey Mustard Chicken 6.00

* * *

* Boston Lettuce, Endive, Radicchio Salad with Dijon Vinaigrette 5.50

Chilled Mushroom Soup 3.75

* * *

Baby Shrimp, Jumbo Lump Crabmeat and Scallop Salad with Dijon and Dill Dressing 14.50

* Papardelle Pasta, Sautéed Chicken, Spinach and Ginger Soy Jus 15.50

Sautéed Coho Salmon with Parsley Crust, Julienne of Vegetable and Caper Jus 16.50

Grilled Marinated Lamb Steak with Couscous and Mustard Jus 15.50

* Sautéed Sea Scallops with Angel Hair Pasta, Asparagus and Curry Jus 16.00

Braised Veal Shank with Tomato, Black Olives, Orzo Pasta and Anchovy Butter 14.50

Sautéed Crab Cake and Rigatoni with Spicy Tomato and Basil 16.50

Roasted Cornish Hen with Potato Purée, Peas and Thyme Jus 15.00

* Vermicelli "Primavera" Style with Herb Jus 13.50

* Sautéed Cod Fillet with Steamed Spaghetti Squash, Red Pepper Coulis 14.50

Grilled New York Strip Steak with Black Peppercorn Brandy Sauce and Macaroni au Gratin 15.50

* <u>Four Seasons Alternative Cuisine</u>
These selections are nutritionally balanced, lower in calories, cholesterol, sodium and fat.
These items meet approval of the Thomas Jefferson University Hospital's
"Dining with Heart" Program.

Anthony C. Clark   Brenda Thompson
Chef de Restaurant   Restaurant Manager

Jean-Marie Lacroix
Executive Chef

Cigar and pipe smoking is not permitted in the Restaurant.
A section is available in the Swann Lounge.

Alternative Cuisine Breakfast

*These selections are nutritionally balanced,
lower in calories, cholesterol, sodium and fat.
Margarine served upon request.*

Home mixed Natural Grains and Fruits
Skim Milk
Carrot Bran Muffin, Natural Apple puree
Brewed Decaffeinated Coffee or Selection of Teas
8.75

Pressed Apple Juice
Cholesterol Free Omelette with Shiitake
and Sun-Dried Tomatoes
Seven Grain Toast, Corn Oil Margarine
Brewed Decaffeinated Coffee or Tea
11.00

Coupe of Mixed Seasonal Berries
Cinnamon Oat Bran Pancakes with Banana Syrup
Brewed Decaffeinated Coffee or Tea
9.25

Continental Breakfast
Choice of Juice
Breakfast Breads or Pastries
Preserves or Honey, Sweet Butter
Coffee, Tea, Hot Chocolate or Milk
9.75

Traditional Breakfast
Choice of Juice
Two Eggs, any style with Bacon, Ham or Sausage
Breakfast Breads or Pastries
Preserves or Honey, Sweet Butter
Coffee, Tea, Hot Chocolate or Milk
12.50

Beverages
Coffee, Decaffeinated Coffee 2.25
Selection of Teas 2.25
Hot Chocolate 3.00
Regular or Skim Milk 2.00
Espresso 2.75

Japanese Breakfast

さけ	(Grilled Salmon)
おんせんたまご	(Onsen Egg)
つくだに	(Tsukudani)
つけもの	(Pickled Vegetables)
のり	(Nori)
ごはん	(Steamed Rice)
みそしる	(Miso Soup)

18.50

and salvation, and American restaurateurs tried to give them both. Even at the restaurants at Walt Disney World, more nutritious items were added to menus, especially after the company's chief executive officer, Michael Eisner, discovered he himself had an intolerably high cholesterol level.

There was a schizophrenia in all this, for Americans still loved the rich foods of the past and the delicacies of the present while depending on restaurant chefs to help them cut their calories. Thus, the same restaurant that might serve fresh New York State–raised *foie gras* would also offer a plate of steamed vegetables sauced with nothing more than a teaspoon of Oriental sesame oil.

It was difficult, therefore, for the proponents of New American regional cooking to maintain their ties to traditional American foods and still offer "healthy alternatives." The fact was, the removal of lard, pork, sugar, and fried foods from a Southern menu robbed the dishes of their authenticity. Chefs could not very well take the Karo syrup out of a pecan pie or the milk out of a milk gravy and get the kinds of flavors that made such foods taste so good. Neither could a chef in Texas or Arizona use fat-free imitation Monterey jack cheese if he were to maintain the integrity of a true stuffed taco. Those who would serve the best American beef knew it had to be marbleized, high-calorie U.S. Prime, and nobody in his right mind could pretend to make a good strawberry shortcake without using real whipped heavy cream and a pastry enriched with butter or lard.

Besides, the public had, by the end of the 1980s, already tired of the overly publicized New American Cooking. And chefs had tired of making it. With that perplexing American dread of ever repeating what had been done before and mindful of the need to create publicity for themselves and their restaurants, most of those young American chefs who had once wholeheartedly embraced with enthusiasm the return to their regional gastronomic roots had begun to desert the expedition and hopped instead onto the next available culinary bandwagon in search of more media attention.

Fashion had come to dictate the direction of American gastronomy and the need to be part of a trend—whether it was a seasonal infatuation with Tuscan trattoria food, reappreciation of French Provençal seasonings, or a completely contrived fusion of Third World cuisines on one plate—took precedence over self-discipline and culinary refinement. A very few exceptions—Larry Forgione of An American Place in New York, Jack McDavid of Jack's Firehouse in Philadelphia, Mark Miller of the Coyote Café in Santa Fe, Jasper White of Jasper in Boston, to name the most prominent—have tried to maintain their links to America's traditional food culture, while others have strayed as far away from regional cooking as it is possible to get, so that it is more likely today to find a line around a California-style pizza and pasta singles' bar/restaurant in Dallas than it is to find customers to support a new restaurant serving fried chicken, mashed potatoes, and pecan pie.

The irony of it all is how the rest of the world has come to regard American food—predominantly in its fast food form—as something wonderful and symbolic of an American lifestyle that may have already begun to pass. Of course, to all those Japanese, French, German, Italian, and Chinese customers, American fast food had the same appeal as blue jeans, T-shirts and cowboy boots. And the promotional potential of an American name was certainly not lost on the Milanese entrepreneurs who opened restaurants with names like Charleston Pizza and Paper Moon. Nor on the owners of a Hong Kong restaurant named California, which features hamburgers, barbecued chicken, and carrot cake amid an atmosphere of TV sets, car headlights, and the pink-and-blue colors of the Eisenhower Era.

Where is the state of American restaurants heading into the twenty-first century?

The all-American hamburger, under furious assault as too fat-laden and cholesterol-rich, was being given strong competition as Americans' favorite food, even though we still average three hamburgers a week or thirty-eight billion each year. In 1985 a National Restaurant Association survey found that pizza was chosen one out of five times by customers at dinner. And the fast food industry was thrown into another gear when Domino's Pizza, started by Tom Monaghan in 1960, perfected a way to deliver hot pizzas to customers' doors in under thirty minutes.

■ New York's "21" Club was in decline when it was sold in 1986 for twenty-one million dollars to a carpet manufacturer named Marshall Cogan, who spent another nine million dollars to refurbish it for a new generation of business people, and even introduced "trim menu selections" for those no longer hungry for steaks, chops, and double Scotches-on-the-rocks.

■ By the end of the eighties most cities in the United States had better, more authentic Italian restaurants, ranging from trattorias to deluxe *ristoranti* like New York's San Domenico and Los Angeles's Rex, serving plates of fettuccine with shavings of white truffles costing up to fifty dollars a plate. There was also renewed interest in French bourgeois cooking, and the influx of both money and people from Hong Kong restored the reputation of Cantonese cooking in the nation's Chinatowns.

The American airline industry had all but given up trying to upgrade its food service, although "special meals" for vegetarians, those on a restricted diet, and those who ate kosher were provided. In 1990 the Department of Transportation reported that the nation's twenty largest carriers spent only an average of $4.25 per passenger on its inflight meals, and that a survey of one hundred thousand frequent fliers ranked food and drink eleventh out of fourteen top concerns when selecting a flight. "It doesn't matter if airline food is bad," a vice president of marketing for Midwest Airlines (which spent a whopping $11.50 per passenger on its meals) said. "People just block it out as an unpleasant experience."

Restaurant Associates was bought out in April 1990 by a Japanese food company named Kyotaru and continued to operate American restaurants like the Publick House in Sturbridge Village, Massachusetts, and the American Festival Café in New York, as well as the food service outlets at the U.S. Open Tennis Tournament and Mamma Leone's in New York's Theater District. RA now has grosses of about $240 million each year.

Joe Baum opened his own restaurant in New York, Aurora (which failed), while continuing to develop several spectacular projects that included the Hudson River Club in the World Financial Center and, in 1987

REX-IL RISTORANTE in Los Angeles elevated the standards and the chic of Italian cuisine and style when it opened in 1981.

bankrolled by the Rockefeller family, the twenty-million-dollar renovation of the esteemed Rainbow Room, which was brought back to a grandeur it had not known since the 1930s. He also restored the Art Deco majesty, the revolving dance floor, old cocktails, and menus that reflected his own nostalgia for the kinds of fancy "restaurant food" he'd championed back in the 1950s. Diners could order anything from lobster Thermidor to baked Alaska, and there were nods of honor to legendary restaurants by including dishes like the Colony's *pigeon en cocotte.*

■　The food press expanded in the eighties—which had become known as the "Foodie Decade"—then began to contract by the end of the decade, with several magazines, notably *Cuisine* and *Cook's* (both of which had championed American food), going out of business. The "celebrity chef" idea lost much of its gloss in the marketplace.

■　When the Colony closed in 1972, its eminence as international society's most indulgent dining room passed to Le Cirque, which opened in 1975 under the ownership of the Colony's former chef, Jean Vergnes, and its maître d', Sirio Maccioni. Later, as sole owner, Maccioni established Le Cirque as the most famous restaurant in the world, both for its cuisine and for its standards of service. Food writer James Villas once characterized Le Cirque as having "drop-dead glamour and four-star food."

■　The Horn & Hardart Company foundered in the 1980s and began dumping all its restaurant assets in 1988, including America's last Automat at 200 East Forty-second Street in New York, which closed its doors on April 9, 1991.

■　After decades of soaring growth, the restaurant industry slowed. The population was growing older, there were fewer young people, and other industries retrenched, causing disposable income and expense accounts to drop by 1990. As a result, menu prices, which had risen rapidly in the 1980s, stabilized or, in many cases, actually dropped, and few entrepreneurs were opening deluxe dining rooms anywhere in the country by 1991.

■　By 1990 the Culinary Institute of America, under the direction of President Ferdinand Metz, in Hyde Park, New York, had graduated more than twenty-two thousand students, many of whom had won medals at the prestigious International Culinary Olympics held in Frankfurt, Germany. With 1,850 students paying twenty thousand dollars for a twenty-one-month course of studies and ninety-five chefs and instructors, the school runs four public dining rooms, including St. Andrew's Café, whose menus are based on the latest nutritional data. Along with several other culinary schools including the New England Culinary Institute in Montpelier, Vermont, and Johnson and Wales University in Providence, Rhode Island, the Culinary Institute of America provides thousands of trained chefs for the American food industry, from *haute cuisine* restaurants to hospital kitchens.

■　Fast food was still a growth industry, but nothing like it had been when the number of fast food stores jumped 78 percent in the decade of the eighties, from 67,290 to 119,880. Too much competition, high prices for ingredients like beef, and shifting nutritional concerns forced the fast food chains to modify their menus. Kentucky Fried Chicken tried to downplay

BY THE END OF THE 1980s, the Culinary Institute of America in Hyde Park, New York, had gained international renown for graduating more than 1,800 fully qualified cooks to meet the voracious demands of a restaurant industry that grew in leaps and bounds during that decade.

its "fried" image by changing its name and logo to KFC and introducing smaller proportioned Lite'n Crispy Chicken with 39 percent fewer calories and 45 percent less fat than their original recipe chicken. Even McDonald's began looking for ways to trim the fat. In 1990 it introduced a 91 percent fat-free hamburger called McLean Deluxe that contained a carrageenan derivative of seaweed used to maintain moisture in the patty. Also, responding to a growing appetite for Mexican food and an increase of 32 percent in the Hispanic population in the 1980s, McDonald's started testing a Mexican

item—an egg-filled breakfast burrito. And, always on the lookout for new converts, on January 31, 1990, McDonald's opened its first outlet in Moscow on Pushkin Square. Serving more than fifty thousand people a day, the Moscow McDonald's had lines bunched up at all twenty-seven cash register lanes that first day. They wound past the mural of a sunset and the Art Deco pillars out the door and down the street. People would wait for hours to get their first taste of a Big Mac (3.75 rubles; $6) and an ice cream sundae (1 ruble; $1.60), although the exchange rate for American visitors brought the price of the Big Mac down to just 60 cents. And in an about-face from the traditions of fast food service, Burger King began offering sit-down service complete with apron-clad waiters and waitresses.

■ Foodies gained a conscience in the 1980s and 1990s. Bothered as much by hunger in America as by the nagging feeling that restaurant-going had become truly an extravagance, many food writers, restaurateurs, chefs, and wine and spirits companies gave generously of their time and money, funding organizations like Meals on Wheels, City Harvest, and Share Our Strength—designed to feed the homeless and the housebound—while charities like the March of Dimes would hold Gourmet Galas featuring the food of America's finest chefs at lavish banquets.

Whatever the fortunes of the fast food or white-tablecloth restaurant are to be in the twenty-first century, it seems sure that they will be reaped by those who from the very start of American food service had a great

IN JANUARY 1990, MCDONALD'S opened its first unit in the Soviet Union, in Moscow's Pushkin Square, where it was soon serving American hamburgers to more than fifty thousand people per day.

gimmick. From the colonial tavernkeeper to the Englishman who first brought waitresses to the West, from John Delmonico to Joe Baum, from White Castle to Alice's Restaurant, the American restaurant owner has always tried to hook a customer in with a good new idea. Sometimes, as in the case of an Henri Soulé, the lure was great food. Other times, as with Messrs. Horn and Hardart, it was the attraction of a new technology.

When the newest technologies and a commitment to good taste were combined with a personality for whom perfectionism was an addiction, the results can be mind-boggling. Which is why it seems appropriate to end the story of eating out in America in Tampa, Florida, at the most remarkable restaurant in the entire world—Bern's Steak House.

For the owner of Bern's—Bernard Laxer—is a man who by his own admission carries everything to extremes, and once told an interviewer, "It's true. I'm a nut." Yet his restaurant could exist only in the United States and seems the apotheosis of the American restaurant story. For Laxer the challenge has always been to find new ways to entice the public to come from all over the world to eat at his restaurant. The son of a Romanian mother who designed dresses and a factory worker father from Poland, Laxer graduated from New York University with a degree in advertising, took a trip to Florida with his wife, Gert, in 1950, ran out of money, worked in a cigar factory, and took a job writing ads for a men's store while he edited a small newsletter called *Garden Notes.* With $1,400 in savings they bought an eight- by fifty-two-foot hole-in-the-wall eatery which they fixed up and called Bern and Gert's Little Midway. Despite its modest breakfast and lunch menus, the couple insisted on making their own doughnuts and squeezing their own fruit juices, and they did well enough to interest thirty-seven investors to bankroll a bigger place on Howard Avenue called Beer Haven. They removed a couple of letters from the sign, substituted others, and called it "Bern's," adding "Steak House" only because the phone company wouldn't accept a single first name as a listing.

Laxer was working twelve-hour days but needed more customers, so he began an advertising campaign that would have done Restaurant Associates proud: He offered a $66,000 steak dinner that included a round-trip ticket to "deepest Africa and a good luck charm." For those who couldn't afford the package, Bern would happily serve you just the steak for $2.50.

Nearly four decades later Bern's Steak House is one of the most famous restaurants in the world. The large, multiroom establishment is garishly decorated (albeit with some very expensive antiques) with gilded plaster columns, red wallpaper, Tiffany lamps, and murals of French vineyards. It is run like an amusement park attraction, and Bern's nearly always has a waiting list for one of his 320 seats.

Laxer's reputation has been built around the single dish that gives the restaurant its name, because he has gone to such lengths to create an aura around his beef that it is impossible not to marvel at the process. Laxer buys only U.S. Prime, then further ages them four to ten weeks in specially built lockers controlled for humidity and temperature. The menu, which is as detailed as the instructions for building a dirigible, lists six basic cuts, from the Delmonico to the porterhouse, available in any thickness a customer

wishes, broiled to any of eight levels of doneness. To read the entire menu would take longer than it does to eat the entire meal: There are two dozen caviars from around the world listed and five different tartares—and Laxer devotes an entire page to explain why "We do things differently here."

The coffee beans at Bern's are hand sorted, the sour cream made specially for him, his breads baked on the premises in pans made in his own metal shops. He designed a special machine just to cut the cheese for his French onion soup (made not with scrap bones but specially ordered veal bones) to a consistent texture and color. He constructed twelve-hundred-gallon tanks in which to allow live fish to swim, and his vegetables and herbs are grown organically on his own eight-and-a-half-acre farm. A recipe may be tested three hundred times before Bern approves its inclusion on the menu.

And then there is something else: Bern's astounding wine list—the world's largest wine list, with more than seven thousand individual selections and a half million bottles, listed and bound into a five-pound volume far larger than the Tampa telephone book and wired to each dining table like a medieval bible.

There are also more than two hundred wines offered by the glass, all kept fresh by a process Bern himself perfected. Yet Bern himself only tastes wines and rarely ever drinks more than a glass. He also fasts in order to purify his body, as part of his belief in holistic medicine.

In an industry of eccentrics and visionaries, Bern Laxer is perhaps the most remarkable of them all. In every way possible he sums up—for better or worse—the American restaurant experience of the past fifty years, from his dedication to serving the best ingredients it is possible for him to get to paying attention to every detail that might please or amaze a customer.

He is a showman on a par with Auguste Lüchow, Walt Disney, and Joe Baum, and never does anything according to the set rules of the game. For one thing, his food costs run nearly double what is considered acceptable to the industry as a whole. He invites all guests to inspect his kitchen. He adds a 12 percent service charge to his checks to ensure his waiters make good money. When customers order a Martini, the vermouth is squeezed out of an eyedropper to the exact degree of dryness desired. He has an "800" telephone number so that in-state customers don't have to spend money for the telephone call. He hires only nonprofessionals, and then teaches them exactly what he wants them to learn and no more. He cares far less about his restaurant's decor—despite the constant jokes made about it—than he does about the food. He serves his steaks on metal dishes that went out of style thirty years ago, and even the red wines are kept at a constant fifty degrees Fahrenheit—far too cool to drink when first opened at the table. And he prohibits smoking entirely in most of his dining rooms.

And then there is Bern's upstairs enclave of alcoves—called the "Harry Waugh Room" after the English wine connoisseur—which he built so that he could more quickly turn over the tables downstairs. Diners leave their table and ascend the stairs where they are assigned a cozy room half-enclosed by highly polished redwood slats. On the table is a metal-jacketed, sixty-five-page menu of desserts, which may be accompanied by more than three hundred eighty-five dessert wines and spirits, available by the glass,

RESTAURATEUR EXTRAORDINAIRE Bern Laxer, shown tending his carefully aged steaks at Bern's Steak House in Tampa, Florida, where he also offers customers the largest selection of wines in the world, two dozen different caviars, and a sixty-five page dessert menu including some of the world's rarest Cognacs and Sauternes right along with more commonplace American cordials.

On the wall of each alcove is a small, computerized jukebox, offering musical selections for any preference. You can even make a request of the live piano player at the Steinway in another room. You simply press another button.

Above your head, on either side of the table, are TV monitors, so that one of you can watch the Tampa Bay Buccaneers play the Minnesota Vikings while your companion watches the *Tonight* show.

Up in his cluttered office Bern Laxer, dressed in old, washed-out khaki slacks and a shirt that seems two sizes too big for his slight, sixty-eight-year-old frame, sits at his computer, works on his wine list, and studies organic farming journals. He may come out now and then to check the kitchen, pick up a scrap from the floor, or peek into the dining room to make sure the customers are happy and the dining rooms are full. And if they're not, well, he'll think of some remarkable way to fill them tomorrow.

THE PHILOSOPHY of Bern's Steak House as printed on the menu

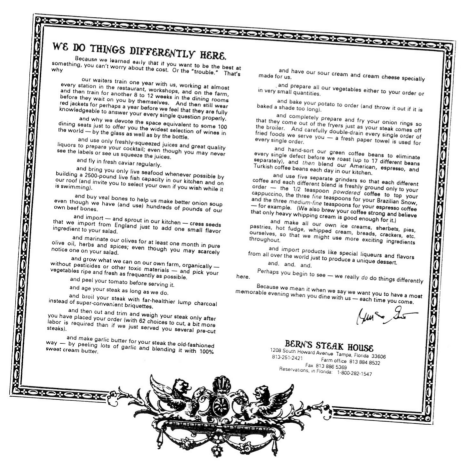

WE DO THINGS DIFFERENTLY HERE.

Because we learned eaily that if you want to be the best at something, you can't worry about the cost. Or the "trouble." That's why

our waiters train one year with us, working at almost every station in the restaurant, workshops, and on the farm, and then train for another 8 to 12 weeks in the dining rooms before they wait on you by themselves. And then still wear red jackets for perhaps a year before we feel that they are fully knowledgeable to answer your every single question properly.

and why we devote the space equivalent to some 100 dining seats just to offer you the widest selection of wines in the world — by the glass as well as by the bottle.

and use only freshly-squeezed juices and great quality liquors to prepare your cocktail; even though you may never see the labels or see us squeeze the juices.

and fly in fresh caviar regularly.

and bring you only live seafood whenever possible by building a 2500-pound live fish capacity in our kitchen and on our roof (and invite you to select your own if you wish while it is swimming).

and buy veal bones to help us make better onion soup even though we have (and use) hundreds of pounds of our own beef bones.

and import — and sprout in our kitchen — cress seeds that we import from England just to add one small flavor ingredient to your salad.

and marinate our olives for at least one month in pure olive oil, herbs and spices; even though you may scarcely notice one on your salad.

and grow what we can on our own farm, organically — without pesticides or other toxic materials — and pick your vegetables ripe and fresh as frequently as possible.

and peel your tomato before serving it.

and age your steak as long as we do.

and broil your steak with far-healthier lump charcoal instead of super-convenient briquettes.

and then cut and trim and weigh your steak only after you have placed your order (with 62 choices to cut, a bit more labor is required than if we just served you several pre-cut steaks).

and make garlic butter for your steak the old-fashioned way — by peeling lots of garlic and blending it with 100% sweet cream butter.

and have our sour cream and cream cheese specially made for us.

and prepare all our vegetables either to your order or in very small quantities.

and bake your potato to order (and throw it out if it is baked a shade too long).

and completely prepare and fry your onion rings so that they come out of the fryers just as your steak comes off the broiler. And carefully double-drain every single order of fried foods we serve you — a fresh paper towel is used for every single order.

and hand-sort our green coffee beans to eliminate every single defect before we roast (up to 17 different beans separately), and *then* blend our American, espresso, and Turkish coffee beans each day in our kitchen.

and use five separate grinders so that each different coffee and each different blend is freshly ground only to your order — the 1/2 teaspoon *powdered* coffee to top your cappuccino, the three *fine* teaspoons for your Brazilian Snow, and the three *medium-fine* teaspoons for your espresso coffee — for example. (We also brew your coffee strong and believe that only heavy whipping cream is good enough for it.)

and make all our own ice creams, sherbets, pies, pastries, hot fudge, whipped cream, breads, crackers, etc. ourselves, so that we might use more exciting ingredients throughout.

and import products like special liqueurs and flavors from all over the world just to produce a unique dessert.

and. and. and.

Perhaps you begin to see — we really *do* do things differently here.

Because we mean it when we say we want you to have a most memorable evening when you dine with us — each time you come.

BERN'S STEAK HOUSE
1208 South Howard Avenue Tampa, Florida 33606
813-251-2421   Farm office 813 884 8532
Fax 813 886 5369
Reservations, in Florida: 1-800-282-1547

Bibliography

THE FOLLOWING LIST OF BOOKS and magazines is intended to direct the general reader and student to the most comprehensive work in the field and may be used as a starting point for the scholar to go further with his or her own research.

Alejandro, Reynaldo. *Classic Menu Design.* Glen Cove, NY: PBC International, 1988.

Baeder, John. *Diners.* New York: Harry N. Abrams, 1988.

Barr, Ann and Paul Levy. *The Official Foodie Handbook.* London: Ebury Press, 1984.

Batterberry, Michael and Ariane. *On the Town in New York: From 1776 to the Present.* New York: Scribner's, 1973.

Belasco, Warren J. *Appetite for Change: How the Counterculture Took on the Food Industry, 1966–1988.* New York: Pantheon Books, 1989.

Berger, Frances de Talavera and John Parke Custis, *Sumptuous Dining in Gaslight San Francisco, 1875–1915.* New York: Doubleday, 1985.

Bernstein, Charles. *Great Restaurant Innovators.* New York: Lebhar-Friedman Books, 1981.

Brody, Iles. *The Colony.* New York: Greenberg, 1945.

Brown, Ellen. *Cooking with the New American Chefs.* New York: Harper & Row, 1985.

Chalmers, Irena, and Friends. *American Bistro.* Chicago: Contemporary Books, 1986.

Claiborne, Craig. *The New York Times Guide to Dining Out in New York.* New York: Atheneum, 1969.

———. *A Feast Made for Laughter.* New York: Times Books, 1982.

Cook, Alison, "The Texas Food Manifesto." *Texas Monthly,* December 1983, pp. 139–152.

Dickson, Paul. *The Great American Ice Cream Book.* New York: Atheneum, 1978.

Egerton, John. *Southern Food.* New York: Alfred A. Knopf, 1987.

Emerson, Robert L. *Fast Food: The Endless Shakeout.* New York: Lebhar-Friedman Books, 1979.

Evans, Meryle. "Knickerbocker Hotels and Restaurants 1800–1850." *The New-York Historical Society Quarterly,* 36 (October 1954), pp. 377–409.

Gage, Crosby. *Food at the Fair: A Gastronomic Tour of the New York World's Fair 1939.* New York: Exposition Publications, 1939.

Greene, Gael. *Bite.* New York: W. W. Norton, 1971.

————. "The Most Spectacular Restaurant in the World." *New York,* May 31, 1976, pp. 43–53.

Gutman, Richard J. S., and Elliott Kaufman. *American Diner.* New York: Harper & Row, 1979.

Heimann, Jim. *Out with the Stars.* New York: Abbeville Publishers, 1985.

Heimann, Jim, and Rip Georges. *California Crazy: Roadside Vernacular Architecture.* San Francisco: Chronicle Books, 1980.

Hess, Alan. *Googie: Fifties Coffee Shop Architecture.* San Francisco: Chronicle Books, 1986.

Hess, John L. and Karen. *The Taste of America.* New York: Grossman Publishers, 1977.

Hooker, Richard J. *Food & Drink in America: A History.* Indianapolis: The Bobbs-Merrill Company, 1981.

Hotchner, A. E., et al. "If You've Been Afraid to Go to Elaine's These Past Twenty Years, Here's What You've Missed." *New York,* May 2, 1983, pp. 34–52.

Jones, Evan. *American Food: The Gastronomic Story.* New York: Dutton, 1975.

Kaytor, Marilyn. *"21": The Life and Times of New York's Favorite Club.* New York: The Viking Press, 1975.

Kirshon, John W., editor. *Chronicle of America.* Mount Kisco, NY: Chronicle Publications, 1989.

Langdon, Philip. *Orange Roofs, Golden Arches: The Architecture of American Chain Restaurants.* New York: Alfred A. Knopf, 1986.

Lender, Mark Edward, and James Kirby Martin. *Drinking in America: A History.* New York: The Free Press, 1982.

Monninger, Joseph. "Fast Food." *American Heritage,* April 1988, pp. 66–75.

Pillsbury, Richard. *From Boarding House to Bistro: American Restaurants Then and Now.* Cambridge, MA: Unwin Hyman, 1990.

Poling-Kempes, Lesley. *The Harvey Girls: Women Who Opened the West.* New York: Paragon House, 1989.

Ranhofer, Charles. *The Epicurean.* New York: Dover Publications, 1971.

Rice, Kym S. *Early American Taverns: For the Entertainment of Strangers.* Chicago: Regnery Gateway, 1983.

Root, Waverley, and Richard de Rochement. *Eating in America: A History.* New York: William Morrow and Company, 1976.

Shaplen, Robert. "Delmonico." *The New Yorker,* November 10, 1956, and November 17, 1956.

Sokolov, Raymond. *Fading Feast.* New York: Farrar, Straus & Giroux, 1981.

Stern, Jane and Michael. *Roadfood and Goodfood.* New York: Alfred A. Knopf, 1986.

————. "Cafeteria." *The New Yorker,* August 1988, pp. 37–54.

Thernstrorr, Stephan, editor. *Harvard Encyclopedia of American Ethnic Groups.* Cambridge, MA: Harvard University Press, 1980.

Trillin, Calvin. *American Fried: Adventures of a Happy Eater.* New York: Doubleday, 1974.

Villas, James. *American Taste.* New York: Arbor House, 1982.

————. *Villas at Table.* New York: Harper & Row, 1988.

Wechsberg, Joseph. *Dining at the Pavillon.* Boston: Little, Brown and Company, 1962.

Williams, Richard L., editor. *American Cooking.* 7 vols. New York: Time-Life Books, 1970–71.

Wilson, Charles Reagan, and William Ferris, editors. *Encyclopedia of Southern Culture.* Chapel Hill, NC: The University of North Carolina Press, 1989.

Acknowledgments

THE GREATEST DELIGHT for a historian is to enlist the help of those very subjects he intends to write about. Pity the researcher who never gets closer to his subject than in the yellowed documents of another age or in the musty haunt where a historic event once occurred. I would very much like to have dined at the original Delmonico's, talked to Fred Harvey at a railroad restaurant, and interviewed Henri Soulé over dinner at Le Pavillon. But they are long gone and must be assessed only through records, reminiscences, engravings, and photographs. How fortunate, then, to have the pleasure of dining out at those very restaurants where America's gastronomic adventure began—places like Fraunces Tavern in New York, Antoine's in New Orleans, Locke-Ober Café in Boston, Arthur Bryant's in Kansas City, Chez Panisse in Berkeley, Spago in Los Angeles, The Pump Room in Chicago, Bern's Steak House in Tampa, and scores of others that are not only still extant but thriving.

But the greatest pleasure has come in meeting and interviewing those figures who have made that history happen, all of whom are still very much involved in the day-to-day operations of restaurants they helped create. For this reason I have been extremely fortunate and very grateful to have enlisted the help of those whose personal anecdotes and assiduous regard for accuracy have made this book far more lively and accurate than it would otherwise have been. Very special thanks go to George Lang, James Armstrong, Joseph Baum, Joseph and Mario Migliucci, Bern Laxer, Pierre Franey, Craig Claiborne, Julia Child, Alan Stillman, Jane and Michael Stern, and Calvin Trillin for enriching this narrative with their direct input.

A deep debt of gratitude is due to Charles Bernstein, editor-in-chief of *Nation's Restaurant News,* whose generosity in allowing me to use the magazine's photo archives was crucial to my research when all other sources failed me. Thanks, too, to the staffs at the Smithsonian Institution, the Library of Congress, and the New York Public Library, the resources of which are not just boundless but so accessible to the public that it is difficult to imagine any more important institutions in a free society.

Thanks for all sorts of reasons to Michael Bartlett, Pam Blanton, Carol

271

Boyd, Alice Brock, Beverly Brockus, Ellen Brown, Gene Cavallero, Irena Chalmers, Sue Chernoff, Valerie Cimino, A. Craig Copetas, Suzanne Corbett, Len Davidson, Byron Dobell, Nora Fine, Andrew Freeman, Paul Frumkin, Marion Gorman, Gael Greene, Bernard Guste, David Haberstick, John Harding, Nancy Wall Hopkins, Rob Kasper, Diane Kochilas, Jenifer Harvey Lang, Andrew Lawlor, Edmund Lillys, Sirio Maccioni, Laura Maioglio, Ferdinand Metz, Jessica Miller, Mark Miller, Ken Aretsky, Tessie Fruge Patterson, Steven Raichlen, Jack Redinger, Barbara Seldin, Richard Snow, Mario Staub, Jara Thomas, James Villas, Jane Wallace, Lisa Cole Wertchafter, and Elaine Whitelaw.

The idea for this book originated with my editor, Harriet Bell, whose enthusiasm has been unflagging and a true energy source for me. Without the encouragement of my agent, Diane Cleaver, I might never have come around to undertaking such a task as this. Thanks to the diligence of my copyeditor, Evie Righter, my textual indiscretions are now few and far between. And because designer Barry Zaid shared my excitement in this project, I am enchanted with the way it all looks.

And to my wife, Galina, who was able to abide every one of my fits and starts, I shall be grateful forever.

Index

Picture Credits

The author gratefully acknowledges the use of photographs from the following sources. Every effort has been made to trace the proper copyright holders of the photographs used herein. If there are any omissions we apologize, and we will be pleased to make the appropriate acknowledgments in future printings.

Antoine's: 33; Author's Collection: 106 (left), 107 (right); Bern's Steak House: 266, 267; Paul Child: 250; Margaret Beck Crist: 45; Culinary Institute of America: 161, 263 (A. Blake Gardner III); Denver Public Library Western History Department: 39; El Cholo Restaurant: 81; The Four Seasons: 190; Four Seasons Hotels: 259, 260; Pierre Franey: 147; Grand Central Oyster Bar and Restaurant: 55; Lou Hammond and Associates: 135; Jim Heimann: 100–101, 102, 141; James Beard Foundation: 148, 149; Judge Roy Bean Museum: 40; Kentucky Fried Chicken, 172; Spencer Krump Collection: 42; George Lang: 225; Lawry's Prime Rib: 142; The Library of Congress: 6, 8, 10 (bottom), 11, 13 (top), 14, 34, 60, 67, 104, 106–107, 109, 110, 112, 114, 115, 116, 127, 129, 154, 162, 182, 208–209; McDonald's Corporation: 264; Museum of the City of New York: 25, 31, 48; Museum of Modern Art Film Stills Archive: 46, 156; Nathan's: 74; *Nation's Restaurant News:* 10 (top), 12, 13 (bottom), 19, 79, 83, 111, 120–121, 139, 165, 166, 167, 168, 170–171, 173, 174, 175, 176, 178, 180–181, 193–194, 196, 198–199, 201, 207, 210, 215, 217, 219, 222, 232–233, 238, 241, 243, 245–246, 248, 251, 255; *New York* magazine: 240; Procter & Gamble: 130–131; The Rainbow Room: 132; Reading Terminal Market: 63; Jack Redinger: 41; Restaurant Associates, 186, 187, 188; Rex-Il Ristorante: 261; The Russian Tea Room: 86; Barbara Seldin: 75; Sign of the Dove: 203; Smithsonian Institution National Museum of American History: 28–29, 56–57, 158–159; Jane and Michael Stern, 242; Stroud's: 85; Trader Vic's: 143; "21" Club: 88, 96, 98–99; Unterfelsen Collection: 17, 20, 22, 24, 27, 36, 51, 62, 64–65, 78, 84, 90, 93, 95, 117, 153; Waldorf-Astoria: 53; Walt Disney Company: 252; White Castle: 123, 124, 125; Windows on the World: 228, 229, 230, 231; Barry Zaid: 69, 71, 77, 113, 118–119, 138.